D0231136

Chris Brasher

Chris Brasher

The Man Who Made The London Marathon

The Authorised Biography

By

JOHN BRYANT

First published in Great Britain 2012 by
Aurum Press Ltd,
7 Greenland Street,
London NW1 0ND
www.aurumpress.co.uk

Copyright © John Bryant 2012

John Bryant has asserted his moral right to be identified as the Author of this
Work in accordance with the Copyright Designs and Patents Act 1988.

All rights reserved. No part of this book may be reproduced or
utilised in any form or by any means, electronic or mechanical,
including photocopying, recording or by any information
storage and retrieval system, without permission in writing
from Aurum Press Ltd.

Copyright acknowledgements for quoted material.

Every effort has been made to trace the copyright holders of material
quoted in this book. If application is made in writing to the publisher,
any omissions will be included in future editions.

A catalogue record for this book is available from the British Library.

ISBN 978 1 84513 637 6

1 3 5 7 9 10 8 6 4 2
2012 2014 2016 2015 2013

Typeset in Fournier MT Std Regular by SX Composing DTP, Rayleigh, Essex
Printed by MPG Books, Bodmin, Cornwall

To the marathon runners who
dream that someday their reach
will exceed their grasp

Contents

FOREWORD

by Sir Roger Bannister

This utterly absorbing biography of Chris Brasher vividly recalls our friendship of over 50 years. He continually surprised me by his complexity. He was so much more than an athlete, although he won an Olympic gold medal. He was part romantic, part idealist, part tough businessman and was capable of some extraordinary acts of kindness. He had a manic energy and single-mindedness that brooked no opposition.

His legacy and crowning achievement was the creation of the London Marathon, the largest in the world, which he fashioned with the support of John Disley in the face of the inertia of bureaucracy. Large sums of money were raised for recreational projects in London and the runners themselves raised over £50 million for various charities. The London Marathon inspired gallant runners of all ages who had never seriously run before to test themselves and Chris was rewarded by the sea of fulfilled faces at the finish who were justifiably proud of their achievement.

As a teenage engineering apprentice in the Midlands he had learnt to escape to 'wild places', the mountains of Wales and Scotland, where he learnt climbing with groups of friends. In his journalistic career he wrote about the mystery of these wild places and the way they rekindled his spirit. This chimed with my own love of the countryside and he even inveigled me to go climbing with him in Glencoe, a risky enterprise three weeks before he and Chris Chataway paced me for the four-minute mile.

Little known was his philanthropy. His wealth helped to save wild areas of Scotland and Wales from invasion by electricity pylons and nearer home at Petersham he helped to preserve the Thames Meadows shown in the famous Turner painting.

Shakespeare described such a man:

The elements were so mixed in him
that nature might stand up
And say to all the world
this was a man.

Marathon Day

'Chris Brasher has done more for the corporate spirit of London than anyone since Adolf Hitler.'

Sir Christopher Chataway

C HRIS BRASHER was annoyed by the phone call that clattered into his sleep at two in the morning. He'd set his alarm in the hotel room to wake him at five. It was Dave Bedford on the line, obviously drunk and mumbling that he wanted to run the marathon the next day. Bedford, the self-confessed wild man who had dominated British distance running in the 1970s and broken the 10,000 metres world record, was calling from his nightclub, The Mad Hatter, in Luton. It was 28 March 1981. These days Bedford is the race director of the London Marathon. In those days he hadn't run a step in a year, but a friend had bet him £250 that he couldn't finish the Marathon.

'Do what the hell you want,' Brasher told him, then turned over and rolled back to sleep.

The phone rang again at four. There was a panic about the tangle of scaffolding being erected at the Marathon finish on Constitution Hill. It was feared that the scaffolding might sever the heads of the mounted soldiers during the Changing of the Guard. Brasher called his sidekick, John Disley, and between them they got the gantry altered.

At 5 a.m. Brasher hauled himself wearily from his bed, bent on hacking through every problem that might threaten his infant marathon, and determined to run the race himself. Some nine hours later, still barking last-minute orders from a crude walkie-talkie, he struggled across the line in two hours fifty-six minutes.

Brasher's first emotion was 'a huge sense of relief'. The days and months leading up to that first London Marathon were chaotic. Ever since he'd roused his wife Shirley from her bed, late on a Saturday night in October 1979, to hear him declaim the *Observer* story that was to launch the saga next day, the dream of the London Marathon had dominated his life.

Brasher had witnessed and run the New York Marathon, and in his paper he laid down the challenge. 'I wonder whether London could stage such a festival. We have the course, a magnificent course, but do we have the heart and hospitality to welcome the world?'

Shirley Brasher reckoned it was a step too far. 'I did not see how Chris could fit one more thing, either paid or unpaid, into his life. I was afraid he would finish himself with exhaustion, me with exasperation and our marriage with sheer pressure.'

In a matter of months, however, Brasher and John Disley, fellow athlete, friend and business partner, had bulldozed through the seemingly impossible task of laying on a mass marathon in the heart of London. Everybody said it was impossible, few thought it could happen, most believed it would end in disaster. But Brasher ploughed on relentlessly.

He'd pop up everywhere, preaching and promoting his dream. He cajoled Ian Wooldridge – the *Daily Mail*'s top sportswriter – to escort him around the course in a limousine. Six hours and several bottles of champagne later, Brasher, confident that Wooldridge's report would command a two-page spread in the *Mail*, picked up a kit-bag. He emerged from a cloakroom with a grin, stripped to his tracksuit and running shoes. He downed a large gin and tonic and then set off to run the nine miles from London to his home in Richmond.

Brasher's heart had sunk with some despair when the leader of the Greater London Council, Sir Horace Cutler, had told him bluntly: 'You won't get a penny from the GLC.' Brasher's response was to whisk Cutler off to New York, champagne and Concorde all the way, to further publicise the race and grab yet more headlines.

Brasher used all the volunteer labour he could muster – raiding running clubs, squads of orienteers, anyone he'd run, walked or drunk with – to handle the overspill of tasks, from the doling out of numbers to the blue line painted round the course. The 'Marathon Office' itself was low-tech and undermanned. It consisted of a desk and two chairs tucked away in the GLC Recreation Office.

Brasher would call on every press man he knew and roped in his good friend David Coleman and the BBC to hype the race. But still, many believed it would never happen. The night before the race Brasher galloped around the broadcasting studios, dispensing his eccentric advice. 'Vaseline all moving parts, ball of foot, heel, groin and where your arm meets your back,' he warned.

Thousands of runners crawled out of warm beds on Marathon morning only to find that the rain chilled their limbs and the Greenwich park keeper, reckoning it was an ordinary Sunday morning, had locked all the changing rooms and lavatories. The trains were gruesomely packed, but somehow 7000 competitors, many dripping beneath black bin-liners, shuffled their way to the start. Among them were a handful of elite runners, hired by Brasher in a series of frantic phone calls to give the race some credibility.

Brasher was everywhere; growling orders, wagging his finger, shepherding the flock of runners who backed up like a football crowd jamming the gates of Greenwich Park. Two hours, eleven minutes and forty-eight seconds later Dick Beardsley from the USA and Inge Simonsen from Norway crossed the line, hand in hand.

In those blister-filled hours when the runners processed around the capital the race had stamped itself on London. The doubters had said it couldn't happen, but the reviews were ecstatic. Thirty-one years later, many thousands have experienced the bubbling enthusiasm, the pain, the satisfaction of raising millions for charity and the euphoria of running the London Marathon.

I was working at the *Daily Mail* when I ran that first London Marathon. I staggered back to my office after the race. There on the front page was a picture of the winners. And there was the headline. It said simply 'The Hand of Friendship'. The race, labelled by Chris Brasher 'the great suburban Everest', was an instant hit. The running boom had become a reality. The finishers limped into their offices next day, proud of their blisters and their medals. The sales of tracksuits, vests, shorts and running shoes soared as never before.

And Brasher, like the London Marathon itself, seemed to be unstoppable . . .

The Man Who Could Never Resist a Challenge

N O ONE GAVE much hope for the man who had scraped into the British team for the 1956 Olympics in Melbourne. Knowledgeable experts reckoned that Chris Brasher was no winner. After all, he had never won a single race in international competition. His closest friends Roger Bannister and Chris Chataway, four-minute milers both, overshadowed him with their seemingly effortless and glamorous victories.

But in the final of the 3000 metres steeplechase, Brasher first overhauled his British team-mates, John Disley and Eric Shirley, then began chasing the leaders. On the last lap Brasher clawed his way to the front and sprinted with his arms and legs flying wildly to win the race by fifteen yards. He had answered the challenge he had set himself, and run the race of his life.

Brasher had hardly got his breath back when the result was announced. He wiped the sweat from his steel-rimmed spectacles and peered up at the scoreboard. His name was not there. The judges had disqualified Brasher for barging the third-placed runner. He was not listed among the finishers.

After a three-hour inquiry the decision was reversed and Brasher was free to celebrate his gold medal with gusto. John Disley, his lifelong friend and steeplechase partner, says: 'Of the threesome,

Bannister, Chataway and Brasher, Chris was the ugly duckling and the only one to win an Olympic gold.'

The 'ugly duckling' was still tipsy when he collected gold the following day. But that one win convinced the 28-year-old athlete of what he had long suspected – that for him anything was possible. It was a win that was to chart the course of his future life.

The athletics world would hardly have noticed Brasher if it hadn't been for Roger Bannister. They had become friends during their university days and when Bannister set his sights on the four-minute mile, Brasher and Chataway were recruited to set the race up for him as pacemakers. On 6 May 1954 at Oxford's Iffley Road track, Brasher and Chataway towed Bannister to instant fame as an icon of the twentieth century. Brasher seemed destined to be remembered simply for playing a bit part in that drama, but the Olympics which came two years later changed all that.

Bannister was there at the track side in 1956, reporting for the *Sunday Times*, and in a piece headlined 'Brasher's Olympics' he wrote:

> Last Thursday a bespectacled, white-faced Englishman became suddenly and joyously free. As Christopher Brasher sank to the track after running the race of his life a burden as heavy as ever Sindbad carried slipped from his shoulders . . .
>
> Few British athletes have plumbed the depths of athletic misfortune in the way Brasher has done over the years. Sore legs, staleness, damaged heels, muscle cramps, asthma during races and infected teeth – Brasher has known it all. He barely made Britain's Olympic team. His unpredictable form made some people regard him as a mild athletic joke, but when ever he failed he always searched himself for the error of approach or training which had made the body give up . . .

Bannister had been disturbed by the victory of the Soviet athlete Vladimir Kuts, a fanatical and, as an army officer, apparently a full-time trainer. Kuts broke the world record for 5000 metres in 1955 and 10,000 metres in 1956, winning at both distances in the 1956 Melbourne Olympics. There were allegations that he was drugged for his races and that he had been hypnotised. With Kuts' domination of the distance events in mind, Bannister wrote:

> Brasher's victory has a significance for athletes all over the world. When Kuts won both the 5,000 and 10,000 metres I sadly felt like writing an obituary for the long-distance amateurs . . . Could any athlete in the future, I wondered, do a normal day's work and still win an Olympic title? But Brasher's victory gave us all fresh hope.
>
> He works a full office day, trains hard, and still has the unbounded energy for a wide range of hobbies including mountaineering. But the Brasher who was once considered for a Himalayan reconnaissance expedition has now climbed his own personal Everest. He has shown the world the self-conquest that can be achieved through running.

Despite Bannister's words there were many who subscribed to the view that Brasher was lucky and the least likely of Olympic victors. 'Well done the old scrubber!' read a telegram delivered to Brasher in Melbourne from his training partners in London. 'Heavy shoulders, thick thighs, solid frame, almost bulldoggish. And typically English, game to the last,' was the verdict of the 1956 British Olympic Association magazine.

It was a view that pertained throughout Brasher's life. Yet this was a man who achieved much – setting the pace in the first sub four-minute mile, winning an Olympic gold medal, and getting the London Marathon up and running.

In the days that followed Chris Brasher's death in February 2003, his wife received a letter. Shirley, who half a century before as Shirley Bloomer had been a champion tennis player, read the conventional view that somehow Chris Brasher had no natural gifts, no flair. The writer described Brasher as the 'least talented' Olympic gold medal winner he had ever come across.

Shirley leapt eloquently to Brasher's defence. In a reply sent on 25 April 2003, she rebutted the charge that this man was the 'least talented' of Olympic gold medal winners:

> I can't agree. Once you are talking in terms of 'world class' – like Olympic finalists or world champions in any sport – every competitor has a natural flair and ability. You cannot achieve that level without it, but natural 'flair' is fickle and counts for little unless there is mental toughness and ability to back it up. It is the mental strength that will decide and therein lays the 'talent'.
>
> Some dictionary definitions of talent actually define it as 'high mental ability'. Above all, sporting top class talent has to 'deliver' on the day under intense pressure. Chris had in abundance all the 'D's' of mental toughness – desire, determination, dedication and discipline – giving the confidence to 'deliver', and that is talent in top class sport.
>
> He chose the best event for his physique and natural talent as well. I think it is a very 'British' attitude to think that 'flair' – which gives an attractive and easy style, but no guarantee of withstanding 'pressure' – is more vital than mental strength in winning at high level in any sport. Maybe it's why we often fail to develop young potential in Britain – we encourage the wrong kind of 'talent'.

The letter to which she was responding had been sent by an author, former MP and, in the days before he went to jail, once-upon-a-time athlete – Jeffrey Archer. Shirley Brasher thought Archer had completely missed the point. What made the man she married unbeatable was that he could never resist a challenge – that's why he won, she said.

Brasher's early challenges, Shirley believed, were thrust upon him. The challenge of a childhood as a shy, bewildered schoolboy struggling with life in a classroom which he hated and which brought on a crippling stutter; the challenge of feeling a fraud when he played a bit part in Bannister's assault on the four-minute mile; the challenge of winning Olympic gold when his track record would write him off as a no-hoper.

Later, said Shirley, Chris Brasher invented, contrived and then rose to his own challenges. When he returned from New York in 1979 after having run the marathon, Brasher posed the challenge: 'Couldn't London stage such an event?' By 1981 he had answered that challenge. Although many considered the race a passing curiosity, a back-of-the-envelope job, within a handful of years the London Marathon had become one of the greatest public sporting events the world has ever seen.

There were more challenges, jostling like runners in a crowded race, each one – big and small – elbowing for Brasher's attention. Skiing across Scotland; the glove-like seductiveness and lightness of the Brasher Boot; the climbing of a mountain; the saving of a meadow; the fortune that flowed from the sports stores; the profits poured into charity that might save the wilderness he worshipped; the racehorses that he dreamt might win. With hard work and the will to triumph Brasher convinced himself that no challenge was unconquerable, he would barge his way through them all.

An old friend, Michael Davie, was athletics correspondent of the *Observer* at the time of the Melbourne Olympics in 1956, and wrote of Brasher's victory:

> Asked why he, a sensible fellow with plenty of interests, had gone on running in the first place after having had a comparatively undistinguished athletics career at Cambridge, Brasher said that everyone else seemed to be packing it in and he thought he would go on and see what happened.
>
> Then, after he became involved in personal and athletic relationships with Bannister and Chataway, and especially after the four-minute mile, he became really committed. He began to resent his role as the third man, at being introduced as the person

who helped Bannister with the four-minute mile or as the friend of the celebrated Chataway.

He became aware, too, that the ability to run faster over a certain distance than anyone else on earth might be due less to natural athletic ability than to the kind of will the runner possessed. Brasher said he found the most interesting thing about human beings to be the degree of control they can develop over themselves . . . How do you react when you are lost on a mountainside, alone and in fog?

It is perhaps because he thinks like this and is this sort of person that Brasher has been capable of producing his best on the right day, whereas other English athletes, who in a formal sense are very much better runners than he is, have been unable to do so.

Brasher had realised after this Olympic gold that he had the ability to take the fable of the hare and the tortoise and transform it into unexpected victory by using application, experience and above all hard work.

'Winning that gold medal,' said Brasher, 'was a vital part of my education. In part it formed my character. It made me believe that if I set my mind to something I could do it. A man's reach should exceed his grasp – and mine always did.'

1

The Shy Boy with a Stammer

*'Half the world is composed of people who have something
to say and can't, and the other half who have nothing to say and
keep on saying it!'*

Robert Frost

C HRIS BRASHER COULD never tell how his stammer started.
He always said he couldn't remember. Something to do
with his childhood, he would reckon. He believed it came
on when he was moved back to England after he had spent the first
seven years of his life with his family in the colonies.

Christopher William Brasher was born in Georgetown, British
Guyana, on 21 August 1928 to Katie and William Kenneth Brasher.
The third of four children, he lived his early childhood in colonial
outposts of the British Empire including Baghdad and Jerusalem,
where his father (usually known by his second name, Ken) was a
pioneer in radio and telephone communications, an electrical engineer
who had worked for Marconi and then for the Colonial Office.

The eldest child in the family was Peter, nearly four years older
than Christopher. Next came Wendy. Christopher was the third and
his younger sister Margaret was born two and a half years later.
The family moved around from country to country, but everywhere they were cocooned in the self-confident club of expatriates
and servants, insulated from the currents sweeping around them

that emanated from the less privileged populations whom they governed and controlled. Ken Brasher, Christopher's father, had been born into a land where British technology was accepted as the best – and in bringing his engineering skills to the colonies he was part of the machine that had made men like him the masters of what was regarded as the greatest empire in the world.

During the topsy-turvy years of his childhood Brasher moved home and country frequently. At this stage the constant changes of location never made the infant Christopher, or Kiki as he called himself, feel insecure or rootless. Surrounded by his family and living in the luxury of colonial splendour, the children found it fun. Christopher's younger sister Margaret was born in Baghdad, but her earliest memories are of life in Jerusalem. She remembers the excitement of the Brasher household chickens being grabbed and stolen by a shadowy passing Arab. Each home offered the promise of a new beginning and, potentially, a new adventure. Brasher, like his brother and sisters, simply accepted that the constant moving was down to his father's career.

After their transfer to Jerusalem, the family returned to England when Brasher was seven in 1935, leaving his father, Ken, to complete his work in the Holy Land. Ken was awarded the CBE, ostensibly for relaying the bells of Jerusalem on Christmas Eve 1936 live to the BBC, but there are those who think that he may have been involved in intelligence work.

Some who recall Ken Brasher say he was gruff and distant – a man of few words and short temper. 'But when he said something,' says Margaret, 'you listened. I was slightly in awe of him.' Margaret has fond memories of her father. She remembers helping him tie tomatoes with string in the garden because his hands were not nimble enough to do it.

It was Christopher's mother Katie – known as Kitty – who set the tone at home. Moyra Bannister, wife of Sir Roger, says that Kitty had drive and charisma and was able to instil unshakable self-confidence in her first-born son, Peter.

The children were educated at home, taught to read and write by their mother and occasional tutors, but right from the start Christopher did not enjoy the same robust health as his older brother. To Margaret he seemed healthy enough, but their mother would plead with a procession of doctors to diagnose and treat the problems the boy had with his chest, which manifested themselves in a constant and irritating cough. From Chris's childhood his mother was concerned with what appeared to be his asthma or hay fever, was almost obsessed by his cough.

Home, for young Chris Brasher, was vaguely somewhere back in England. And wherever he and his family wandered he was never far from a world which had been 'Made in England'. The power and the influence exerted by the British made it appear that they had invented much of what he knew as a child. They had devised, and appeared to be the best at, all the great games – rugby, soccer, cricket, golf, horse racing, mountaineering, skiing. They had developed radio and television, tourism, the Boy Scouts, postage stamps. Their heroes had explored the far reaches of the Earth, and they had won the war to end all wars against the Germans.

But perhaps the frequency with which his family moved, and the uneasy feeling that home was somewhere far off, had something to do with the fact that Brasher later in life could remember little of his early childhood and spoke only rarely of it. 'I paid the penalty for that sort of nomadic life when my mother came back to England in 1935,' Brasher remembered. 'To all intents and purposes I was part of a one-parent family as my father was still working in Palestine.'

The Brasher family moved first to Bristol and, at the age of seven, Christopher stepped into a land where Stanley Baldwin was Prime Minister and street parties up and down the land celebrated the Silver Jubilee of King George V and Queen Mary. The follow - ing year the king died and the Berlin Olympics were dominated by the black athlete Jesse Owens, both through his prowess on the track and his undermining of Hitler's Aryan fantasy. As seemed inevitable for a colonial child returning from the Empire in the thirties, Brasher was packed off at the age of eight to Oakley Hall Preparatory School on the outskirts of Cirencester.

'I was sent to boarding school which I thought at the time was barbaric,' he said later. 'Suddenly, not only had I shifted country but was moved from my family environment to a school where I practically knew no one. I was desperately unhappy. I was feeling insecure and scared and I'm sure that that's what started me stammering. The one thing that's forever engraved in my memory is having to endure morning school assemblies.' The headmaster, remembered Brasher, would throw chalk at the boys and shout at them if they said they couldn't do anything.

'At these assemblies we had to take it in turns to read verses from the Bible. I used to sit there on a bench shivering in my shorts, praying that it wouldn't be my turn this week or tomorrow and realising that a tumbrel was getting nearer and nearer. Any other boy could read a verse in thirty seconds but it would take me five minutes to stutter and stammer my way through it. I used to scour that Bible looking for the shortest verse. I can remember it was "Jesus wept." I might just have managed that.

'Certain letters were worse, like Ws and Ps. It was sheer agony. My stutter was extremely noticeable and it is a measure of how bad it was that from the age of eight my mother took me to see every quack in the business who promised a cure. One of these so-called doctors told me always to carry a small pencil and to twiddle it in my fingers to help me relax. There was lots of advice on breathing. Another told me to stand in a room by myself practising saying PPP and WWW. None of these things worked of course.

'The amazing thing was that I didn't suffer any bullying as a result. In fact my stutter didn't seem to manifest itself nearly as much with my friends and it was only when there was an adult around or at a formal occasion. What did work starting to reduce my stammer was achieving a good position, some status in the school. In my case, that came through sport.'

It was little wonder that the short, shy boy who turned up at prep

school was afflicted by a stammer. Oakley Hall was a small establishment of some fifty boys when Chris Brasher went there. Its
prospectus advertised the benefits of fresh air for children and easy
train connections to London from Cirencester station.

Quentin Letts, now a journalist and broadcaster with the BBC
and the *Daily Mail*, and a grandson of its then headmaster,
remembers Oakley Hall well. 'It was run by my grandfather C.F.C.
(Francis) Letts and his indomitable wife Eveleen, an intellectual
who had been one of the early female undergraduates at Oxford.
Eveleen Letts was a magistrate and a power on the town council.
She took few prisoners. C.F.C. Letts (practically everyone used his
initials or referred to him as Major) was a cricket-mad classicist and
co-author of the Latin text book Letts and Jackson. He was a
subaltern on the western front in the Great War in the Rifle Brigade
and a kindly, slightly eccentric fellow.'

Boys at the school used to tell, or embroider, stories about their
headmaster. One such legend revolved around his habit of sneez-
ing with great ceremony and deafening volume. On one occasion,
during the Second World War, when he was accompanying
London-bound boys to and from Paddington station at the start
and end of term, he sneezed under the station's echoing roof. Such
was the din, according to his pupils, that people scattered to take
cover fearing the onset of an air raid. The headmaster was a heavy
smoker and his suits often had cigarette burns on them. He was
moustachioed, bespectacled – a great believer in ripping yarns, religion and sport.

Oakley Hall was formerly a grand Victorian villa. Its pillared
drawing room – known as Big School – was the assembly area. This
was where the boys would have 'Morning Call Over' and where
Brasher lived in torment at the prospect of reading the Bible aloud.
The fireplace at one end seemed to stretch from wall to wall, and
would be stoked high in the winter; here, the boys, nearly always in
shorts, would warm their bare knees. Children normally arrived at
the age of seven or eight. The boys first went into the baby

dormitory and progressed through various other dormitories. 'Baby dorm' was next to the matron's day room, where malt and vitamin supplements would be dispensed after breakfast to those boys whose parents had paid for them.

The malt had the consistency of melted glue and a distinctive smell of hops which boys from Oakley Hall can still remember, accompanied for those who grew up in the baby dorm by the odour of Dettol. The matron's room also had a roaring fire and she was a dynamo of energy, sewing, darning and keeping up a flow of non-stop chatter to the children. Homesick boys could blink back their tears here and pull themselves together in readiness to battle through another day.

Shirley Brasher, Chris's widow, remembers well how challenging life was for children of that era: 'Boys in the prep and public schools in the 1930s and 40s were tested and marked for every subject on a regular basis. Often the results were read out weekly and pinned up on a notice board for all to read. In sport, too, it was always very clear who was thought good, bad or indifferent – academically or through sport every boy needed to meet the challenge of somehow securing a special identity that might pick him out from his fellows.'

Oakley Hall's playing fields were devoted to ball games. The boys played organised sports every day except Sunday. In keeping with the educational ethos of the day, it seemed essential to find ways of exercising these young men with their surging hormones, to find other outlets for their energy. Sport tired the boys out, gave a focus to the day and certainly was given as much importance as any academic lesson. For many, sport was a way to give boys an identity. In a small school there are not very many pupils to pick from and soon enough even Brasher was selected for the cricket team, the soccer team and the rugby team. But the big event was the annual sports day held in summer on the paddock field – a well turned out arena with a circular running track, its lanes defined by white limewash and its boundaries by little flags.

There was a high jump, a long jump and an obstacle course, as well as a handicap race in which the school's slowest runners were given an advantage. All the boys took part in what the school called a 'steeplechase' – a point-to-point cross-country race which was refined into the Olympic event that Brasher was to tackle later. There were relay races for the houses – Nelson, Drake, Wellington and Wolfe – and individual races for the 100 yards. There was a competition for throwing the cricket ball. At the end of the day, cups were handed out by the headmaster to the applause of attending parents. The ever attentive Kitty, still worried about her young son's cough, was a regular visitor at sports day, and Brasher, the small, shy, nervous, even alien boy, threw himself with gusto into sport of any kind.

Brasher's older brother had been sent to Oakley Hall too. Brasher major, as he was always referred to, went to there in 1933, but he overlapped with his brother for just one term. In 1936, while Brasher minor was still in the baby dorm, Peter left to go to Clifton College in Bristol and a career as a doctor. Academically, Peter had done well. He seemed to have no interest in sports but his reports were held up as an example to Christopher. When Peter turned up at Clifton College he was so bright that he was moved up a year. It was an example Christopher found it tough to match.

Nonetheless, the school magazine, which was often dominated by reports on the school's sports, makes countless references to the athletic achievements of the younger Brasher. Here, for instance, is his profile as a soccer player featured in the Oakley Hall magazine of Christmas and Lent term 1939–40: 'C.W. Brasher, inside left, a keen and determined worker, excellent in the field but has no kick, could not pass with his left foot.' And again, in the same magazine: 'C.W. Brasher wing three quarter, spirited player, handicapped by size, a useful scrum half.'

Brasher was also keen on boxing, where he found some avenue for his energy and the signs of aggression that were prompted by his size and stammer. Fighting as a lightweight and beaten in the final in the Lent term of 1940, Brasher still manages to win some praise: 'Most elusive, his footwork is first class.'

The Easter term of 1940 finds Brasher fighting as a featherweight and once again the report is encouraging. 'Brasher was quicker and perhaps produced the most scientific display of the day,' it says. 'Brasher was superior in speed, the footwork was excellent and he had a good left.' But, even so, the diminutive Brasher was beaten again and again; and although he often made the final he was having a hard time of it.

Brasher also tried his hand at rugby football. The magazine's report from the Christmas and Lent term 1938–9 notes that, playing wing three-quarter, he is 'very small but keen and plucky and was always up with the ball. Should be a useful player one day.' By the summer of 1941 Brasher was playing cricket. Again, this time in the handwriting of Major Letts, comes the judgement: 'Brasher is a promising bat and an active fielder but his catching is poor.'

In time these sporting achievements brought the young Brasher enough kudos to be made a monitor, a sort of prefect, and in the summer term of 1941 he was made junior prefect in charge of day boys. What excited the young Brasher, though, was nothing to do with being promoted to monitor but the seductive thrills of adventure and the outdoor life. From the start Brasher loved scouting and was an enthusiastic member of the troop at Oakley Hall. Most of the activity of scouting – the pitching of tents, the making of fires, the cooking, the wide games – took place in a small, heavily wooded area just beyond the paddock field and known as 'the wilderness'.

For the rest of his life the term 'the wilderness' was replete with meaning for Brasher. He wrote about it and talked about it, and he never lost the romance of camping in the open air. 'Here's where I learned to light a fire at school,' he would say. 'We were only allowed two matches.' The wilderness was normally out of bounds and right beside it was a swimming pool – not so much a pool as a hole, a gloomy affair hidden by old laurel bushes. Swimming was conducted here without trunks, and sometimes on hot summer nights the boys would be allowed to run down from their tents or their dormitories to have a short swim before returning to their beds.

Brasher played his team games with more enthusiasm than skill; it was in running that you could more accurately chart his progress. In the summer term of 1937 there is the first recorded appearance of Christopher Brasher in a track and field event. He ran in the obstacle race in the under-10 age group. The race was actually won by Dick Letts, the son of the headmaster, who had invited Brasher to stay with him in the half-term holiday, but second in that obstacle race came Brasher.

In the summer term of 1938, Brasher got his first recorded victory in a competition. Once again it was the under-10 obstacle race, but this time Brasher won. In the school handicap in that same year he came third and by 1939 managed to win the under-12 obstacle race; in 1940 he managed third in the 100 yards.

When sports day was over the children disappeared for a couple of days for their summer half-term break. Boys who lived overseas were normally sent to their friends' homes. Sometimes, as sports day drew to a close, parents would wander around Oakley Hall's formal gardens admiring the weeping elm and the evergreens that included a large cedar whose canopy would keep you dry in the fiercest of downpours, or the magnificent mulberry tree from whose dark fruit Eveleen Letts would make a sloppy jam.

The house itself had a circular front lawn surrounded by a gravel path not unlike a small running track. The boys used to play games of tag in the gardens, running around the gravel path. They were always running everywhere and forever being scolded and told to slow down. When they paused for a moment to catch their breath the distinctive sound to be heard was of pigeons cooing. The school tuck shop was a small wooden shed over which loomed an impressive horse chestnut tree. Outside the chapel there was a cannon, over which the children would clamber, reliving some of the great battles of the Empire.

The school chapel, built after the Great War as the first memorial chapel in the country, is still standing. Its pews were built to suit short legs, children's knee sizes, and it still smells of furniture polish and probity. Oakley Hall's religion was steeped in the Book of Common Prayer and the Authorised Version of the Bible, with the boys turning to say the Creed towards the altar. The old headmaster would take the service in his Cambridge gown. This towering figure who terrified Brasher so much seems to have been an inspirational and effective teacher. His experience of life in the trenches had given him a generally benevolent view of childhood which he seemed to pass on to his pupils.

The big breakthrough for Brasher came with the weather. Brasher always said that he discovered he could run quite well during the winter of 1940, when he was twelve years old. Certainly the winter of 1939–40 was one of the coldest on record, with persistent chill weather that lasted from 22 December right through to January. Temperatures were the lowest for at least 100 years in many parts of Europe. There were strange wartime theories that this cold spell was caused by the intense military activity in the North Sea, which was responsible for disturbing the sea temperature and therefore the climate.

On the night of 23 January a temperature of minus 23.3° C was recorded at Rhayader in Powys, a record low for that date. The Thames was frozen for eight miles between Teddington and Sunbury and ice covered stretches of the Mersey, the Humber and the Severn. At Folkestone and Southampton harbours were iced over. Central London was below freezing for a week and there was skating on the Serpentine on thick ice.

The snowfall lasted until 29 January. In Cirencester, freezing rain fell for two days and nights in temperatures of between minus 2 and minus 4° C. Telegraph poles and wires were broken, unable to cope with the weight of the ice. Birds were unable to fly because ice had built up on their wings. Roads and pavements were transformed into treacherous skating rinks.

All this was faithfully recorded in the Oakley Hall school magazine. Here is the entry for Christmas and Lent Terms 1939/40:

> The silver thaw or ice rain as some people call it which occurred on the night of January 27th will not easily be forgotten. All night long branches could be heard breaking and crashing to the ground and when we woke it was to find outdoor movement practically impossible owing to ice. Roads and paths were littered with fallen boughs. Every blade of grass, every branch, every strand of wire carried a thick icicle which tinkled musically at every movement through them. It was only possible to go to chapel at all by the upper route and even then it was far from easy . . .
>
> We did however sustain one loss. All the goldfish, grown fat and well liked in the twenty years, in which they had lived in the fountain, were frozen to death. We miss them very much and so far we have been unable to replace them.

It was not until 4 March that games could resume. By the time that day came, Brasher had made a remarkable discovery – he had unearthed something that he could be good at. His size didn't matter, the fact that he couldn't kick a ball or catch didn't matter, what mattered when the ice came was that in long-distance runs he could win, he could beat the others.

The boys, in an attempt to burn off their excess energy, were forced out to run on the icy paths and roads – most of them reluctantly, their teeth chattering, their fears of falling making them run hesitantly. In his first long-distance race, over about three miles, Brasher hung on to the bigger boy in front. For the first time in his life he experienced the quivering flicker of triumph. He came home second, beaming with pride. It had seemed easy. It was a thrill that was to stay with him for ever. He had, that March day in 1940, fallen in love with cross-country running.

It worked wonders for his stammer. This cure would succeed

where all the quacks had failed. Along with this, Brasher had started to discover that reading about his heroes could give him even more encouragement and inspiration.

Brasher made good use of the library, particularly at times like this bitter winter, whenever the weather was bad, or when the pupils would be incarcerated because some epidemic had broken out at the school. Here Brasher could escape into a world of make-believe, a world that was inhabited by his heroes, and where he could play the hero himself. He was picking up volumes by Dumas, Buchan, Henty and Thomas Hughes. He'd read and re-read *The Thirty-nine Steps*, *Bulldog Drummond* and *Tom Brown's Schooldays*. His favourite hero was Richard Hannay, John Buchan's great creation. He relished the thought that like himself, Hannay had been born in the colonies, in Hannay's case Rhodesia. He admired the fact that Hannay was an all-action hero with a stiff upper lip and a miraculous knack for getting himself out of sticky situations.

But what most excited the young Brasher were the comics that were passed round from hand to hand at that time by the boys. These were not the picture-strip comics of the post-war generation; heavy on text, they carried full-length stories. With their stories of overcoming great odds, they stimulated a fantasy dream world and became highly addictive to the young Brasher.

The best of these comics were based almost entirely on glorifying the British Empire. They were incredibly patriotic; there were countless examples of British heroes overcoming fearsome odds. Here the sportsmen and athletes would journey to the ends of the earth and prove that Britons reigned supreme. Their heroes were clichéd but they certainly stimulated the patriotic imagination. The target readership was essentially Boy Scouts with attitude; young men who could somehow make do and improvise, overcome any hardship, rout the opposition, take on any challenge, and do it all essentially by fair means not foul.

As George Orwell wrote in an essay in *Horizon* magazine,

It is probable that many people who would consider themselves extremely sophisticated and advanced are actually carrying through life an imaginary background which they acquired in childhood. If that is so, the two-penny weeklies are of the deepest importance. Here is the stuff that is read somewhere between the ages of twelve and eighteen by a very large proportion, perhaps an actual majority of English boys. And there is being pumped into them the conviction that the major problems of our time do not exist, that there is nothing wrong with the *laissez-faire* capitalism, that foreigners are unimportant comics and that the British Empire is a sort of charity concern that will last forever.

Memories of the British Empire may be fading fast, but these comic-book heroes never die. They certainly lived on in the imagination of Chris Brasher. Decades later he used to remember in vivid detail the details of their fictional adventures he had read at Oakley Hall and at Rugby School. One of these heroes was known to the boys as 'Wilson of *The Wizard*'. Brasher used to speak fondly of Wilson, whose exploits fascinated him and whose character inspired him.

'Wilson' was a boys' comic strip about the adventures of William Wilson. It was originally published in DC Thomson's *Wizard*, but other episodes appeared in the *Hornet* and *Hotspur* comics. The stories, which made an indelible mark on Brasher, featured a series of unlikely achievements that Wilson seemed to perform with effortless superiority. Wilson the athlete would leap from the crowd to run a four-minute mile; Wilson the climber would be the first person to get to the top of Mount Everest, reaching the summit ahead of a German team to claim the honour for Great Britain, and, of course, doing it without the aid of oxygen.

The fictional Wilson was apparently born in Yorkshire in 1795 and settled on Axmoor in the West Country. What appealed to the young Brasher, already in love with cross-country running, was that Wilson lived an extremely simple life in a cave on a diet of rabbits, fish, nuts and berries and washed in fresh stream water every morning. Wilson could be spotted chasing deer and foxes just for the hell of it. He had befriended a hermit who gave him the secret of eternal life – a potion made from herbs, which endowed him with great athletic strength. The hermit told him that the secret of great endurance was to slow down your pulse and increase the capacity of your lungs.

Wilson's running outfit was an all-over black body suit and he always ran barefoot. The fictional hero's exploits, however, extended well beyond athletics. When the England cricket team were tragically killed in a plane crash en route to Australia, Wilson was flown out to captain the side and led them to a glorious Ashes triumph. On another occasion he got involved in a bare-knuckle boxing challenge and had to beat the US champion, as well as a sinister plot by the Mafia. He romped up the Great Pyramid of Cheops in eight minutes and vaulted over a twenty-foot prison wall using only a flag pole.

But above all, Wilson was a product of wartime Britain when people were yearning for super-human heroes. Like the pilots, the 'Few', in Winston Churchill's phrase, who patrolled the skies to fight and die for their land, Wilson exemplified British grit and the stiff upper lip. His make-believe golden era as an athlete began in 1938 at the British Championships, when the real-life Brasher was just ten years old. Wilson, the fictional champion, reeled off laps of fifty-seven seconds in the mile and broke the tape at three minutes forty-eight seconds. Nor was he just a middle-distance runner. He once defeated an American arch-rival in the US decathlon championships in Philadelphia, winning all ten events.

For the young Christopher Brasher, of course, the marathon was an event that he could only dream about. He had read true stories of those who had run the distance, like Dorando Pietri, the legendary hero who had collapsed and nearly died at the 1908 London Olympics. But the fictional Wilson of *The Wizard* won this race with ease at the 'Athens Olympics' in two hours twenty minutes, despite starting late.

Brasher was to have many heroes. But all of them embodied some facet of Wilson – barefoot, running in black, living in the wilds, doing the impossible with effortless ease. As the teenage Brasher flogged his way through the fields and lanes, determined to be the school's best cross-country runner, it was Wilson who sent his legs and his dreams spinning.

Inevitably, for the adolescent readers of *The Wizard*, Wilson became a Spitfire pilot. He was apparently killed during the Battle of Britain in 1940 but he swam thirty miles to the Dutch side of the English Channel, where he found the clothes of a dead RAF officer on the beach and borrowed his identity to avoid unnecessary press intrusion.

When Brasher left Oakley Hall at the age of thirteen he didn't follow his brother Peter to Clifton College. Less academically gifted than his brother, Chris Brasher departed the school with a much more important legacy. He had discovered that his couple of matches could ignite the flames of his passion both for running and for modelling himself on the heroes who could achieve remarkable things. Not only had Oakley Hall succeeded where the quack doctors had failed in getting rid of his crippling stammer, it had also enabled him to discover what made his heart sing and what came easily to him in life.

Decades later Brasher would say, 'When I tell people that I used to have a really bad stammer they say that explains why I am so aggressive.' Oakley Hall, the long-vanished boarding school, had managed to turn out a boy who had learned to channel his aggression, to dream the dreams of a breed, equally long vanished, that was born for Empire and action, and whose obsession for school sports would help him survive in the tough world of Rugby School.

2

Rugby and the Challenge of the Crick

'Champions aren't made in the gyms . . . Champions are made from something they have deep inside them – a desire, a dream, a vision.'

Muhammad Ali

HAVING STUMBLED ACROSS the key to status at Oakley Hall Preparatory School, where he made a few friends, lost a little of his terror of overpowering adults and all but freed himself of his stutter, it must have been a shock for the young Christopher Brasher to find himself yanked out of that cosy world to step into the cold, towering grandeur of Rugby School.

Brasher minor went to Rugby in 1942. He took the Common Entrance exam to get in, though what may have made the choice of Rugby irresistible was that its headmaster was a friend of the Brasher family. 'The headmaster at Rugby school was Hugh Lyon,' says Margaret Brasher. 'He was known to the family as "Uncle". I think he was related distantly on my mother's side. We used to spend time at his seaside house – aunts, uncles, cousins; we all used to pile in.' Margaret describes the holiday home in Fairbourne, north Wales, as 'very primitive'.

When Brasher started at Rugby the senior boys could not wait to get out and fight before the war against Germany was over. But the thirteen-year-old new boy's thoughts were on seeing how he might survive all those new rules and new routines, all the new, anonymous faces. Hampered by poor eyesight, lack of confidence and height, asthma and that persistent cough, he had found a refuge in cross-country running. It had worked in Cirencester, but could it work here?

For his first few painful days he would wander through those stony corridors, with echoes ringing that would remind him of the homesickness he thought he'd left behind in Oakley Hall. Here, once again, he was in a strange environment where he knew nobody, where he had to find his feet again. Rugby was founded in 1567 by Laurence Sheriff, who had made a fortune supplying groceries to Queen Elizabeth I. One of the nine great English public schools, proudly defined by the Public Schools Act of 1868, it was among just a handful of such schools to boast of producing the ideal of the Victorian gentleman, and one of the first to recognise that it was creating a blueprint for the men who were to run the British Empire at its height.

Its most famous and innovative headmaster, Thomas Arnold, set the tone for generations at the school. The novel *Tom Brown's Schooldays*, written by Thomas Hughes, a Rugby old boy, immortalised Dr Arnold and the school, and was to influence many thousands of boys who dreamed that they could share Tom Brown's adventures and grow up to be a hero like him. The main difference from Oakley Hall for Brasher was that Rugby was a huge school, big in reputation and history, and it wasn't going to be easy to make his mark. Brasher soon made a decision that he would turn his back on team games where you needed an eye for a ball – cricket and rugby – to concentrate on the two sports where he had found some initial success, boxing and cross-country running.

Boxing was an individual sport and would provide an outlet for his aggression. He was a plucky fighter, as all his prep school write-ups confirmed. But it was in cross-country running that he felt he could really make a mark. He showed promise from the start. He had what the headmaster at Oakley Hall had identified as 'pluck', and it was clear from his contemporaries that he had an ability to train.

As a member of School House, located in Rugby's main buildings completed in 1815 around the old quadrangle, the thirteen-year-old entered the very heart of the school. Brasher's contemporaries remember him as making little impression apart from his enthusiasm for cross-country running. He was very much a loner. Some boys at public schools are hero-worshipped but not, it seemed, Brasher. He didn't shine academically or socially. Cross-country running seemed to fulfil him. But even when he had established himself as a member of the 'first eight' – a team consisting of the best eight runners in the school – he did not emerge as a natural leader of men. It seemed, even by this age, that Brasher had learned a degree of independence and a little detach_ ment. He appeared to know his own mind and embrace it.

But in cross-country running, the school magazine, *The Meteor*, charted his progress continually. His first efforts after going up to the school in 1942 are recorded in a notebook entitled 'School House Runs 1937–49'. There, in fine handwriting which makes more than a nod to copperplate, a pupil at Rugby, N.V.E. Seymer, recorded every run in which the boys of School House competed. Seymer himself added a touching and charmingly modest footnote to his meticulous reports of the season in 1943.

'Lastly,' he wrote, 'I must be the first holder of this book not to get even a fifteen.' (The school ran two teams of eight, so Seymer didn't even make the second team.) 'I'm sorry about this but I think you can blame earache.'

On Thursday 1 April 1943, five days before the end of term, Seymer reported that the boys managed to find an hour or so to squeeze in their handicap. 'Even then,' he wrote, 'the school was allowed to see *Desert Victory* at The Plaza at 1 o'clock, and lunch was 12.15 so we couldn't start the run until 4 o'clock. An hour is ample for the whole race.' Seymer managed to get a final entry list of thirty runners. The day was windy but fortunately not wet, he noted. The event was run in the traditional Rugby way – a hare and hounds chase, modelled on hunting.

In the early nineteenth century cross-country was practised in all public and many preparatory schools in Britain and its origins linger on in the names of many British athletics clubs – like the Thames Hare and Hounds – that were founded in the nineteenth century. The course was set by paper-chasing. A few runners, the 'hares', would have a start on the bulk of the field, the 'hounds', and lay a 'scent' by scattering a paper trail behind them which the hounds would follow. Racing would take place between the hares and the hounds and between the hounds themselves.

Brasher's running was faithfully recorded by Seymer, and his times in the cross-country handicap races were good. 'Brasher's run was exceedingly good for a person of his tiny stature and a new boy last term. Pim is also new but much older, over 15, Brasher won quite comfortably although I put him back 4 minutes,' reported Seymer. 'I'm very glad he did as he has practised far harder than anyone else and been over the course three times beforehand.' Concluding this report on the 1943 cross-country running season, Seymer notes, 'There is considerable talent at the bottom of the House. I expect Brasher will one day be writing in this book.'

By 1944 Brasher was employing his cross-country stamina on the track, and on sports day he had finished fourth in the Under-16½ mile. In the spring of the following year Brasher was still trying to make his way as a boxer but although he made the finals of the bantamweight competition, he was beaten by P.G. Hurst; the school magazine account of that fight says, 'Brasher fought back hard and well but Hurst was the winner from the beginning.' By 1945 Brasher had abandoned boxing in favour of running. The school magazine, *The Meteor*, picks him out as one of the characters of the running eight with a hint of things to come. 'C.W. Brasher has quickly established himself as a most determined and gifted runner. If his performance improves as his legs grow he should become a record breaker.'

Brasher tackled the track again on sports day in 1945. This time he ran the mile in the open class and came third in a race that was won by G.T.E. Wilson in a record-breaking 4 minutes 35½ seconds. Again Brasher gets a mention among the April 1946 characters of the eight: 'C.W. Brasher, Schoolhouse, a strong elegant runner with plenty of staying power and an unorthodox but easy arm action. His ability has brought him to the front in every race.'

Brasher would remember few of the luminaries who addressed the boys at Rugby. They bored him. But there was one visitor to the school that he never forgot. His first memory of seeing sporting greatness was in the form of Sydney Wooderson.

Wooderson was a record breaker, a giant of an athlete, though he certainly did not look the part. Some commentators described him as looking less an athlete than 'a man who looks as if he has been mugged for his ration book'. But as Brasher was to learn, looks can be deceptive. Sydney Wooderson, dubbed The Mighty Atom, was an English athlete whose career was at its peak in the 1930s and 1940s. He was one of Britain's greatest middle-distance runners and had an amazing sprint finish. Slightly built and bespectacled, his appearance disguised immense reserves of strength and an overwhelming turn of speed.

Wooderson always ran in the black running vest and shorts of Blackheath Harriers. His effortless speed over the mile must certainly have aroused memories of the amazing Wilson, who in the comic-book fiction surpassed Wooderson's mile record just a year after he had set it. In fact, Wooderson set the world mile record of 4:06.4 at London's Motspur Park on 28 August 1937. This record stood for nearly five years.

Wooderson shared with Brasher the handicap of poor eyesight, which ruled him out of active service during the Second World War, though he experienced his share of danger in the National Fire Service during the Blitz and served later in the Royal Electrical and Mechanical Engineers as a radar operator. In an attempt to keep wartime morale high, Wooderson would visit schools and sports grounds to speak and give an exhibition of his running prowess.

What most impressed schoolboy Brasher was that even on the track, Wooderson looked a most unlikely champion. Bespectacled, slight and only five feet six inches tall with hair immaculately groomed, he looked as if the merest breath of wind might blow him over, but his long stride enabled him to outkick the best with an explosion of pace in the final lap. When representing Britain as an international on the track he was rarely defeated. Wooderson was shy and unassuming in public. He spent most of his leave during the war racing around the country. His status by then was so iconic that, says author Richard Holt in *Sport and the British*, 'The small, thin, dowdy, bespectacled man in Blackheath's all-black strip represented the courage and endurance that defeated Hitler's armies.'

Wooderson was the epitome of the suburban commuter, a solicitor's clerk. Brasher took one look at the puny figure, his hair Brylcreemed back, his short-sighted eyes peering through thick horn-rimmed wire glasses, and declared: 'If he can be a champion, so can I.'

It wasn't the only moment of inspiration for the boy who had glimpsed what he might achieve through running. Ever since William Webb Ellis allegedly picked up a football and ran with it in 1823, the game of rugby football had been the most famous export of the English public school. But in Brasher's eyes, Rugby's contribution to sport was far more profound. Besides being the birthplace of England's rugby football, the school was also a guiding impulse behind the modern Olympic Games. Rugby School was a driving inspiration to the man who founded the modern Olympics, the Paris-born Pierre Frédy, Baron de Coubertin.

Coubertin was first and foremost an educationalist. In refounding the Olympics his goal was to improve education all over the world through sport. He had originally despaired of the condition of his country's youth during the Franco-Prussian War of 1870 and was determined to do something about it. What better, he believed, than to model his remedy on the great public schools of Britain? The idea of using sport to transform the lives of young people, a principle that was later to be enshrined in the Olympic charter, is rooted in the grounds of Rugby School, and in the ideas and ideals of its legendary headmaster Thomas Arnold. Coubertin first read *Tom Brown's Schooldays* in translation at the age of twelve. It was said the book never left his side. Forty years after Arnold's death, Coubertin made a pilgrimage to Rugby to see for himself what he had read about in the pages of Thomas Hughes's novel.

Anything to do with sport, and in particular running, fascinated Brasher, but he still loved to pore over books in the library that sang the praises of heroes who had won the British Empire through battles and cunning. Brasher was hooked on volumes by Eric Shipton, tales of Scott and the Antarctic, and one of his favourite books was *Sweet Thames Run Softly* by Robert Gibbings – a travelogue which later inspired an expedition on the River Thames.

He was still very much into the derring-do of adventure books and his favourites remained the tales of John Buchan. His hero, Major Richard Hannay, provided much later in life a framework for the make-believe world that oiled the workings of many expeditions with Brasher's friends. By 1945 Brasher was ploughing his way through *War and Peace*, for which he wrote a book review for the school magazine, and André Maurois' biography of Disraeli.

One volume in which Brasher took great pleasure and interest was *Narrow Boat*, written during the war by L.T.C. Rolt and published in 1944. The biographer of many great civil engineering figures, including Isambard Kingdom Brunel and Thomas Telford, Tom Rolt was also one of the pioneers of leisure cruising and an enthusiast of both vintage cars and heritage railways. Brasher read *Narrow Boat* when he was seventeen and its influence was both clear and long-lasting.

Brasher tramped the canals near Rugby that Rolt had written so romantically about, and here he first toyed with the idea of becoming a civil engineer, noting that Rolt had started his life as an engineering apprentice. In *Narrow Boat* too, Rolt sowed the seeds of Brasher's campaigns for the environment – fighting for a past that was being rapidly despoiled by advanced technological development.

Books and films fired Brasher's imagination, and anyone who could take on a challenge inspired him. One of his contemporary heroes during those years at Rugby was Douglas Bader, perhaps the most famous Second World War fighter pilot Britain has known. This was the man who overcame the loss of both legs to command a fighter squadron during the Battle of Britain. Shot down and imprisoned by the Germans, his numerous escape attempts provided inspiration for thousands of schoolboys. Yet there was a darker side to this great British inspirational figure.

According to later biographers like S.P. Mackenzie, Bader could be arrogant, selfish and breathtakingly rude. He treated subordinates appallingly and was thoroughly disliked by many of those beside whom he worked and flew. Losing his legs at the age of twenty-one seemed to be the key that transformed him into a difficult, tenacious and aggressive war hero. But Mackenzie believes these qualities had their origins earlier in his life, springing from Bader's harsh and unhappy childhood. It was this, Mackenzie believed, that forged Douglas Bader's character and left him with an unbreakable will of iron.

He was clearly Brasher's kind of hero, and Brasher spoke often of his admiration for the man and what he had achieved. After Brasher's death, his widow Shirley found an exercise book he had used when he was eighteen years old. In it Brasher had written: 'How wonderful to be able to do something for your country, like Douglas Bader. What would I be able to do?'

'He didn't answer that question,' says Shirley, 'and it was hardly on a par with the Battle of Britain, but I think he did achieve "something" with the London Marathon.' Brasher was young, fit and, like many of his generation, he fantasised about being a Spitfire pilot. Eager to emulate his heroes, Brasher dreamed of being a Douglas Bader with legs.

From 1945, at the age of sixteen, Brasher had kept a sporadic diary, reviewing the books he had read, the films he had enjoyed and his training and racing for cross-country. A faded light-blue cardboard-bound volume, foolscap-sized, lined to keep the handwriting neat, dog-eared, it reads like a personal confessional. It was discovered by his son, Hugh, after his death. Here is Brasher writing about a visit to the cinema on 10 February 1945:

> I've just seen *The First of the Few*, the film about Leslie Mitchell designer of the Spitfire. Leslie Howard played Leslie Mitchell, Rosamund John as Diana his wife and David Niven as Geoffrey Crisp, his friend and test pilot. Leslie Mitchell was a man who believed in something and then devoted everything, including his life, to attain his purpose. He was not egotistical, he saw that something had to be done to contest the Germans' growing power . . . He did it with all his power and will, he worked to the verge of collapse. His body and health were secondary considerations. The main lesson of his life is that he worked all his life to save his country, although he received hardly any support from the government.

The diary also gives a remarkable insight into Brasher's approach to cross-country running. On 16 February 1945 (a Friday) he finds a notice pinned up after Chapel and he can scarcely contain his delight at being selected for the first eight: 'Gosh, wasn't I excited? My first taste of real success. The morning was one long line of congratulations. I had to do my Physics prep in the afternoon but I was so jittery that I couldn't concentrate.'

The following day, Brasher is about to undertake his first race as a member of the first eight. He writes: 'I was frightfully jittery and nervous up till the end of third lesson; in fact I could hardly write properly. I hardly ate any lunch. After lunch I lay on my couch, ate glucose tablets, and read *War and Peace* to keep my mind off the match . . .'

The cocktail of terror and anticipation is something that is known to every athlete who dreams of pulling the best out of his body when threatened. Brasher battled to bring this surge of adrenalin in check – to tame the hormone that sends your heart racing, swells your lungs and prepares your guts for fight or flight. It would be ten years before he was able to control these 'jitters', and then, to his delight, he found he could reach for victory way beyond his grasp.

As he lined up on this February day in 1945, Brasher wrote of his opponents from Uppingham School in Rutland:

> They looked terribly tough. We lined up across the road and started off at a colossal lick. Soon I was one but last with Maitland just behind me. After that I began to catch up until I was lying about 20th at the turning near Dunchurch. I think I could have done much better if I had started off faster. Also I think I was a bit over-trained. I said to myself 'Try to come in 17th', and so I did. If I had set myself a higher target and had more confidence in myself I would have done *much* better.

Brasher learned the lessons well, and the self-analysis of his performance worked. By the end of that term he had established himself as the second-best cross-country runner at Rugby. By the beginning of the following year, he was the best.

Later diary extracts show Brasher's attitude to his career:

> Weds, March 6th, 1946: What am I to do for a career? I face what is probably the greatest decision of my life and I am only seventeen and a half. It's hard but it has got to be faced. We have had two wars in a lifetime and now mankind has GOT to straighten itself out . . . Civil engineering benefits mankind to a certain degree but you get wound up with materialistic considerations so that the divine soul, the inward mind, gets set aside and covered up with the materialistic side of life.

Here in his diary, Brasher quotes Rolt:

> There are two courses open to each man in his brief lifetime: either
> he can seek the good life, or he can struggle for wealth and power:
> the former emphasises spiritual, the latter material values. After
> the war the choice will still be ours, and if it be the good life the
> land awaits our coming. If, on the other hand we continue to
> pursue our material obsession, the urban bureaucrats are ready
> to plan our lives from cradle to grave and we shall become the
> slaves of a scientific technocracy.

For page after page, Brasher copied out the thoughts of Rolt in
Narrow Boat and his journey through the canals of Britain. In this
book Rolt hammered home his message: 'The factories and the
mean streets of our industrial cities may represent the wealth of
England, but the greatness of the English tradition was born of our
fields and villages, and is dying with the peasant, the yeoman and
the craftsman.' Brasher faithfully reproduced every word and the
echoes stayed with him.

'Here, in my hand so to speak, I have a life,' wrote Brasher in
this diary in March 1946. 'What am I to do with it? We have got to
get a clear relationship with God so that in all our petty differences
the issue ahead may not be clouded over. We must united strive for
ideals.'

But two months later, on 17 May, he writes, 'Sometimes when I
read what I have written before I feel it is all bosh. I get moods and
then suddenly my whole line of thought is broken. I am too
material, trivial little details bother me.'

Brasher wrestles with the books he is reading, and where they
grip him he pins down their thoughts. He rapidly devours the
volumes of Henry Williamson, naturalist and visionary author,
whose work includes *The Flax of Dream* and *Tarka the Otter*. Here
too, in 1946, is the first mention of Robert Browning and his poem
Andrea del Sarto. This meandering work in blank verse tells of a

failed hero, an artist who has lost his inspiration. For Brasher it was the source of his favourite quotation, lines which he never forgot:

> *Ah, but a man's reach should exceed his grasp,*
> *Or what's a heaven for?*

Brasher was also beginning to grow up, and like any other seventeen-year-old boy he took an adolescent interest in the opposite sex. P.H.B. Lyon, headmaster of Rugby – the Brasher family's 'Uncle Hugh', though his nickname among the boys at Rugby was the Bodger – was a well-known poet and winner of the Newdigate Prize, awarded to students of the University of Oxford for English verse; it was an honour he shared with one of Brasher's favourite authors, John Buchan. As the number of boys at the school under his headship crept towards 700, it was the odd appearance of girls (not yet members of the school) that excited boys like Brasher.

In a tradition set by the great Dr Thomas Arnold, the headmaster would treat Rugby's senior boys as gentlemen so that they might share with him responsibility for moral tone as well as discipline. That didn't stop Brasher from fantasising about the headmaster's daughter, Elinor – a girl half a dozen years older than Brasher who must have known him quite well from those family holidays in north Wales. The girl was renowned for her beauty and sent many a heart racing in School House. As Elinor Bruce Lyon, she went on to become a popular children's author in the 1950s and 1960s, writing adventures in what was labelled the 'camping and tramping' genre.

On fine summer days Brasher and his companions would find a patch of grass on which to lie and soak up the warm sun. When Elinor came to visit her father or others in the school she would take a short cut that involved her leaping over a shallow ditch. As she leapt, Brasher would remember fifty years later, the boys could catch a glimpse of her frilly underwear. 'I used to lie in the sun', he said, 'for hours waiting for that to happen.'

Once he was established in the first eight, Brasher was renowned as one of the best cross-country runners in the school; he trained hard and won most races. And although he was never appointed 'Holder of the Big Side Bags' (as the captain of the running eight was known in Rugby argot – a reference to the origin of the sport in paper chasing), one of his great ambitions was to win Rugby's famous Crick Run.

As an organised sport, cross-country running is recognised to have its genesis in the thirteen-mile Crick Run, held at Rugby School nearly every year since 1838. Not only was the Crick Run the first such event of its type in the world, it is still a major annual event in the school's calendar. Brasher, by 1946 almost certainly the best distance runner in the school, had set his heart on winning it.

Even transatlantic papers talked glowingly about the glories of the Crick. Here is an article from the *New York Times* published on 23 January 1885. It's in the flowery language of the period but gives some indication of how highly the Crick was rated:

The Supreme Test of an English Lad's Endurance
The Annual Chase of Hounds after Hares.
A killing pace over bog and through hedge and ditch.
Rugby, Warwickshire December 29th.

We are not exactly in season for one of the great events of the Rugby year viz The Crick Run which is to the young deerfoots of Tom Brown's famous school what the Matterhorns once were to the Alpine climber, but we may recall it. Many of the lesser paperchases – The Cottonhouse, The Barby Village and even the formidable Harborough Magna are within the reach of most boys whose lungs and limbs are in tolerable condition. But the great Crick Run, thirteen miles from point to point and seven of them over ploughed fields and meadows, is a trial which like the Victoria Cross on a soldier's breast or the string of scalps adorning an Indian's brave wigwam, shows that he who has achieved it must have proved his mettle.

Anyone who should stand on some gloomy December evening at the great gate of the School, would need no great stretch of fancy to recall many famous worthies, living and dead, who have started from this very place on the long struggle across country which was a foreshadowing of their success in the greater race of life.

Boys who could tackle the Crick, take it on and win it – or even aspire to win it – were regarded as gods within the world of Rugby. There is plenty of evidence, both from write-ups in the school magazine and the recollections of his contemporaries, that Brasher trained harder than most. He knew this race, he knew the course, but doubts were raised by fellow runners as to whether he could manage the distance. He had been tipped in the school magazine as someone who should become a record breaker. He was proud of his ability that brought him to 'the front in every race'.

But a sad note, recorded in handwriting at the time of the race, told a different story:

> Brasher was not expected to stand the distance and he did not. This may have been because he was not strong enough or because he had eaten something which did not agree with him. Anyhow he was sick twice on the way round and came in a long way behind the winner in a very bad condition. The winner was a complete outsider although a member of the eight, D. Jarrold, Tudor House and second came Staik accompanied by Kinman. On the whole School House showed good form except for Brasher's misfortune. Unfortunately Brasher is not staying on next year to win the Crick. He is leaving at the end of the summer term.

Over half a century later Brasher, only days from death, was still haunted by the fact that he hadn't won the Crick. As he lay there, his mind wandering, he would recall, 'I should have won the Crick but I didn't.'

He told the story of how his aunt had turned up in the days before the race. 'Rationing was still going on in Britain,' he said, 'and I think eggs were limited to one a fortnight. But my aunt brought a food parcel including a couple of eggs.' Always looking for an edge, an advantage, Brasher decided that he would save the eggs and eat them for breakfast on that cold December day to get him around this ordeal of a race. He ate the eggs but they were bad and upset his stomach.

The stomach upset was enough to shatter his self-confidence for the run ahead. The bristling sensation of dread drained him. His guts were twisted with an attack of diarrhoea, but even so the school doctor passed him fit to run. Brasher went to the start line a dehydrated and shivering wreck. And so, what should have been the crowning glory of his brief and otherwise undistinguished career at Rugby, ended with failure and what he regarded as humiliation. Much later in life he claimed that he had started the race but couldn't continue; the record shows that he did start but finished dismally far behind the leaders.

Added humiliation came when, visiting one of the other nearby public schools to run against its cross-country team, he was reported by one of its teachers for smoking after the race. Brasher was furious that a member of staff from a different school had reported him to his Rugby masters – particularly as he had run well in the race. Nevertheless, it didn't stop him from getting six strokes of the cane, and there were mutterings about whether he should be asked to leave the school altogether. Brasher did not object to the thrashing – once away from home a good beating was accepted as an essential part of the process of turning out a public school gentleman. What rankled with him was the attitude of the teacher who had reported him. He regarded the man as a 'sneak'.

Brasher's older brother, Peter, had passed through Clifton College with flying honours on his way to becoming a doctor. There was no such vocation in prospect for Christopher. Inspired by Rolt and his romantic view of the canal network, Brasher had toyed with the idea of being a civil engineer. His father, Ken, decided that something had to be done to secure his future, and helped Chris to choose a path that he believed would shape the future pattern of his son's life.

3

As Free as a Lark

I'm a rambler, I'm a rambler from Manchester way
I get all me pleasure the hard moorland way
I may be a wage slave on Monday
But I am a free man on Sunday
                    Popular song composed by Ewan MacColl

'WHAT ARE YOU GOING to be when you grow up?' was never a question that the young Chris Brasher gave much time to. There were always people telling him what to be; parents, teachers, friends all seemed to have their opinion of who he was and what he should do. But Brasher was quite happy living in the present. He never thought much beyond the next race, or beyond the next adventure story that fuelled his imagination.

When Brasher's father pronounced that Christopher would be wise to follow his footsteps and get a steady job as an engineer that would look after him in the future, Brasher shrugged and agreed. 'My father was a big man and he drummed into me that I had to have a profession. So I became an engineering apprentice. He didn't share any dreams I had, but I didn't know any better.'

This move meant that Brasher sidestepped conscription, or what is usually referred to as national service. National service conscription in Britain was introduced in 1939 and it continued after the Second World War. The process was formalised in peacetime by the National Service Act, which became law in May 1947, and from January 1948 every young man aged eighteen or older was expected to serve in the armed forces for eighteen months, a period increased to two years after the war in Korea.

This was a major disruption for young lives to suffer and caused many people's plans and ambitions to be knocked sideways. The only escape, it seemed, was to fail the compulsory medical test, or to be in a 'reserved occupation'. John Disley believed that Brasher had won the ballot held among new recruits to become one of the 'Bevin boys' who would work in the mines rather than serving in the forces, but that Brasher failed the medical because of his eyesight and then took up the engineering apprenticeship. Margaret, Chris's sister, remembers him telling her that he did not get called up because his papers, along with those of others in his age group, 'got lost', and that Chris used to joke about it.

Armed with his Higher School Certificate, Brasher seemed destined to become an engineering apprentice and he was sent in 1946, on the advice of his father, to the sprawling Metropolitan Vickers factory in Trafford Park, Manchester. Here they manufactured engineering parts that kept half the world running – switchgear for trams in Buenos Aires, turbines for Bombay, they made it all. There Brasher became one of two thousand boys running errands for seventeen hundred skilled men and women who worked for Vickers.

Brasher was paid £2.10s a week. His digs cost him 30s a week, which included breakfast, sandwiches for lunch and a large dinner. He worked five and a half days a week, and his working day stretched from half past seven in the morning until five o'clock in the evening. The apprentices started on the lowest rung, so Brasher became a tea boy, wiping grease from tools, carrying messages and taking illegal bets from his foreman to the bookie. In winter he cycled to work in the dark. At the end of the day he cycled back to his digs in the dark. The factory was so massive he hardly ever saw the winter sun. Brasher and the other apprentices would wait for the hooter that signalled he could clock off and he had just forty-two minutes at midday for lunch. It began to dawn on him that this was no way to live.

One day in February 1947, during a cold and snowy winter almost as harsh as that of 1940, Brasher climbed into the bowels of a massive turbine casing to clean it out and, unseen by his foreman, crawled out the other end. He slipped through the factory doors and hid himself on top of an air raid shelter. There he lay in the winter sunshine gazing up at the sky. For a moment all was silence, then he heard a lark. 'The bird was singing a glorious song,' wrote Brasher later, 'soaring, dipping and free.' Brasher looked at the lark and realised that he felt imprisoned. The bird was free and he was a prisoner. 'That was the moment I decided this was not the life for me. From now on I would seek freedom. And freedom, as I had read, lay in the hills.'

The following Friday, when Brasher was supposed to be at an apprentices' day-release class, learning about the mysteries of magnetism, he played truant and caught the earliest train from Manchester to the north Wales coast, where he got off at Llanfairfechan. There he started a very different apprenticeship: an apprenticeship with the mountains and the beauty of Snowdonia.

He had armed himself with a Bartholomew's ½ inch to 1 mile map and he took with him his father's First World War prismatic compass. He had a rucksack and boots (with wide welts he had fixed on with 'clinkers', a large-headed soft metal nail). He stuffed a whistle in his pocket because he had read somewhere that six long blasts, followed by a minute's silence and then repeated, were an emergency signal to call for help. He had equipped himself with these essentials because he had pored over every detail of the books – with evocative titles like *Everest 1933* and Kirkus's *Let's Go Climbing* – that were strewn beside his bed.

As he set out from the train he clambered up the broad shoulder of Drum and then along the ridge towards Foel Fras. He looked further south, screwing up his eyes as he tried to unravel the unfamiliar Welsh names, over Carnedd Llewelyn and Carnedd Dafydd, striding along the main ridge of the Carneddau. He kept tramping, alone and all day, and then as the sun was setting came to the summit of Pen yr Ole Wen and looked down on where he hoped to end his route – the youth hostel at Idwal. There, far below in the valley, were food, companionship and a bed. But first he had to get down from the summit.

To begin with he found it easier to climb up than to climb down. But soon enough he found that there was no way down at all, just a precipitous drop. Not for the first time in his life, Brasher was lost. What had seemed so easy on the map was baffling to him on the ground. He made his way left and then right, threading his way down through the rocks, his heart thumping with fear. He had eaten all his food. The sun had vanished from the sky, the stars had appeared and the cold air was biting into his tired body. He pushed on, feeling a mixture of exhilaration and terror, the ice crunching under his feet, cursing the fact that he was completely inexperienced as a walker or climber.

He had misjudged the distance and it was deep into the evening. In the dying light he had difficulty reading the map, which was printed on linen with its contours shaded brown, but he calculated there was only a mile left now to the youth hostel and its food and rest. Brasher could see it now, down in the pass, far below him in the trees, and he began to hurry. The way was steep and then suddenly vertical and once again he was frightened. He was alone and, feeling very young, he half remembered some of the stories he had read at school, tales of great deeds performed in the mountains of the world. He recalled that Franz Lochmatter, the greatest of all Alpine guides, had been killed coming off the Weisshorn when he was within sight of his home. Slowly he crept back from the vertical cliff, edged sideways and inched his way down.

Terror gave way to exhaustion when at last he saw the lake and found the road leading to the hostel. He went in, to be greeted by a woman called Joan, the assistant warden, and the bliss of a hot dinner. Decades later, when Joan Hughes lived next door to his cottage in Nant Gwynant, Brasher was to write emotionally in the *Observer* of his first experience in the mountains:

> It may seem strange that anybody should seek to be alone and frightened but both these feelings are important to me and I believe to the soul of this nation. To be alone is very different from being lonely, which is something that I have felt only when there are millions of people around me in a big city. I can be alone with myself or with one compatible companion or even with a small group, a nucleus of like minded people, in a wild and empty world and occasionally that wild and empty world should frighten me, must take me back to my roots, back to those far off days when my ancestors first hunted for existence.
>
> Now we live in a world in which most of us are living in layers packed to suffocation in an underground train, or lonely and isolated in a tower block. I am reminded of that fascinating and terrible film that shows rats in a courtyard. At the start all is orderly; there are pathways and feeding areas and sleeping quarters and the ratty society is disciplined. Then as more and more rats are introduced into the courtyard their society starts to break down, terrible crimes are committed. Are we not in danger of making this rat experiment into human reality? That is why I believe wild empty places are so important.

That soaring lark had woken Brasher up to the prospect of freedom and opened a new chapter in his life – a passion that was to be with him for the rest of his days. The welcome he found, the cosy log-fire warmth of that youth hostel, had created in him an insatiable appetite for wandering the hills. It echoed the memories of the wilderness where he had pitched his tent as a prep school boy. He knew now what he wanted to do with his life.

Brasher seized on hill walking just when it was becoming a

popular form of recreation in post-war Britain. In the early years after the war, the unions were already seeking cutbacks in the time that people had to work in the factories. By 1947 they were negotiating for a 46½ hour, five-day week. Affordable equipment and improved public transport ensured that the hills became a playground for ordinary people. Anyone who had the taste for wandering and enjoying the outdoor life could get there and back in a day or two.

North Wales had long been the haunt of upper-class Oxbridge gentlemen, drawn to the area as a practice ground for climbing in the Alps. The hotel at Pen y Pass, now a youth hostel, and later the Pen-y-Gwryd hotel, became the focal point of mountaineering and rock climbing in Snowdonia. After the Second World War the push to keep areas of Britain special and to protect them from post-war development led to the establishment of the National Parks and Areas of Outstanding Natural Beauty. Long-distance routes – these days called long-distance footpaths – were opened, the first, in 1965, being the Pennine Way.

Snowdonia, where Brasher had his first wilderness experience, is regarded as the finest mountain range south of the Scottish Highlands. It stretches nearly fifty miles, from the northern heights of the Carneddau looming over Conwy Bay to the southern fringes of the Cadair Idris massif overlooking the tranquil estuary of the Afon Dyfi and Cardigan Bay. As Brasher had discovered, the physical fitness he had developed at Rugby School made his rambling much more enjoyable, and with a compass and an adequate map he eventually learned to dodge trouble in the hills and began to hone the ability to navigate efficiently in all conditions, including ice, mist and darkness.

Brasher was bored out of his mind in the Vickers factory, but weekend camping and youth hostelling in Snowdonia and the Derbyshire Dales became his life-saver. Occasionally he would go along to watch Manchester United or Manchester City play football on Saturdays, but he did not really enjoy life as a spectator. And a year of engineering was more than enough for Brasher; he wanted action, to test himself in the hills.

Academic and bright, Brasher's father Ken had been to one of Cambridge's most ancient and beautiful colleges, St John's. Brasher had already made up his mind to quit his apprenticeship and vowed to start lobbying his father to see if it might not be possible for him to get into St John's and study something other than engineering. To enter Cambridge in the 1940s you had to pass the Higher School Certificate in Latin. Brasher had fallen behind in Latin at Rugby but he seemed determined to remedy that during his year as an apprentice. Margaret, his sister, recalls that there were pleadings whenever Chris was home of: 'Where are my Latin books, Ma?' as he made frantic efforts to catch up.

For Brasher, one of the attractions of Cambridge, and particularly of St John's College, was its Master, Sir James Wordie, who carried with him a gigantic reputation as an Arctic explorer. Wordie was a remarkable man who had left his mark on the history of polar exploration. Although quiet and unassuming, he was well known in exploring circles as the chief of the scientific staff on Sir Ernest Shackleton's *Endurance* expedition between 1914 and 1917.

Wordie had played a leading role in the legendary adventure of the *Endurance* after the ship had been crushed by the ice of the Weddell Sea, and the members of the expedition had spent months in improvised camps on the pack-ice. When the expedition reached Elephant Island, Wordie remained with the main party while Shackleton made his extraordinary open-boat journey to South Georgia for help.

By the time Brasher first met him in Cambridge, Wordie had already played a large part in the planning of the first ascent of Mount Everest in 1953. He was from a wealthy and ancient Scottish family and after studying geology at Glasgow University he went to Cambridge, where he met several of the survivors of Scott's disastrous last expedition to the South Pole.

Wordie was elected a fellow of St John's College in 1921, and was successively tutor, senior tutor and president before being elected Master of the College in 1952. So he was ideally placed to infect many generations of undergraduates with his own passion to explore remote parts of the world. Among many other achievements that caught Brasher's eye, Wordie was a founder member of the committee of management of the Scott Polar Research Institute and chairman, from 1953 to 1956, of the British Mountaineering Council. He had a son, John Wordie, also at Cambridge and three years older than Brasher, who was a keen cross-country runner.

Brasher went up to Cambridge in 1947 to study geology (Wordie's chosen subject). The decision to read geology rather than engineering was taken after vigorous arguments between father and son, and Margaret Brasher vividly remembers that Chris seemed to pluck the subject out of the air as if he had just thought of it, which seemed to come as a surprise to their father. Margaret also believes that Ken 'pulled a number of strings' to get Chris into his chosen college.

Given the taste that Chris had picked up for camping and youth hostelling, he was already anticipating that James Wordie's reputation might lead him to field trips and the mountains. To make up the geology syllabus, Brasher threw in maths as a 'half subject'. He was taught maths by the astronomer Fred Hoyle, but confessed that after five minutes of listening to Hoyle speak he didn't have 'a bloody clue what he was talking about, though you envied his brain leaping about from place to place'.

Brasher went up to the university at a time when it was packed with 26- and 27-year-olds who had survived the war or served in the forces. They all seemed terribly keen to get on with their work and their lives and after a couple of weeks of beginner's keenness, the nineteen-year-old Brasher discovered that most lectures, which were optional, were a waste of his time. He believed that he was better off doing background reading of his own and in his own time.

He also found it both fun and challenging to take in lectures in totally different subjects by people he had heard or read about and who were recommended to him by other students. He loved being exposed to others' minds, going to hear others' stories and their exploits.

Soon enough Brasher rediscovered his other great passion, his love of cross-country running. Having cycled to and from work in Manchester and spent his weekends rambling and scrambling, he had retained much of his schoolboy fitness. The University Hare and Hounds Club had primitive headquarters down by the Granta pub in Cambridge, totally separate from the Athletics Club at Fenner's. With his talent for distance running, Brasher became captain of the Hare and Hounds Club and president of the Cambridge University Athletic Club, where he usually competed over three miles.

He was not alone at Cambridge in being an accomplished sportsman. Among the students were John (J.G.) Dewes, who opened the batting for England, and the captain of the England hockey team. In 1947 eight Oxford and Cambridge men played rugby for England, and at St John's College they had six of the Cambridge rowing eight.

Cambridge in October 1947 still treated cross-country running as a 'half-Blue sport', the only concession offered by the Blues Committee being that the first man home for each team could be awarded a full Blue (the token that you had been awarded colours against the university's rivals at Oxford). In 1947, Oxford's Peter Curry, who was leading the annual cross-country race between the two universities, glanced back in the closing stages and saw that four other Oxford runners were far enough ahead of the chasing Cambridge duo – Brasher of St John's and Max Jones of Clare – to secure victory for Oxford. The four Oxford men crossed the line together holding hands – all claiming that they should be entitled to full 'Blues'.

That 1947 result caused considerable controversy. At the time Sandy Duncan and Harold Abrahams, of the Amateur Athletic

Association (AAA) – the latter being the winner of the gold medal in the famous 1924 *Chariots of Fire* Olympics – tut-tutted that this was no way for university runners to behave. Brasher and Jones crossed the line together fifth equal, claiming that as the first finishers for Cambridge they should get a full Blue too. All six did indeed collect their full Blues. The Blues Committee were in disarray. It was an indication that even the Oxbridge runners were flexing their muscles and refusing to accept the authority and traditions of the pre-war athletic officials.

As well as cross-country, Brasher became a Blue on the track at three miles and he joined the Achilles Club. Achilles was an exclusive gathering, drawing its athletes from both Oxford and Cambridge. It was rich in both tradition and international achievements and it was here that Brasher first came across Roger Bannister and Christopher Chataway.

Bannister was born in 1929 and won the odd sprint race at his primary school in Harrow before he and his family moved to Bath. There he joined the City of Bath Boys' School, where he won the school's annual cross-country race three times in a row.

Subsequently Bannister, still blushingly shy at school, moved to the University College School, London, where the headmaster had been educated at Rugby and attempted to encourage Bannister to play the game with little success. His father, Ralph, who had won the mile race himself at school, took the schoolboy Bannister to gain the inspiration he needed from seeing Sydney Wooderson battle against the Swede, Arne Andersson, at the White City in 1946.

Bannister took the entrance exams for both Oxford and Cambridge and at the age of seventeen was offered a place at both universities to read medicine. Bannister went to Exeter College, Oxford in the autumn of 1946. Having never previously worn running spikes or run on a track, almost immediately he went off to inspect the Iffley Road running track. Within two years he was selected as an Olympic 'possible' for the 1948 London Games, but declined as he felt he was not ready to compete at that level.

Bannister was brought up reading Arthur Mee's *Children's Encyclopaedia* – full of British imperial history and stirring deeds of heroes. Clearly the social values and the shared Oxbridge education of Brasher and Bannister played a part in their friendship. But it was their shared passion for distance running that brought the two of them along with Chataway together.

Educated at Sherborne School, the boys' public school in Dorset, Chataway had shown a blazing natural ability as an athlete right from the start. He played a fine game of rugby and was tough enough at Sherborne to captain the school at boxing. In the school library he read about the epic series of races over the mile and 1500 metres between the Swedes Gunder Haegg and Arne Andersson in the 1940s; and while still at school he wrote to the Amateur Athletic Association asking them for coaching advice.

After leaving school he joined the Army as an officer cadet to do national service, where his running and rugby continued with success – in 1950 he broke the inter-services mile record with 4:15.6. In 1950 Chataway went up to Magdalen College, Oxford to study politics, philosophy and economics. Although his first job on leaving Oxford University was with Guinness, already he was aiming for a political career.

Brasher met Bannister and Chataway in Varsity matches, on the track and in cross-country. Bannister and Chataway were aware of Brasher's existence as a rival middle-distance runner in the Cambridge team. Brasher ran in the Cambridge cross-country team against Oxford every year between 1947 and 1950. Bannister ran in the same match in 1948 and 1949, and certainly knew Brasher at this time; after his national service, Chataway ran for the Oxford cross-country team in 1950, 1951 and 1952. Neither Chataway nor Bannister can remember when they first met Brasher, but as they did so in a team context that is not remarkable.

All three became members of the Achilles Club, Bannister in 1947, Brasher in 1948 and Chataway in 1951. But in his early days at Cambridge Brasher made little impact in terms of track running, although he was usually good enough to be in the first two or three in the university's matches against Oxford.

In 1948, for instance, he had run the two miles in 9:06.5 and the three miles in 14:36.8. In 1949 he had been a member on tour of a combined Oxford and Cambridge team, first against Princeton and Cornell and then against Harvard and Yale. After these races, his sister Margaret remembers being sent for by her headmistress, a Mrs Butler. Margaret was afraid that she had broken some rule, but was relieved and thrilled to learn that her brother's victories had been reported in the press. 'I was so proud,' she says, 'and in the headline they called him "Barrel-chested Brasher".'

In June barrel-chested Brasher came second to his Oxford rival and fellow Achilles Club member Philip Morgan in the two miles. He had a rare victory over Morgan in June 1951 at the Kinnaird Trophy in Chiswick, managing to beat him over three miles in a time of 14:29.6. But it wasn't until Brasher took up the steeplechase that his name came to be reported more widely.

Brasher's training was to alter radically once he and others from the Achilles Club fell under the eyes of good coaches. But the Corinthian approach to their sport was still very much in evidence when Achilles arranged a tour to Greece and Rome led by Tommy Macpherson. The tour took place in July 1950 and Achilles turned out a strong side featuring a number of future Olympians, including Roger Bannister and Brasher himself. The Achilles team were royally received, lodged in the best hotel in Constitution Square and entertained both by the British Council and by the Greek government, in the person of Prime Minister General Plastiras.

The two-day meeting against the combined team of the leading Greek clubs, Pan Athenaeum and Pan Ionian, was held in the classical-style stadium built for the 1896 Olympics. Unlike a modern stadium, its straights seemed to go on for ever and the bends were very tight. Spectators sat close to the track on terraced stone benches and Greek classical statues were scattered everywhere.

The evening before the meeting, the Achilles team ran around the stadium for the benefit of the Greek press and a bevy of spectators. Once competition began, there were audible gasps of admiration as Achilles' long-legged Ray Barkway showed perfect style over the high hurdles. The Greek press went overboard with reference to the twinkling feet of sprinter Norris McWhirter, who captained the Achilles team on the track, and the elegant Bannister, who was running the 1500 metres. The Achilles members spent their spare time having fun, with a whirl of beach parties, attractive girls and drinks receptions.

Despite the number of banquets and the amount of wine that was consumed, Achilles completely dominated the events and were given a great write-up by the Greek press. Whilst at this meeting, Brasher had had his first rather eccentric introduction to steeple-chasing.

'It was in Athens,' he recalled, 'on tour competing against what was virtually the Greek national team.' He had run the 5000 metres on the first day. He won it and in the evening someone took a casual look at the programme to discover what was taking place on the second day. The athletes found there was an event called the steeplechase.

'What's that?' asked Brasher. 'How far is it?' In Brasher's day, no such event was included in the matches between Oxford and Cambridge.

'We're not sure,' they said, 'but the distance is 3000 metres so you'd better run it.'

Somewhat bemused by the event and its distance, Brasher arrived at the stadium the next day and set off into unknown territory.

'You had to make a ninety-degree turn to get to the water jump on the outside of the track,' he said. 'On the corner there was a statue of a Greek god and on the first lap I couldn't quite understand why these Greeks seemed to be swinging on something to help them get over this jump. The second time around I realised that at the appropriate place on this statue there was a phallus which you grabbed hold of to swing yourself over the water jump.'

It was certainly an unrecognised technique, but he won the event anyway.

The team then left for Rome to meet an Italian university squad, only to find that the Italian students had failed to raise a full team. However, they provided lavish hotel accommodation for Achilles – and, noted McPherson, 'laid on entertainment in the form of ladies of spectacularly easy virtue. When one of the ladies hinted that the team could expect to be presented with a bill for services rendered, we students made our excuses and left.'

As well as enjoying this first taste of international athletics, Brasher soon became a leading member of the Cambridge University Mountaineering Club (CUMC). He cultivated the friendship of James Wordie, and was sent on an expedition to Baffin Island in the Canadian Arctic during his first long vacation in 1947. When the expedition leader, Professor W.A. Dear, met a representative of the Canadian Defence Board to fix the logistics of the trip, he left Brasher outside smoking so heavily that Dear was asked if Brasher would be up to the rigours of the far north. Dear replied that anyone who could beat Oxford at distance running should have no trouble.

The Canadian government provided the team with a Canso, a plane that could take off from land or water, and they landed at Pond Inlet where they picked up two Inuit guides who were said to know the territory well. The purpose of the expedition was to explore a geological line of weakness in the rock below. The team got their navigation hopelessly wrong. The expedition found a line of weakness beneath the ice, but it was apparently forty miles south of the area Brasher and his team were exploring.

Brasher also went to Spitsbergen with W.V. Harland, a lecturer in the geology department. This trip was similarly full of mishaps. 'A disaster came when we were sledge hauling up a glacier and a snow bridge over a crevasse collapsed. Five of the team fell thirty or forty feet. Nobody expected the group to be back for a week.'

There was little hope of rescue and Brasher had lost his glasses. Harland had injured an ankle. Hampered by his injury, he would set off straight after breakfast, an hour before the team, and arrive in the evening an hour after they had set up camp, walking in considerable pain for three days. According to Mike O'Hara, a later president of the Cambridge University Mountaineering Club, after that fall into the crevasse Brasher ran and skied his way back to base camp to raise the alarm.

Even despite such mishaps, Cambridge University Mountaineering Club had a fine reputation in the post-war years and provided plenty of climbers who were to help in the conquest of Everest in 1953, though the climbing community in this period was still tiny compared with today. Pre-war books on the subject were avidly devoured by anyone interested in climbing, but the usual method of getting news about climbing and its development was by word of mouth.

Brasher soon became the secretary and then president of the CUMC. Though the British Empire was fading fast when he arrived in Cambridge at the beginning of October 1947, an uncomplicated spirit of adventure was still abroad. The Mountaineering Club was founded in 1905 and although all the climbers knew that mountains were dangerous, no one had ever heard of risk assessments.

As president of the club, Brasher was chosen to lead climbs. According to the Everest mountaineer George Band, Brasher was not an accomplished climber, but nevertheless his years in office were extremely successful, mainly thanks to his enthusiasm. There were just twenty members of the club in his first year, but by his second year there were one hundred and twenty. He would hold club meetings wherever he could find a lecture room and hired an impressive list of speakers.

Once a year the club brought out a handsome booklet, entitled *Cambridge Mountaineering*. Priced at 5s, it was full of reports and photographs of members' climbs and highlights of the speakers' appearances. Published by Charles Elphick of Biggleswade, it carried wonderfully nostalgic and evocative advertisements. Here you could read about the delights of the Fish Hotel in Buttermere – handy for climbing in the English Lake District – or the Cairngorm Hotel. You were encouraged to buy your boots from Timpson Boots for Climbers in Manchester, and if you wanted to read the latest climbing literature you could take your pick from W.H. Murray, J.H.B. Peel or Tom Longstaff. The CUMC tie, green and white with crossed ice-axes and a coiled rope, was available from A.G. Almond Ltd.

Brasher would invite many of the heroes whose books he had read at school to lecture to the club – people such as Eric Shipton, who was originally appointed to lead the 1953 Everest expedition. When Shipton turned up to give his talk he was between jobs and he asked Brasher if it would be possible to apply to Cambridge to read geology. Brasher knew just the man who could fix it and got in touch immediately with Sir James Wordie.

'Eric Shipton's visiting us here at St John's,' said Brasher, 'Could you see him tomorrow morning at eleven?'

The next morning Shipton turned up and was so keen on showing maps of the terrain around Everest to the young members of the CUMC and suggesting routes that could be climbed that when the appointed hour came round, he told Brasher that he was far too busy to keep his appointment with Wordie and turned the meeting down.

This may not have gone down too well with Wordie. The following year he was one of a group of four people who chose to sack Shipton as leader of the Everest expedition and appointed John Hunt in his place.

Brasher handed over the presidency of the club to Kim Smith, and Smith was in turn succeeded a year later by George Band, at twenty-four the youngest of the team recruited by Hunt to conquer Everest in 1953.

'In my day, most of the undergraduates joining the CUMC had

done very little if any climbing with ropes,' said Band. 'I was lucky, because while doing national service in the Royal Corps of Signals at Catterick, there was a climber, Tony Moulam, who started a small climbing club. So when I arrived at Cambridge, the first club I joined was naturally the CUMC. The president then was Chris Brasher, possibly elected for his proven leadership as captain of the Hare and Hounds, rather than for his actual prowess as a climber.

'But we had some outstanding and unforgettable lectures – Bill Murray on the Scottish Himalayan expedition; Tom Longstaff setting the altitude record on Trisul and being avalanched on Gurla Mandhata; Bernard Pierre being led by Gaston Rebuffat up the north-east face of the Badile.

'Chris announced in 1950 that in the summer he would be organising a CUMC Alpine Meet in the Dauphiné, and all we had to do to join was to give him a cheque for £34. I was relying on a none too generous government grant and knew it would be difficult to raise that sort of money. Fortunately, I discovered that the aluminium plant in Fort William took on students to tend the red-hot furnaces when their regular manual workers took their summer holidays. So I signed on for six weeks, at the then princely sum of £11 per week.'

With his mountaineering duties and his afternoon training with the Hare and Hounds group, Brasher often found that work and lectures were a problem. In the cosy warmth of the lecture room he would find a corner and drift off to sleep. Of lectures given by Bertrand Russell at four in the afternoon after Brasher had completed a seven-mile run over the old Roman road just outside Cambridge, his only memory was a high-pitched, monotonous voice that lulled him into a torpor. Brasher confessed that he never heard a Bertrand Russell lecture all the way through. He would wake from these catnaps, legs stiff from the run, but refreshed for the next outing.

In his final year, 1951, inspired by the book *The Roof Climbers of Cambridge* – an account of nocturnal climbing on the colleges and

buildings of Cambridge published in October 1937 under the pseu-
donym 'Whipplesnaith', and which formed a sort of 'guidebook' to
the routes on to the roofs of the town's ancient buildings – Brasher
and his cronies had worked out a plan to decorate every pinnacle of
the university with balloons filled with hydrogen to celebrate the
end of exams. The Cambridge University Mountaineering Club
smuggled big hydrogen cylinders into college. Brasher took responsibility for the highest climb, the Wedding Cake, an ornate
pinnacle in St John's New Court.

'As dawn broke,' Brasher remembered, 'there was a marvellous
sight of coloured balloons all over it and on King's College Chapel.
But sadly by seven o'clock there wasn't one to be seen, just little
bits of string and rubber. The group had bought ordinary balloons
and the hydrogen had diffused through the rubber.'

Before Brasher left Cambridge he met, while taking a party of
climbers to north Wales, the man who would have a profound effect
on his life and career.

John Disley, who was to become Brasher's steeplechasing
partner, climbing companion, business associate and friend, was
already an established athlete. He lived in Wales and was also good
enough at climbing to have become an instructor. The first time
Disley came across Brasher was in a climbing hut, and while Disley
couldn't see Brasher, he could certainly hear his bellowing voice.

'I actually heard Brasher before I saw him,' says Disley. 'It was
in Helyg one morning in 1949. I was lying there in bed when I heard
an abrasive voice harassing some poor CUMC member on how to
make porridge. I now know that Chris's knowledge of porridge
making was practically nil, but then, as I discovered later to my
amusement, he felt obliged to change any plan that he hadn't
actually made himself. He was at that time the president of the
CUMC, so he was laying down the law about the perfect way to
make porridge. It was all a load of nonsense, but he probably felt it
necessary to establish authority in the kitchen in the morning before
the rock faces were reached later in the day.'

This meeting was to change both their lives. It knotted together their athletic, climbing and business careers, weaving a friendship that was to last for the rest of Brasher's life.

4

The Cinderella of Track Events

*'I like Cinderella, I really do. She has a good work ethic.
I appreciate a good, hard-working gal. And she likes shoes.
The fairy tale is all about the shoe at the end, and I'm a big
shoe girl.'*

Amy Adams, actress

CHRIS BRASHER'S MEETING with John Disley in 1949 meant that he had found someone who shared both of his guiding passions. Brasher was ebullient, extrovert and had a breadth of vision – it was impossible to ignore him. Disley was unassuming, methodical, appraising, a quiet man who got things done.

But in other ways they had much in common. They shared a love of open spaces – the hills and mountains – and they shared a hunger for cross-country running and athletics. Above all, they both fell in love with that Cinderella of track events, the steeplechase.

John Disley was born in Corris, Wales on 20 November 1928 and by his teenage years was beginning to emerge as a top-class athlete. In 1949, he won the first of his four Welsh mile titles in Abertillery Park in a modest four minutes thirty-two seconds. But within two years of winning this title he was to become Britain's first world-class steeplechaser when he set four British records at two miles and five at 3000 metres.

In September 1951 Disley broke his own British and Commonwealth record for the 3000 metres steeplechase, clocking 9:11.6 at a meeting at London's White City. Trained as a schoolmaster, Disley ran for London Athletic Club and gained nineteen British vests between 1950 and 1957. He first ran cross-country at Oswestry High School in Shropshire, but he had never seen an athletics track until he went to Loughborough College as a student in 1946.

Until 1963 there was no steeplechase in the Oxford v. Cambridge match and at most athletics meetings the event was considered an unfashionable bolt-hole for those who could not make the team in more glamorous events. In imperial Britain the standard steeple-chase distance was generally two miles, though the continentals wanted to make it 3000 metres to fit in with their metric measure of distances.

In 1948, the year that Brasher joined Achilles, the Olympics came to London and the final of the 3000 metres steeplechase took place on 5 August. There were no British representatives in the final. They'd all been hammered in the first round, and it was dominated by Swedish runners whose country stayed neutral through the war. The Swedes provided the first three: Tore Sjostrand, Erik Elnsater and Gote Hagstrom.

Britain's Geoff Tudor, captain of Oxford University Cross-Country Club in 1947 and one of the Achilles men taking part in those Olympic Games, had been knocked out in the heats. Tudor's account gives a colourful indication of the training methods used at the time.

'Clearly,' he said, 'we were unprepared and probably under-trained for such a demanding event as the steeplechase.' He'd arrived in Oxford late in 1945 after early release from war service and he spent more time playing hockey for his college than on the cross-country course. The harsh winter of 1947 started to bite on 28 January when Tudor, playing hockey for Christ Church, battled on through a blinding snowstorm. After that, snow and ice meant that it was impossible to get to the running track.

'The thaw didn't arrive until 10 March,' noted Tudor, 'just twelve days before the varsity sports at the White City. We just rolled up our sleeves and ran. We didn't even have proper cross-country shoes at first. I remember one race when three times I had to stop to retrieve a shoe stuck in the mud. The general approach was still not far removed from that depicted in *Chariots of Fire*. Towards the end of my time at Oxford we had Geoff Dyson as a part-time coach.' In 1946 Dyson was appointed chief coach to the Amateur Athletic Association, and visited Oxford to run training sessions for the Oxford University Athletics Club at the Iffley Road track. 'Dyson encouraged us to pass the pain barrier with his battle cry: "You're not tired. You only think you're tired,"' said Tudor. 'In those days at Oxford, we battled on.'

Tudor's preparation for the upcoming Olympics was wonderfully casual. In the long vacation he would take long walks and play table tennis. Occasionally he would turn out and run a half-mile or a mile. Between his athletic endeavours he would play tennis, cycle and do a little gardening. In 1947 Tudor was nominated by Britain's international selectors to train for the 3000 metres steeplechase in the 1948 Olympics. He had never run in the event and couldn't remember if he'd even seen one.

Amazingly, it was late November before Tudor had his first try over steeplechase hurdles and it was only at the beginning of January 1948, the Olympic year, that he was sent to Herne Hill to get steeplechase coaching from Bill Thomas – the famous coach who'd trained Jack Lovelock, the Oxford-educated New Zealander who won the 1500 metres at the 1936 Games. In April Tudor was whisked off to train at Butlin's Holiday Camp at Clacton and managed to fit in one twelve-mile run with his Achilles friend Peter Curry.

On 14 May Tudor ran a steeplechase event for the first time. By July he was running in the AAA Championships, coming in second to Peter Curry. By the end of the month he was racing in the Olympics. Tudor completed his race in 10:10.9 (his time supplied to him by Norris McWhirter and his twin brother Ross, who by this time were running a fact-finding agency in London) and he left a few days later for his wedding and his honeymoon in France and Belgium.

Tudor's Corinthian approach to the Olympic Games of 1948 contrasted deeply with that adopted by athletes competing in the Games that followed, in 1952 and 1956 – particularly with Brasher's preparations for the 1956 Olympics. But it was very much the sort of approach and training that Brasher was involved in while he was running for Achilles at Cambridge.

It was in 1950 that Brasher first saw John Disley in action in a steeplechase at the White City. Brasher thought the event was rather elegant and certainly more interesting than twelve and a half laps of straight running on the track and began to take the steeplechase seriously.

Brasher was a double medallist at the World Student Games, held in Luxembourg in 1951. In the 1500 metres he was beaten into second place by the local hero, Josy Barthel, 3:52.6 to 3:54.0. In the 5000 metres, however, Brasher led a British clean sweep of the medals, winning by some ten seconds in 15:07.6.

Brasher stayed on for a fourth year at Cambridge, doing part two of his degree in two years. He got a third-class degree but shortly after he went down in 1951, he too was named as an 'Olympic possible' for the 1952 Games in Helsinki.

Brasher left Cambridge with two job offers stuffed in his pocket – one as an oil geologist in Iraq for what he saw as 'a vast salary' and the other as a management trainee for Mobil. He was offered the high-paying job in Baghdad, where his father had worked, but the glamour and temptation of running in the Olympics was seductive. So he took the lower-paid job in London to concentrate more on his running.

Mobil Oil, he found to his delight, were extremely generous with their time off for international competition, although his day-to-day training had to be slotted into lunch hours or evenings after work. It was during those snatched hours that Brasher first fell under the spell of coach Franz Stampfl.

Stampfl was a Svengali-like figure who seemed to be able to inject his athletes with the conviction that they had within them the power to win, no matter what. Cultured and Jewish, before the Second World War Stampfl had been an art student in Vienna, where he had reportedly been a javelin thrower, an international skier and all-round athlete. He fled after Hitler annexed Austria at the outbreak of war and tried to volunteer for the RAF.

Stampfl shipped up in Britain as a 25-year-old. Amongst his closest friends in Vienna were the Ronay family, who had come to England in 1937. David Ronay, who was Jewish, and his Catholic wife Ilona had five children: Deszo, Marcel, Pip, Charlotte and Illa. Illa, the youngest of the Ronay children (she was ninety-two in 2011), remembered that Stampfl was reckoned to be 'one of the family'. A rare photograph features Marcel and Pip Ronay with Stampfl in Vienna, probably taken in 1936.

'The boys,' said Illa Ronay, 'including Franz Stampfl, lived in a flat in Notting Hill Gate.' Only when Illa arrived in England from Vienna on 5 November 1937 did Stampfl move out of the Ronay family home to make room for her.

Tall, rugged and handsome, with the chiselled look of an athlete, Stampfl had a mop of dark, curly hair and spoke good English with a lilting Viennese accent. He was dressed like a middle-class gentleman of the 1940s, rarely without a tie and a waistcoat, and he hid his hair beneath a beautifully tailored, check flat cap often worn at a jaunty angle. Above all, having studied art in Vienna he had the air of an intellectual. Full of self-confidence – some even said swagger – he was used to stimulating debate over music, art, sport, poetry and politics with other students of his native city.

Despite the efforts of Harold Abrahams to find Stampfl a job in athletics coaching, when war broke out Stampfl found himself interned as an enemy alien.

In 1940 Stampfl was shipped to Canada aboard the liner *Andorra*

Star. The ship was torpedoed and only 400 of the 2400 internees and crew survived. They drifted in the sea for nine hours before being picked up and subsequently Stampfl was sent to Australia. 'If there was any wavering doubt in my mind,' Stampfl said, 'the war convinced me that the mind, body and soul must be cultivated into one dynamic force to achieve sporting greatness.'

As soon as the war was over Stampfl returned to Britain. He moved first to Belfast and then to London, where his coaching services were valued by such clubs as Belgrave Harriers, Blackheath Harriers and South London Harriers. Oxford University paid him a small retainer to train their team and in between he held court at the Battersea Park track, where a hundred or more athletes would pay their shilling fee – 'a bob a knob' – for his hypnotic and inspirational advice.

Stampfl prided himself on having brought to Britain the ideas of Czech hero Emil Zatopek – winner of the 5000 metres, 10,000 metres and marathon at the Helsinki Olympics in 1952 – and German coach Woldemar Gerschler. He liked to be thought of as the man who put science into British sport. 'I must say this much,' he said. 'The first person to introduce these methods in England in 1938 was me. I introduced biological and physiological approaches to running mechanics and to throwing, and today they are generally accepted throughout the world.'

It was a highly debatable claim. Nevertheless Stampfl was a charismatic and highly inspirational figure and soon established himself as a freelance athletics coach. Every evening he ran training sessions at the Duke of York's barracks in Chelsea. Stampfl was the man who could guide Chris Brasher to the Olympics in this unfashionable event – the steeplechase.

Long walks and the occasional game of tennis were no longer good enough in the international world of steeplechasing. By the following year, under Stampfl's guidance, Brasher was no longer simply a 'possible' but had improved enough to make the team for Helsinki. But he found the heats of the 1952 Olympic steeplechase terrifyingly fast, with five runners breaking nine minutes. The third heat was won by the American Horace Ashenfelter in a very quick 8:51.2.

In the final, Ashenfelter seized the lead on the final bend and sprinted away to an easy victory in a world record time. With the Cold War raging between the United States and the USSR, the American press went wild with the story that Ashenfelter was an FBI agent who chased down his Soviet 'enemy'.

John Disley's third-place bronze was a lone success for the British team. Watched from the stands by his sister Margaret, Brasher finished eleventh out of twelve. He hit a hurdle and fell over.

Chris Chataway, another Achilles team-mate of Brasher's, would run his heart out in the 5000 metres, only to fall in exhaustion on the last lap and finish fifth. Margaret well remembers Chataway tripping over the edge of the track in that last lap, but what she recalls most vividly of the Games was the legendary horse Foxhunter, ridden by Harry Llewellyn, coming into the Olympic Stadium on the final day of the show jumping, clearing all the obstacles with a clear round, and securing Great Britain's only gold medal from those Olympics with victory for the three-day eventing team.

One of the favourites from the Achilles team was Brasher's colleague, Roger Bannister, picked to run in the 1500 metres. According to Brasher, the fit and wonderfully talented Bannister was nevertheless going through mental turmoil as the final of his event approached. Somehow Bannister appeared trapped between the Corinthian approach of those like Geoffrey Tudor and the more scientific approach of post-war coaches like Stampfl and Dyson, who swore that hard work and hard racing were everything.

Just prior to the Helsinki Games, five of the world's athletics authorities were asked to give their forecast of the probable results of the 1500 metres. Three predictions, those by Dr Roberto Quercetani of Italy, Fulvio Regli of Switzerland and the McWhirter twins of Great Britain, put Bannister in first place. 'That,' said

Bannister, 'is the burden that was on me. That's what I was facing.'
Challenged by this pressure, his own natural nervousness, and the
new dread that another semi-final round had been introduced into
the event only a few weeks before, meaning three races in three
days, Bannister found it almost impossible to sleep in the Olympic
village.

The sleep problem is recalled clearly by both Chataway and
Brasher. Chataway shared a room with Bannister and said, 'It was
terribly self-defeating. Looking back now I think he was defeated
purely in his own mind and he could have won that final quite
easily. But Roger was absolutely devastated by the thought of an
extra round in the 1500 metres and I can remember him lying on
that bed. It was a square box of a room with iron bedsteads. We had
strung a blanket up across the window to try and keep out the
unrelenting Scandinavian daylight.

'With us was Nick Stacey who was very funny. He maintained an
absolute non-stop cabaret act throughout. Nick had this wooden
box in the corner of a room on which he would practise the victory
ceremony. Some days Avery Brundage, the Olympic President,
would be approaching his rostrum and Nick would say: "Well it
was nothing sir really, pure luck sir, pure luck."

'Then other days he would be punching the air proclaiming: "By
God that showed them!" He got this Coca-Cola bottle and he
reckoned that the best way to stop himself having wet dreams and
wasting precious energy was to tie the bottle to the back of his
pyjamas. But Roger was taking it very badly. He was lying on his
bed moaning the entire time and there was much talk that he might
be ill in some way.'

Both Brasher and Chataway thought that Bannister's real
problem was a mental one. By the time he lined up for the 1500
metres final, the man who had been tipped as the favourite for the
race found that anxiety had given way to fear, and fear had been
elbowed aside by panic. Bannister had defied advice, gone his own
way, trained by his own methods and raced his own races. He

hungered for the victory that would justify everything. But he knew that if he failed, the press, the public and even the athletics authorities would turn on him.

By his own admission Bannister had hardly the strength to warm up for that 1500 metres final in Helsinki. In the last lap, both Barthel of Luxembourg and Bob McMillen, the American athlete from Los Angeles who was to win the silver medal, went charging past Bannister, who was lying second when they started their sprint. For Bannister the race was over. The pain that gripped him was much more than the usual exhaustion that followed the end of a race. Lactic acid mixed with despair, disappointment and anger was for him the bitterest of athletic cocktails. Bannister was beaten into fourth place, the worst place to be, out of the medals. It was a lesson not lost on Chris Brasher.

Brasher's verdict on the race was analytical. 'Roger knew then that it was going to be four years before the next Olympics and that he was going to be too busy working as a doctor. He knew he would never find the time to commit himself to go for an Olympic victory again.'

The press, which had torn into Bannister for his failure, were kinder to Chris Chataway. He was seen as the man who ran till he dropped. 'Chataway's failure in the 5,000 metres perhaps did as much to restore British credit as a virile country – if anyone persisted in doubting it after 1939 to 45 – as any victory would have done,' reported *The Times* on 4 August in an article headlined 'The True Spirit'.

But, said Brasher, 'I believe that it was the headlines that screamed his failure that set Roger Bannister on the quest for the first four-minute mile. 1954 was the year of the Empire Games and the European Championships. Roger knew that neither an Empire Games title nor a European title could quite make up for a lost Olympic title, but the *four-minute mile* – there was a target to go for. It was an ambition that would surely be unique in history.'

On the way back from Finland, according to Brasher, he

introduced Chataway and Bannister to Gerschler, the German coach who, while working at the University of Freiburg in the Black Forest, had pioneered scientific interval training. This – added to the use of stimulants, as was later discovered – had led to Josy Barthel's surprise victory over Bannister in the 1500 metres.

'I introduced them at the airport,' said Brasher. 'Roger was fascinated by the details of the interval training that Josy Barthel had been using. We realised that we could train a lot harder without any fear of going stale.' The lightly trained university athletes were amazed to learn how strenuously Barthel had prepared. Brasher and Chataway, said Brasher, even asked Gerschler if he would take them on as their coach and adviser. The German replied that he would be happy to do so, but only if they were prepared to visit him in Freiburg to undergo scientific assessment of their condition and potential. Brasher turned down the offer, but he and Gerschler exchanged letters for some time expounding their training theories.

'Anyone who had seen Zatopek win had to know how he did it,' Brasher said. 'You had to learn what made it possible. We had to wonder what this sort of training might do for our own running.'

For Brasher the Olympics had provided other role models. He had witnessed Chataway, lauded for his 'pluck and courage', as the man who never gave up in the teeth of defeat. And Brasher had glimpsed that for Zatopek, particularly in that man-killer of an event, the marathon, hard work could bring undreamt-of rewards.

Brasher had come second to last in his steeplechase final in 9:14.0, but he wasn't dejected. He was excited by his first taste of the Olympics. His friend Chataway toyed with the idea of giving up athletics after the Games. Bannister knew too that his commitment to his career ruled out further Olympics, though he still dreamed of the four-minute mile.

But Brasher couldn't wait to get back to Britain and start training harder than ever with his coach Franz Stampfl.

5

The Four-Minute Pacemaker

'Doctors and scientists said that breaking the four-minute mile was impossible, that one would die in the attempt. Thus, when I got up from the track after collapsing at the finish line, I figured I was dead.'

Sir Roger Bannister

TALK OF THE mythical four-minute mile reached something of a crescendo in the second half of the twentieth century. In the 1950s, Raymond Glendenning was the BBC's leading sports commentator, his gravelly, authoritative voice known to millions through his radio broadcasts. A daunting figure, a little overweight with a wide drooping wartime pilot's moustache and Brylcreemed hair, he surveyed the sporting world through horn-rimmed spectacles and a cloud of smoke from his ever-present cigarette.

But his was the voice of sport and in 1951 at a Brains Trust, a round-table conference of a dozen of Britain's sportsmen chaired by Glendenning, he asked a young Roger Bannister the question about which people were already speculating in bars and dressing rooms throughout the land.

'What are the prospects,' boomed Glendenning in his plummy broadcasting style, 'of a four-minute mile by a Britisher?'

Bannister answered: 'I would say that there is a reasonable

possibility of our doing it. If you can find the man who can run a mile in 4:04 like Wooderson, it's reasonable that you will find someone who can go below that when he has someone to run against. He must know what he is aiming at and who will do his pacemaking.'

Chris Brasher was convinced that the quest for the four-minute mile became a reality during the Olympic Games of 1952 in Helsinki. He said of Bannister's defeat in the 1500 metres by what he described as 'an unknown chunky little runner from, of all unlikely places, Luxembourg', Josy Barthel: 'It is hard now to realise how traumatic that was. One must recall the conditions of 1952: the continuing austerity, the apparent inability of Britain to recover from the war, the complete lack of any sporting successes abroad. We the British with our customary introspection were wondering whether the war had not drained us of all ambition and will.'

There was, said Brasher, just one hope. 'A tall, pale Oxford medical student who seemed to have perfect control of himself. After all, hadn't he refused an invitation to take part in the 1948 Olympic Games at Wembley because at nineteen, he thought he was too young?'

'Immediately after the Helsinki Games in 1952,' said Chris Chataway, 'Roger Bannister wrote me a letter saying he would like to make two attempts on the four-minute mile later that year. He asked if I would pace him saying that nobody could do it on their own, and that he felt extremely comfortable running behind me.'

'I feel I could do it with you,' Bannister had added.

'But with the Games over,' said Chataway, 'I was absolutely finished. I had made arrangements to go with a relative in his car across France to stay in Switzerland. I had never been abroad or on holiday and it was a big thing. So I said no.

'But it was clear that Roger immediately saw the breaking of that mile record as providing the vindication of his athletic career.' It was evident from the letter, said Chataway, that

Bannister wanted to do it. 'He talked not just of breaking Gunder Haegg's record but specifically of running the four-minute mile, and it was obvious that he was well aware of how significant such a run would be.'

Haegg was the Swedish runner who had set the world record for the mile in 1945. He set thirteen world records in races from 1500 metres to six miles; and with his friend and rival Arne Andersson trimmed the record for the mile half a dozen times, ending with Haegg's 4:01.4. This was the fastest mile in the world until Bannister broke the four-minute barrier in May 1954.

With Chataway temporarily out of the picture as a pacemaker, Bannister wondered if he might break records before the year was out, and his thoughts strayed to Brasher and to a bright young middle-distance hope called Brian Hewson. He decided to enlist Hewson's help in a match between the AAA and the Combined Services at Uxbridge in mid August 1952.

In the event Bannister slowed dramatically and though he won the race in 4:13.8 he was almost caught by the chasing pack. He concluded that he had passed his peak for the season and that the speed and fitness he had enjoyed before the Games had vanished and would have to be rebuilt.

Bannister and Brasher understood well that any miler was limited by lack of oxygen and that in order to keep his oxygen requirement to a minimum he would need to run at precisely fifteen miles per hour to achieve the target of the four-minute mile. The ideal pace would be four even laps of sixty seconds each. So if time was the object of the race, other competitors would have to be ignored unless they were willing to co-operate in setting and achieving a predetermined schedule. This was why pacemaking was so important to these runners in the seasons that followed the Helsinki Games.

In 1953 Mount Everest would be conquered by Edmund Hillary and Tenzing Norgay. The two were paced and pushed to the peak by British teamwork. The news that at last two humans stood at the top of the world was delivered to the public on the eve of the coronation of a young Queen Elizabeth II. Two million people camped on the streets of London and millions more were glued to their flickering black and white television sets, watching as the 27-year-old Queen was carried in her golden coach to Westminster Abbey. Her coronation ushered in what the press were heralding as a new Elizabethan Age.

Brasher and his friends Chataway and Bannister believed that in this new era anything was possible. With rationing ending in Britain in February and Stalin breathing his last in Moscow, the long shadow of the war seemed at last to be lifting. In America a fresh-faced Jack Kennedy was marrying the glamorous Jacqueline Bouvier. At Wembley that old wizard Stanley Matthews, Britain's greatest football hero, at last gained an FA Cup winner's medal with Blackpool's victory over Bolton. At the Oval England's cricket team under the captaincy of Len Hutton regained the Ashes from Australia for the first time in nineteen years. At Buckingham Palace Gordon Richards, the finest jockey in the sport of kings, was knighted.

To mark coronation year, Britain's biggest-selling Sunday newspaper, the *News of the World*, came up with an idea that caught the excitement of the battle for the four-minute mile. It announced that it would sponsor a mile race open to the finest athletes in the world. The story the paper was after was the epic of the first man to break the four-minute barrier. They hoped it would be an Englishman. And so too did the McWhirter twins, Ross and Norris, statisticians and pedlars of sporting facts.

Brasher had first come across the McWhirters as sprinters in the Achilles team at Oxford. Norris McWhirter had captained the team to Athens and Rome in which Brasher had his first encounter with the steeplechase. They were friends of Chataway, too, who was working as a management trainee with Guinness. In May 1951, Sir Hugh Beaver, then the managing director of Guinness Breweries, went on a shooting party in County Wexford, Ireland. He got involved in a fierce argument over which was the fastest game bird in Europe – the golden plover or the grouse.

That evening he was annoyed that there was no reference book to settle arguments about such records. He raised the issue with his promising trainee. Chataway recommended the McWhirters, who had left Oxford to run their fact-finding agency in London. The brothers were commissioned to compile what became *The Guinness Book of Records*.

'No other journalists were as well informed about the athletics scene as the McWhirters,' said Brasher. 'Their passion for statistics was legendary. They fed everything to Bannister and to others like Harold Abrahams and Franz Stampfl. They were always trying to wind up Roger to go for the first four-minute mile.'

The McWhirters shared Brasher's belief that Bannister was Britain's best hope. They knew too that perfect pacing was one of the keys to breaking the barrier and they pored over their statistics, making lists, plotting how the puzzle might best be solved. In the 1950s pacemaking was strictly illegal under the AAA's laws: no athlete was supposed to enter a race unless he intended to complete it and try to win it. But the rule was difficult to enforce and was becoming increasingly blurred as athletes strove to break records. What the pacemakers – the hares, in the parlance of the old paper-chasing days – had to do was set up a reasonable show of running to finish and attempting to win. It was always difficult for officials to judge if a man was pacemaking or simply running in front in an attempt to win the race. If he didn't drop out and kept going to finish, it was virtually impossible to disqualify a pacemaker. If he wasn't stupid enough to actually admit he was pacemaking, the officials were likely to turn a blind eye.

Bannister and Chataway lined up together in the mile at Oxford on 2 May 1953 for the annual match between Oxford University and the AAA. On that May day Chataway, who had taken an afternoon off from the last-minute panic of revising for his final exams, had agreed to run as hard as he could for the first three laps. Then it would be up to Bannister to make a dash for home.

When the bell clanged at 3:05.2, Bannister strode past his tiring friend, who pulled off the track after only a few more yards. With a brilliantly fast final lap of 58.4 seconds, Bannister hit the tape at 4:03.6, a new British record. John Disley, Chris Brasher's climbing friend and Olympic bronze medallist in the steeplechase, was second in 4:15.4. But the man missing from this equation was Brasher, who might provide the perfect pacing.

After Bannister's new record, the British public were hungrier than ever for someone to break the four-minute barrier. The McWhirters were on the phone all the time relaying information to Brasher, Bannister and Chataway.

'The McWhirters were always stoking up his fears,' said Brasher. 'The danger was that the record might cross the Atlantic before Roger could manage it. There was a sense of desperation and hurry. We all knew Roger could do it but time was running out.'

Norris McWhirter said that Wes Santee, Bannister's American rival from Kansas, was threatening to run the four-minute mile first, and was planning a serious attempt on the record in Dayton, Ohio on 27 June 1953. Santee had run 4:02.4 on 5 June 1953, the fourth fastest mile ever. And he wasn't the only rival threatening to break the four-minute barrier. On 12 December 1953, the Australian John Landy was to run 4:02.0.

'Leave it all to us,' said Norris to Bannister. He added that he would fix up something with Brasher. Because of the time difference between Britain and America the McWhirters decided to stage the event secretly the following Saturday, just hours before Santee was scheduled to race. They called Brasher by phone and asked him to take part in a special invitation mile in the unlikely surroundings of the Surrey Schools AAA Championship at Motspur Park.

'There were only three of us in the race,' said Brasher. 'There was Roger of course, the Australian Don MacMillan (who had come ninth in the Helsinki Olympic 1500 metres) and me. We decided to pace the whole thing, get Roger round in four minutes if we could. It was all a bit mad and had been fixed up on the hoof very quickly. MacMillan reckoned he was fit enough to manage three laps but that wouldn't be enough, so we got to thinking and came up with what we thought was a fiendishly clever idea.'

This ploy was typical of Brasher. Anything fiendishly clever seemed to strike a chord with his sense of ingenuity. 'It was brilliantly simple really. While MacMillan and Roger covered three laps I would take it easy and jog round for two. We hoped that just when MacMillan ran out of steam they would be coming up to lap me and I would take over and tow Roger round at full pace.'

As a solution to the pacing problem it was resourceful, beautiful – outrageous even. A strategy that Brasher had hatched with Norris McWhirter, it very nearly worked. The race went pretty much according to plan. MacMillan galloped through the first two and a half laps before he tired badly, leaving Bannister briefly out on his own. But coming up to the bell he caught the waiting Brasher, who was so full of running and excitement that he was able to shout encouragement to Bannister over his shoulder as he ran.

When Bannister made his strike for the tape the school children, most of whom were politely sitting cross-legged on the grass by the track, cheered wildly, caught up in the thrill of it all. The first three-quarters of a mile had been run in 3:01.8. Urged on by Brasher's shouts, Bannister ran the last lap in 60.2 seconds to cross the line alone in 4:02.0, missing the magic four-minute mile by only two seconds – but still running the third fastest mile in history. Five hours later, in Dayton, Ohio, Santee ran 4:07.6. The prize was safe for a little while longer. Significantly, Bannister's race was never mentioned in the programme of events (which was against AAA's rules), giving the authorities plenty of scope to ignore it.

When the British Amateur Athletic Board met a couple of

weeks later to consider ratification of several new British record marks, they were faced with the problem of what to do about the bizarre Motspur Park mile. They issued the following statement:

> The British Amateur Athletic Board does not accept the 4 02 mile by R.G. Bannister at Motspur Park on 27 June as a record. The Board wishes to draw attention to the fact that it has unfettered discretion whether to accept or refuse to recognise a record. The Board has carefully considered all the circumstances and regrets that while it has no doubt that the time was accomplished it cannot recognise the performance as a record. It has been compelled to take the view that it was not done in a bona fide competition according to the rules.

'And so we come to that winter of 1953 and 54,' said Brasher. 'Bannister is in his last year as a medical student at St Mary's Hospital, Paddington; Chataway working as an under-brewer at the Guinness brewery in Park Royal; and myself working as a junior executive for an oil company.

'Both Chris and I were training under Franz Stampfl, the Austrian who had come to Britain in the 1930s, and a man of vast imagination and almost overpowering personality. Seeing that Roger's vulnerable point was his lack of strength, we inveigled him into joining us on Friday nights in the Duke of York's barracks in the King's Road, Chelsea, where more than 100 athletes enjoyed themselves in the gym under Franz's regime.'

In the winter of 1953 Chataway, Brasher and Bannister were meeting Stampfl regularly. Chataway and Brasher discussed their training with him in detail. Their previous light regimes were replaced by interval training, which might in an evening mean ten times 440 yards in 60 seconds, with a two-minute rest period in between, or four or five half-mile runs, again with only a short breathing space.

Some time in March 1954 the date for the attempt was set for 6 May, said Brasher. 'And the tactics were decided upon as well: even-paced running with the first two laps by me, the third lap by Chris and then Roger stretching out for the tape.

'I can remember one particular evening a week or two later when, after a hard session at the Duke of York's, we went for a cup of tea at the Lyons tea shop in Sloane Square. Franz asked if I could manage two and a half laps and if Chris could manage three and a half, leaving Roger to burst for the tape with 220 yards to go. I had doubts, but Stampfl had a way of exorcising such doubts from the mind of an athlete.'

There was one other strange interlude in those weeks before the attempt. Something was wrong with their training. However hard they tried, the trio simply could not run ten repetition quarter-miles in an average of under sixty seconds for each quarter. In exaspera-tion, Brasher told Stampfl: 'We seem to be marking time.'

Stampfl thought they needed some relaxation. 'So Roger and I went climbing in Glencoe,' said Brasher, who promised that they wouldn't try anything too difficult.

'How big are the mountains?' asked Chataway.

'Small,' said Brasher, 'but they could test us. We'll go up Clachaig Gulley and tackle Jericho Wall. It's pretty steep but it's no Everest.'

Brasher and Bannister set off for Scotland in a 1950s Le Mans Aston Martin DB2 that was built for speed rather than passenger comfort. The athletes took it in turns to crouch down on an in-flated lilo in the luggage space between the two bucket seats. Brasher had managed to cadge a lift from his climbing compan-ion John Mawe, a doctor. Mawe had observed that there was 'nothing worse than for a couple of athletes like you to be cooped up like this'. After some ten hours they approached Glencoe. A light drizzle was falling as the athletes went for their first stiff-limbed walk.

On 18 April 1954, Mawe, Bannister and Brasher set out to climb

Clachaig Gulley. A few hours earlier a climbing companion, David
Thomas, had gone alone up the gulley and found it very wet. After
the first waterfall he peeled off his anorak and pullovers and stuffed
them into his rucksack. Later Brasher led Bannister up the 'red
chimney', but the going was cold and they were drenched when
they reached the top.

Brasher had been growing increasingly anxious about Bannister
and the effect that the chill factor might have on his finely tuned
athletic body. The weather was so cold and wet that he feared
Bannister might catch pneumonia. Scrambling over the summit,
Brasher barked to Thomas, who was waiting for them at the top,
that he should give all his dry clothes to Bannister immediately for
the 'good of British sport'.

'How could I refuse?' said the bemused Thomas. Three weeks
later, when Bannister eventually broke the four-minute barrier,
Thomas was able to pride himself in having played a small part in
his success.

It was a crazy training programme with the race so close but
three days later, after another cramped ten-hour car journey, the
trio of Bannister, Brasher and Chataway, timed by Stampfl, ran their
ten quarter-miles at an average of 58.9 seconds each. The trio had
eventually achieved their training target and the attempt on the
four-minute mile could go ahead.

'Roger went to work on the morning of the race,' said Brasher.
Bannister took a mid-morning train from Paddington and was
joined in the compartment by Franz Stampfl. It seemed to be a
chance encounter, said Brasher, 'But it was a vital meeting. Franz
used his persuasive powers to convince Roger that he was capable
of 3:56 and that the wind could not slow him by more than half a
second a lap at the most.'

Neither Chataway nor Brasher could remember afterwards how
they got to Oxford but the trio assembled at the Iffley Road track
at about five o'clock that Thursday evening. 'The wind still blew,
gusting fitfully,' said Brasher. 'We warmed up and then went back

to the old wooden changing rooms. It was obvious that the secret was out – that Roger was going to make an attempt that evening. There was a BBC film camera in the middle of the track and the well-known faces of every athletics correspondent.'

A small army of sports writers and photographers had been mobilised to turn up at Iffley Road by McWhirter, who had also tipped off BBC Television to cover the meeting. The wind and the rain made the record attempt seem crazy. 'Back in the dressing room,' said Brasher, Roger was making his decision. It was he who had dreamed of reaching beyond a man's grasp.'

Ten minutes or so before they lined up for the start, the rain stopped. As they lined up for the start, Bannister glanced at the flag which flew from the church overlooking the Iffley Road track. It fluttered gently in the breeze. The wind had dropped and the six o'clock sun was strong enough to cast shadows on the track.

A false start from Brasher and then they were away, Brasher taking the lead as pre-arranged. Brasher remembered: 'And then there we were on the starting line. "I can remember the relief at the gun," Roger told me. "It was a relief that the race had begun, that here we were, actually running, that there wasn't a howling gale or pouring rain, how lucky we were."' Bannister and Chataway tucked in behind Brasher, gliding in his slipstream. After five days of rest the trio were schoolboy fresh. Brasher ran the first 220 yards in a fraction over twenty-seven seconds, which was fast. Bannister misheard the crackling speakers and in panic shouted 'Faster, faster,' at Brasher.

'I don't think I heard him,' said Brasher, 'but in any case without getting up on my toes and sprinting flat out I was going as fast as I could. You do not sprint and survive at that stage in a mile race. The wind hit us in the back straight, but the pace I remember was flowing sweetly and automatically. At 1 min 58 sec for the half-mile the pace was fine.

'Here,' said Brasher, 'I must confess that in the days before the race, at times of day-dreaming, I had imagined myself completing my two and a half laps and then, as Chris Chataway and Roger swept by me, latching on behind and being towed around until I unleashed my finishing burst and won the race!

'It explains much about the mind of an athlete – a mind will wander into the realms of fantasy beyond the reach of his body, a mind will occasionally command the body to reach into that fantasy. On that evening my mind could not command the body to move any faster at that pace.

'We went into the back straight, my task was done: but where in the hell was Chataway? Then he swept past with Roger behind him. Maybe it looks magnificent on the film, but it was hard and Chris Chataway was tired. He kept the pace going, passing the bell for the last lap in 3 min. 0.4 sec.'

Bannister had to complete the last lap in fifty-nine seconds to break the barrier. He kept his nerve and clung to Chataway until just 300 yards from the finish, then he struck. All long arms and legs, stride massive, hands pumping with power, his hair streaming behind him. 'The arms of the world were waiting to receive me if only I reached the tape without slacking my speed,' said Bannister. He finished and sagged like a beaten heavyweight in the arms of Achilles sprinter Nick Stacey.

'Then,' said Brasher, 'came that famous announcement by Norris McWhirter in which he listed every record we had broken, from the Iffley Road track to the world record, before announcing the time as: THREE . . . at which point the roar drowned him.'

For the record it was 3:59.4, with Chataway second in 4:07.2, William Hulatt third in 4:16.0 and Brasher fourth, untimed because the crowd were all over the track. There were two Oxford men in the race as well, Alan Gordon and George Dole, an American, but the crowd prevented them from finishing.

While Bannister signed autographs and thanked the head groundsman, Walter Morris, for preparing the track, Brasher was in no doubt about the significance of what they had achieved. He told the reporter Terry O'Connor, working for the London *Evening*

News, with an understandable air of triumphalism: '*Well, we did it. That means Landy and Wes Santee can never break the four-minute mile first.*'

So confident had Brasher been that the record would be broken, before leaving London for Oxford he had reserved a table for a celebration that evening at Clement Freud's club above the Royal Court Theatre in Chelsea, and, he said, 'lined up three girlfriends to share the dinner'.

Afterwards, in the small hours of that night, Brasher remembered, 'we stopped in Piccadilly Circus to ask a policemen the way to a nightclub that was, reputedly, still open. He peered into Chris's old pre-war Austin, saw the three of us jammed in with our current girlfriends, and said: "You gentlemen are not gentlemen if you take these ladies to that club." And then he started to take out his note-book and I thought: "We can't be booked for asking the way."

'But instead of writing in the book himself, he handed it to us, saying, "Perhaps I can have your autographs, gentlemen."'

It was when the morning newspapers were delivered to the nightclub that the full impact of what the three of them had achieved struck home and Brasher began to have misgivings about the part he had played in the drama. There was a story blazoned on every front page, and not just in Britain. The *New York Herald Tribune* declared that Bannister had achieved the track's wildest dream:

> The four minute mile – this has been the holy grail of foot racing. This is the vision that has governed men's minds, fired their imagination, inspired more dreaming and more argument, more speculation and prophetic debate than the way of an eagle in the air, or the way of the serpent on a rock, the way of a ship in the midst of the sea, the way of a man with a maid.

Next day Bannister needed a suitcase to carry all the telegrams and messages of congratulation. He had become a household name, a national institution overnight. He was learning rapidly that the pressures of training could be as nothing compared with the pressures of fame. The British had a new folk hero and the press and the public swelled with national pride.

Brasher was left with mixed feelings at his part in the four-minute mile, although he was later to write:

> Twenty-four hours after it was all over the three of us went for a walk over Harrow Hill as the light faded. There was in that hour or two a closeness, man to man, such as I had never experienced before or since. We had trained together and fought together. We had been rivals and one man had proved himself incomparably the best. Yet there was no resentment – just a sweet relish of the past, a companionship of the moment and resolutions, idealistic all of them, for the future.

Within days Brasher had decided to put his thoughts on paper about how the four-minute mile could be achieved. On the back of foolscap sheets of Mobil Oil manifests, noting the names and cargoes of oil tankers and dated March to May 1954, are Brasher's own handwritten notes. There is much about the methods used by Emil Zatopek and details of the sessions that he and Stampfl arranged in the build-up to the race. These notes were to provide the raw material for many articles to come about that day in May.

Six weeks later John Landy became the second man to break the four-minute mile, setting a new world record on 21 June 1954 at an international meet at Turku, Finland. Having received help from Chris Chataway, Landy achieved a time of 3:57.9, ratified by the International Association of Athletics Federations (IAAF) as 3:58.0. That record stood for more than three years.

In August that year Brasher rejoined his old friends, Bannister and Chataway, to run in the Empire Games in Vancouver. There was no steeplechase in these Games and Brasher was selected alongside

Bannister, David Law and Ian Boyd to run in the mile for England. John Disley represented Wales in the same event. Both Brasher and Disley failed to make it past the heats, Brasher finishing sixth in heat two in 4:15.4 and Disley fifth in heat one in 4:09.0. The meeting in the final of the world's two fastest milers was dubbed 'The Miracle Mile' and the 'Race of the Century'. It was heard over the radio by 100 million people and seen on television by millions more. Bannister hung back in the early laps while Landy surged ahead, Bannister finally taking the lead in the last lap to defeat Landy in 3:58.7. Both men broke four minutes.

Following the Games, Brasher and Chataway took a few days' break to explore parts of British Columbia. It was here, says Chataway, that Brasher showed the first signs of what was to become an entrepreneurial career.

'He was very excited by the concept of self-service petrol stations. It sounded pretty impractical to me, never got anywhere. But it was a hint of things to come. We also got tied up for a while syndicating British and European sports results to a sports radio channel. We got £25 a time. I was more well-known than Chris, so I got £15, and Chris got £10. It didn't last long.'

When his four minutes of fame were over, Bannister disappeared into the corridors of St Mary's Hospital, to emerge nine summers later, after years of medical training and two years of Army conscription, as a consultant in neurology. He said he never dreaded the burden of that four-minute fame in any sense. 'It's a passport to communication with people who might otherwise find it difficult,' he told Brasher. 'And for me it's become a sort of responsibility that one is at times a piece of public property.'

But for Brasher, failing to make the final in the Empire Games and his bit part in the four-minute mile was never going to be enough. 'It left me feeling something of a fraud,' he said. 'Any fame I had was a result of Roger's generosity in giving as much credit to us – Chris and I, his pacemakers. In reality I was a very ordinary athlete with very little to my own personal credit.

'So a feeling grew that I, too, must concentrate and I must give up all my other activities and devote myself for one year to the climbing of my own particular pinnacle – an Olympic title.'

6

No Fags, No Mountains, No Women

'So you wish to conquer in the Olympic Games, my friend? You will have to put yourself under discipline; to eat by rule, to avoid cakes and sweetmeats; to take exercise at the appointed hour whether you like it or not, in cold and heat; to abstain from cold drinks and from wine at your will; in a word, to give yourself over to the trainer as to a physician.'

Epictetus, Greek philosopher

IN 1954 CHRIS BRASHER was desperate to become successful in his own right. He had seen what his close friends could achieve. 'Roger Bannister had his four-minute mile,' he wrote, 'and Chris Chataway had beaten the great Russian Vladimir Kuts in a world record time. Me, I'd done nothing. But we honestly believed that if you have a dream and you work to make it come true, then you can really change the world. There is just nothing you can't do.'

So in May 1955, just a year after Bannister made history, Brasher decided to make his own sacrifice for the Melbourne Olympics. He gave up smoking twenty cigarettes a day plus pipe tobacco and he turned his back on mountain climbing and girls. He forsook them all for a year and two months and hoped that fate would be kinder to him than it had been in Helsinki. His sights were set on the steeplechase – where he was up against his friend and his greatest rival, John Disley.

Disley's was the dominant influence on British steeplechasing throughout the 1950s. Before 1950 the steeplechase was considered to be rather foreign, an event of which the Scandinavians alone knew the secret. Yet this so-called foreign event is probably the oldest race in the British athletics calendar. It was devised in 1850 at Binsey near Oxford when Exeter College students settled a wager by racing on foot around the local meadows. This race was unlike the early paper-chases, where the pack had to follow a trail of shredded paper; it was a true 'steeplechase' in which the competitors ran from landmark to landmark, from steeple to steeple. If there were streams to ford or gates to leap over, the runners would press on as best they could.

It was not until the 1950s that British steeplechasing began to improve. In September 1951 Disley had broken his own British and Commonwealth record for the 3000 metres steeplechase, clocking 9:11.6 in a meeting at the White City, London. Among those he beat was Chris Brasher, who was back in fifth place. Disley had taken the bronze medal in the Helsinki Olympics in 1952 while Brasher trailed in one from last. Brasher was determined to make up for it four years later, and working with his coach, Franz Stampfl, he was improving a lot.

On a foggy night in October 1955 at London's White City, with less than a year to go to the next Games in Melbourne, Eric Shirley, a tough Finchley Harrier who had been born in a workhouse and experienced a rough childhood, won the 3000 metres steeplechase in a new British record of 8:47.6. Disley was second in 8:50.0 and Brasher just behind him in 8:52.6. Britain could now boast of three athletes in the world's top ten, and they could look forward with confidence to the 1956 Olympics.

On 12 January 1956, ten months before the opening ceremony of the Olympics, Brasher wrote a letter to *The Times* from his home in Kensington Mansions that was to spell out much of his attitude to sport and the coming Games. In this letter Brasher expressed his annoyance at the suggestion, put forward by British officials still wedded to the 'amateur' ideal, that state-aided athletes, of whom the Soviet Union had plenty, might be excluded from the Olympics:

> If those athletes in my own event who come from behind the Iron Curtain were excluded on these grounds from going to Melbourne, I for one would immediately cease training. One of the major reasons for still competing would have disappeared.
>
> These reasons are as complex and very akin to the reasons why people climb mountains. . . . An athlete knows that he will be competing against the athletic elite of the whole world, not against only certain classes of people from certain countries. The winner of a gold medal at Melbourne has proved to himself that he is the best athlete in the world at that event.
>
> That athlete knows the standards that are required . . . no athlete wants excuses made on his behalf by the press or the public. He does not mind if his opponent has been playing hooky with the amateur laws, for who can effectively define these laws. He does not mind if his opponent has no real job or profession except that of sport.
>
> I still believe that a man who uses his brain during the day and has an interesting job can become a better athlete than he who spends all his time in sport. Mental development is just as important as physical development.
>
> In any one year approximately three quarters of Great Britain's athletic team come from the London area. Are we better specimens physically or mentally than the northerners or Scots? I and some of my friends trained by permission of the Territorial Army, the Chelsea Football Club and the London County Council, but if we lived in Manchester or Glasgow most of us would have retired long ago because of lack of these training facilities.

Living in London and trained for four years in Cambridge, Brasher had enjoyed the coaching and the tracks of an Olympic contender. He knew that athletes like Eric Shirley did not share the privileges of upbringing that he had enjoyed. The injustice of it annoyed him, he strongly felt that the 'best man should win'.

But early in 1955 Brasher was faced himself with the fear of losing the man who masterminded his training – his coach Franz Stampfl.

Bathing in the inevitable fame which followed the breaking of the four-minute mile barrier, Stampfl was applauded and sought after as one of the world's leading trainers. He had spent many years during the war interned as an enemy alien in Australia and it was to that country that his eyes now wandered looking for a job as a coach.

It was Stampfl who had inspired Brasher to drop all other interests – to break up with his girlfriend, give up cigarettes and mountain climbing – in order to focus on the Olympics. 'Franz is the only coach,' said Brasher, 'who makes you feel an utter heel if you don't complete his schedules. I was determined not to leave anything to chance. If you were prepared to go out and die, Franz was the man to prepare you.'

Bill Rawlinson, then president of Melbourne's Sports Union, heard that Stampfl had married an Australian, Patsy, and was looking to settle in Melbourne. He approached a former Olympic swimmer, Sir Frank Beaurepaire, with a request to fund a salary to enable the appointment of Stampfl as 'advisor in athletics' at Melbourne University. Stampfl's recruitment by the university was considered a great coup by Australia, but a blow to the British athletes who relied on him.

Stampfl's coaching relied on constant physical and physiological tests. He was meticulous in checking temperature, humidity and the weather conditions under which the athletes trained; pulse checks would be taken at set times each day and blood pressure kept constantly under surveillance. Performance, Stampfl believed, would improve in proportion to the amount of training the athlete could handle. 'It's like building up immunity to poisons,' he explained. 'Give a man a big dose and he is dead but gradually step up the doses and he won't die. There's no guesswork to it.'

But the coach's psychological value to his pupils was even more powerful. 'Men are lifted from their mediocrity by their imagination and the wealth of experience they can portray in their vocation,' said Stampfl. 'I myself can be inspired by listening to music, by looking at great paintings, or be enraptured by superb dancers. I thrill at the fantastic rhythm of their bodies swaying in perfect harmony and the sheer magic of seeing them as lonely men dominating a vast audience. Night after night they must pit their skill against the odds. When I leave the theatre I am like a boy wanting to be a dancer and entertain others as they did me. It is not possible for me, but the inspiration need not be lost.'

This inspiration is what Brasher needed most. He still dreamed of his fictional hero, Wilson of *The Wizard*. He knew that he could never achieve athletic heights with the 'effortless superiority' that Chris Chataway seemed to exude, but he was convinced he could do it through hard work. Stampfl would motivate him to do the hard work.

'I pass on the experience to my athletes,' said Stampfl, 'and tell them that one day they will enter an Olympic stadium all alone with thousands of eyes watching. They must prepare thoroughly for this moment. I teach them independence. They must be complete masters of themselves and resist the overwhelming feeling of loneliness which captures them. I try to make their minds so strong that they are blessed with an inward feeling of complete superiority for there must be no mental breakdown or all physical training will be in vain. I will try to lift them up above themselves for immortality may be only a few minutes away.'

The problem for Brasher was that Stampfl was leaving to go to Australia. It was a dilemma that both wrestled with and both tried to solve. Brasher believed that nobody could replace the bond that he had made with Stampfl – and they came up with an ingenious solution.

Stampfl would record his coaching instructions, every session that Brasher planned, on to spools of tape which would then be shipped to the other side of the world and replayed on a tape recorder. Brasher would get these sessions by listening to Stampfl's uniquely hypnotic voice. Closing his eyes, he would imagine himself back in the Lyons Corner House or on the track at the Duke of York's Barracks as he listened once again to Stampfl. He would replay the tapes and get the sessions right. For Brasher, this worked.

It worked, too, for Chataway. To judge by results, Stampfl's voice as it emerged from the speaker was almost as powerful as his physical presence. In March 1956, when Chataway drifted into a period of almost giving up on his running, a spool of tape arrived from Melbourne. It outlined Chataway's training schedules and kicked him back to the track. His subsequent performances were better than ever.

Loaded with passion, Stampfl's recorded messages were almost impossible to ignore. His mesmeric accented English would pour out a mix of inspiration and technical details in a seemingly endless stream:

'Try ten times 440 yards interval running from sixty to sixty-one seconds with a recovery lap of two minutes. Then next, three times a three-quarter mile each in three minutes fifteen seconds, but this time you can have fifteen minutes between . . . There is nothing a man can't do if the spirit is there . . . Do nothing on the day before the race. Let me know how you get on and I'll send you more.' The tapes worked well enough, but as Brasher discovered there is no substitute for the presence and eye of a good coach.

The AAA title in the Olympic year of 1956 was won by the ever-improving steeplechaser, Eric Shirley, who added the championship record to his British one with a time of 8:51.6. John Disley was a good second in 8:53.4 but for Brasher it was a disaster; he came a distant third.

Brasher had imposed upon himself an austere winter of vicious training under Stampfl and appeared to be in superb condition by the summer of 1956. So it was a shock to find himself draped across the track at the end of these AAA championships being violently ill after running a pathetically slow time, way behind Disley and Shirley.

'I had never felt so bad, I was absolutely shattered,' said Brasher. The worm of self-doubt twitched in his mind. Had all that hard work failed to transform him into a real athlete? Was he still the 'hoax' that he feared he might become after his bit part in the four-minute mile? The answer was to come in the lilting tones of Stampfl, relayed to him from the other side of the world. 'Immortality may be only a race away,' said the hypnotic voice. 'Inspiration is everything.'

More prosaically, Brasher knew he needed rest. Under Stampfl's guidance every race, every training session had its own point and purpose. Brasher believed that the results would come, hard work would bring its reward; but now his own single-mindedness, his stubbornness, was about to wreck him. 'I knew I hadn't under-trained so I must have over-trained,' he declared.

He needed a rescue plan. And it came from the Corinthian style of training that had brought Roger Bannister to the brink of greatness. For five long days before his four-minute mile, Bannister had done no running. He had paced the hospital corridors, walked in the parks, gathering himself like a coiled spring for the test to come. Like Bannister, Brasher's recipe for regaining his form was to stroll around golf courses and parkland, squirrelling away his mental and physical strength. Three weeks later this strategy was put to the test.

Among the Olympic selectors there were huge doubts about his form. It was obvious to them, and to the athletics commentators in the press, that unless Brasher could prove himself fully fit the selectors would drop him from the Games. He had one last chance to pluck out a performance that would get him into the Olympic team, to prove that all that training and sacrifice was worthwhile, otherwise he would sink into obscurity. He needed all the help that he could grab, and it was his old friend John Disley who threw him the rope.

At the last possible moment in August, Brasher was dragged through a 61.2 second last lap by Disley in the match between Great Britain and Czechoslovakia to record 8:47.2. Disley regained his British record with a time of 8:46.6. Disley's pacemaking was to prove an unselfish act of colossal significance. Without his assistance Brasher would have had little chance of making the team for Melbourne. Eric Shirley, the third member of the steeplechase squad, would for years shake his head in disbelief that Brasher had made the Olympic team. Without Disley's help, said Shirley, Brasher wouldn't have stood a hope.

'Sixteen seconds improvement in three weeks,' beamed a delighted Brasher. The confidence began to seep back into his sinews; he began to believe once more that if you have a dream there is nothing you can't do. By the time November came, Brasher had convinced himself that he was showing the best form of the three. Disley, Brasher knew, was short of training due to a bout of virus pneumonia. Shirley, he convinced himself, was 'over the hill', suffering from too much training.

Six weeks before the rest of the British Olympic team travelled, Brasher left for Melbourne with his friend Chris Chataway. There were inevitable mutterings among others in the team. Shirley, for instance, reckoned that these Oxbridge athletes had been given preferential treatment; nobody else, he said, could afford this sort of acclimatisation. Shirley was a salesman and had to take two weeks' holiday from work to compete in Melbourne; at that point Brasher had never beaten him in a race. But Stampfl was already installed as Australia's national coach in Melbourne, and Brasher wanted to spend the final six weeks under the watchful eye of his coach and mentor.

As the Melbourne Games approached, the world was plunged into turmoil. Russian tanks rolled into Budapest to crush the Hungarian revolution. Back in Budapest the Red Star was torn down from parliament buildings and replaced with the Hungarian national flag. In Melbourne hundreds of Hungarian expatriates, who had moved to Australia in previous years to escape the communist regime, were gathered at the airport when the bulk of the Hungarian Olympians landed. Many people suggested that, with the world entangled in conflict, the Olympics should be cancelled.

Avery Brundage, president of the International Olympic Committee (IOC), was still determined to hold the Games. 'The Olympics belong to the people,' he declared. 'They are a contest for individuals and not of nations.'

Little by little tension subsided. When the opening ceremonies were staged, 105,000 Australians filled the stadium and for the track competitions a capacity crowd turned out.

By 1 p.m. on the day of the opening ceremony, 22 November 1956, the Melbourne grandstands were filling fast. It was unbearably hot. Those with hats were the lucky ones; those without started fashioning their own newspaper hats of all shapes. Umbrellas were pressed into service to shield people from the blazing sun.

The Duke of Edinburgh's motorcade did a circuit of the arena. A Boy Scout gave a smart salute. 'God Save the Queen' echoed around the concrete amphitheatre. The biggest roar, however, was for the Hungarian team. Emil Zatopek, the Czech, one of Brasher's great heroes of the Helsinki Games in 1952, suddenly flung his hat wildly in the air in spontaneous delight as he passed the Duke of Edinburgh's box.

Brasher, despite the energy-sapping heat, enjoyed the spectacle of the opening ceremony. Stampfl had convinced him that he was in the form of his life, already acclimatised to this Australian summer. His eyes sparkled with pride at the promise of the British women's team, crisp and smart in their red and white uniform.

In the arena for a moment there was absolute stillness. The Duke of Edinburgh broke the silence: 'I declare open the Olympic Games of Melbourne celebrating the sixteenth Olympiad of the modern era.' The stadium burst into sound: a trumpet fanfare, cheering and then a great roar of pride. Soldiers raised the white Olympic flag bearing the five symbolic rings and from a hundred places around

the outside of the arena thousands of pigeons were released. The
stadium was rocked by a twenty-one gun salute.

From the north-eastern entrance Ron Clarke, the former world
junior mile record holder, appeared with a torch held high above his
head. Athletes broke ranks and raced across the ground for a closer
look as the flame passed down the back straight. Clarke came into
view again on the balcony high above the stadium. He leaned
forward, pitched the torch into the cauldron. A choir of twelve
thousand voices sang the Olympic hymn and the 'Hallelujah'
Chorus. John Landy strode to the rostrum and pronounced the
Olympic oath on behalf of the 3500 assembled athletes,.

United in the Olympic Stadium for the opening ceremony were
Bannister, Chataway and Brasher. The old team were back together
and just as the four-minute mile had produced an explosion that
was to change their lives, so too did what was to happen next.

7

No, No, No, Not Brasher

'Fear is the strongest driving force in competition. Not fear of one's opponent, but of the skill and high standard he represents; fear, too, of not acquitting oneself well. In the achievement of higher performances, of beating formidable rivals, the athlete defeats fear and conquers himself.'

Franz Stampfl

ON 14 NOVEMBER Brasher's gruelling hard work in Australia started to pay off. He raced at Geelong, just fifty miles from the Olympic Stadium, against the man who everybody fancied to win the 1500 metres gold medal in Melbourne, the second man to have broken the four-minute mile barrier and the man who was currently the world record holder at that distance – John Landy.

Brasher was dismissed by the press and the pundits as a makeweight in this Olympic warm-up race. Although held over an unusual distance, two miles, it featured a number of high-class competitors. All eyes were on Landy, the favourite, when the race started. Looking and behaving like the strongest man in the field, he had an imperious air in the early laps, as if just waiting to unleash his sprint and collect the prize.

For most of the race Brasher was tucked away, an inconspicuous fourth. With a couple of laps to go the restless crowd looked for a spurt from Landy when suddenly Brasher, overtaking the leaders, surged to the front, urged on from the trackside by Chataway and Stampfl.

Stampfl yelled at Chataway: 'Tell him to go now!' Brasher heard the shout and thought to himself, 'Who, me? Go now against this field? They must be mad.'

But go Brasher did, with the sound of Stampfl's tapes echoing in his head. He hurtled home by fifteen yards in 8:45.6, breaking the Australian all-comers record held by the Hungarian Sandor Iharos. Landy slumped from the body blow of Brasher's sprint – and finished, well beaten, tenth out of the field of thirteen. Reporting on the race was Harry Carpenter, then of London's *Daily Mail*:

> What a service bespectacled Brasher has done Britain. He may have killed John Landy's bid for the Olympic 1500 and 5000 metres. Australia's hero Landy, who holds the world mile record at 3 min 58 and has crashed the four minute barrier six times, is no longer the bogey man he once was.
>
> And so, a week before the Games open, in Brasher we have a major athletic sensation on our hands.

Stampfl knew that Brasher was in the best shape of his life. He had done every session that Stampfl had hurled at him, his spikes were featherlight – he'd even taken the precaution of having crude contact lenses made in case there should be rain on the day of the final. Brasher was taking no chances, not with his opponents, not with the weather.

The lenses were colossal, agonising to insert, so Brasher hoped he wouldn't need to wear them. There is a story, which Brasher told often, that he used to store them in glass tumblers beside the bed. One evening a visitor to his room picked up what he thought was a glass of water and downed the lot – lenses and all.

In any event, on 27 November there was no rain and Brasher wore his black steel-rimmed spectacles when he lined up with

Disley and Shirley for the heats of the steeplechase. The first heat was fast and qualifiers for the final needed to run inside eight minutes forty-eight seconds. Horace Ashenfelter, the winner in the Helsinki Olympics in 1952, was eliminated while the world record holder, the Hungarian Sandor Rozsnyoi, and Disley finished their heat together, neck and neck in 8:46.6.

In heat two, Shirley came through strongly to win in 8:52.6. Brasher's heat was slower, and he qualified looking comfortable in 8:53.8. All three members of the British team had made the final and the race, said the experts, was going to be fast. Disley had run one of the swiftest times in the heats. Shirley had won his heat. But Brasher was the slowest of the British trio to qualify.

That time didn't bother him. 'The object of a heat is to make the final,' he would say later. 'The slower, the better.' He had learned the hard lessons of training too hard too close to a race when he had almost failed to make the British Olympic squad. Now, with two days' rest he would use every technique to get the best out of himself.

Back in 1952 he had seen his friend Roger Bannister torturing himself with the agonies of the Olympic final to come. Brasher had witnessed the sleepless nights, the terror of the newspaper headlines, the fear of failure. He remembered too those other November days long ago when he was a schoolboy, and how that stomach-churning dread had haunted him when he failed to win the Crick Run at Rugby.

But now things were different. Chataway remembers Brasher stretched out on a bunk, relaxed and reading *The Seven Pillars of Wisdom* by T.E. Lawrence, ever searching for that sandgrain of inspiration. He had read the book often. There on the pages were words that would resonate for Brasher. 'All men dream but not equally,' Lawrence wrote. 'Those who dream by night in the dusty recesses of their mind wake up in the day to find it was vanity, but the dreamers of the day are dangerous men, for they may act their dreams with open eyes to make it possible.'

And Franz Stampfl was forever at Brasher's elbow, whispering in his ear. The hypnotic voice that could lull him into a trance, that could convince him that like Wilson he could find a heaven by reaching beyond his grasp, would come every time he closed his eyes.

Sometimes the hours were endless, and Brasher would wistfully long for the consolation of a cigarette. But he'd go for a stroll, breathe a little deeper, polish his contact lenses, reach for another book. He'd watch the clock, but he knew it was his time. He was ready.

On 29 November, as they jogged to the line together, John Disley wished Brasher good luck and said, 'If I don't win, I hope you will.'

The start came as a shock. Neither of them had expected the first lap to be so furious. Norway's Ernst Larsen tried to break away from the field right from the gun. For a moment Brasher panicked and wondered if he could keep up. This seemed worse than his pacemaking in the four-minute mile, with Bannister urging him, 'Faster, faster, Chris.'

But after a suicidal one thousand yards, Larsen faded a little, and it gave the breathless Brasher and Disley the hope of closing up. It was a tight-knit pack that swung into the last lap. Each knew that they were in with a chance if they could raise a sprint; each knew that you would have to fight your way to the front with opponents like these.

At the bell, Rozsnyoi was at the front with Larsen and the Russian, Semyon Rzhischin, hard on his shoulder. Brasher and Disley clung on to the backwash of the chasing runners. As the bell clattered for the final 400 metres the challengers declared themselves; they swung their heads, looking straight into the eyes of their rivals, daring them to make a move.

The pace had been fast throughout the race but now soared to a punishing level. As the runners gathered themselves only the strongest survived. The Hungarian clung on to the lead but he was helpless to prevent his stride from shortening. Watching the faltering, staccato steps Brasher knew that this was his opportunity.

Going round the first bend Brasher and Larsen struck elbows; it was like oars in the Boat Race, momentarily touching, looking for the clear water home. As they came to a hurdle at the start of the back straight Brasher surged with desperation. He squeezed between Rozsnyoi and Larsen. Abruptly, he was three, four, five yards up on the leader, Rzhischin, before any of them could counter-attack.

The crowd and the runners were expecting the blow to come from Shirley or Disley, as were most of Brasher's supporters. But like a galloping racehorse Brasher took the bit, whipped himself and showed no signs of slackening. The chasing field was stretched out far behind him and with every yard he gained a few precious inches. As he reached the finish he seemed to be out on his feet.

Brasher ran himself out exactly on the tape before slumping on the track just beyond it. He had won in a trance. He had somehow taken fifteen yards from his pursuers. John Disley helped him to his feet.

Even remembering the race some forty years on, Brasher marvelled at the sounds and images that were swirling through his mind. 'Marvellous occasion,' he said in an interview with journalist Pat Collins. 'Never known anything like it. You're standing outside yourself looking on at something which is precisely the race you'd dreamed about. All you can hear is screaming inside your head, loud beyond belief. It's filling the Albert Hall, Beethoven's Ninth – the Ode to Joy. You're drowning in sound, there's something inside you that wills you to do it. It's irresistible, quite irresistible.'

The influence of Stampfl on Brasher's inspired run in this particular race is unmistakable. As Brasher lay on the grass of the infield, a mixture of triumph and pain overwhelmed him. This was the climax of his life. He knew that he had done it. He knew that all the sacrifices he had made, all the preparations he and Stampfl had gone through, had changed his life. He got shakily to his feet and threw a consoling arm around his friend Disley. He nodded at the

congratulations of the runners but he felt weak and played out from
his effort.

After about ten minutes he shuffled towards the start to collect his
tracksuit. And that was when his golden world ended. Brasher was
walking towards the stadium exit when the loudspeaker announced
the result of the 3000 metres steeplechase. First – Rozsnyoi,
Hungary; second – Larsen, Norway; third – Laufer, Germany.

Brasher stopped to listen. For a moment he couldn't believe what
he heard. He thought he might be hallucinating. He approached
the nearest track official.

'They got that wrong, didn't they?' he asked.

The official asked him his name.

'Brasher?' he said. 'You're disqualified.'

Alarm and anger poured energy back into his legs. Brasher
marched across the arena to the jury of appeal. 'I can still see them
lined up there,' he said. 'Scarlet blazers, white trousers, the chairman was David Burghley, the Marquis of Exeter. The secretary was
Don Payne, another Englishman. They told me I had been disqualified for obstructing Larsen at the top of the back straight. I
couldn't believe it. All the photographers came clustering around
as I made my case to Burghley. He didn't like the attention.'

'Perhaps you would like to leave us for the moment,' said
Burghley.

'So I went to the one hundred metre start and met our team
manager Jack Crump. I'd just finished telling him what had
happened when Don Payne came over and said, "Mr Crump, I have
to tell you that your athlete has put in a protest against his
disqualification. Would you formally like to support that protest?"'

'Oh, Don,' said Crump, 'what should I do?'

Payne stuttered, 'Well,' he said. 'As secretary of –'

Brasher broke in before Payne could complete his sentence.

'Yes,' said Brasher. 'He would like to support it.' Both men, said
Brasher, appeared terribly embarrassed. 'You see they felt that the
British sense of fair play was under challenge.'

Brasher left the stadium, head down, muttering, and disconsolately walked to the dressing rooms. On the way he passed by a stand serving free Ovaltine drinks to competitors. There at the stand stood Rozsnyoi, Larsen and Laufer.

'What's this all about?' they said. 'You won, didn't you?'

'It couldn't happen today,' said Brasher. 'Far too much at stake. They'd all be thinking about their equipment bonuses and how much the shoe companies would pay them for winning a medal. But in those days the vision of Baron Pierre de Coubertin really did mean something. You know that line of his about the youth of the world shall assemble? Well, we'd assembled and we discovered who was the best man on the day. And we'd all accepted it.'

The steeplechase final had finished at nine minutes past four. It wasn't just the British press who seemed baffled. Dozens crowded around Brasher asking what had happened and why he'd been disqualified. Rozsnyoi seemed as astonished as any of them. Laufer, the German who was promoted from fourth to third, told Brasher immediately that he didn't want his medal. He'd throw it back in their faces, he said.

The jury of appeal could not meet until nearly 6 p.m. and it was to be another hour before Brasher knew his fate. The jury sat in judgement. Larsen assured them that nothing and nobody had impeded him and Brasher himself told them that it was one of the cleanest races he had ever experienced. The hearing lasted just fifteen minutes, and at around seven o'clock the disqualification was overturned and Brasher was finally confirmed as the Olympic steeplechase champion. Rozsnyoi took the silver and Larsen the bronze while Laufer returned unrewarded, and uncomplaining, to Germany.

Brasher went back to the Olympic village, to the room that he shared with Chataway. Together, two years earlier, they had paced Bannister for his four-minute mile and now they talked deep into the night. Around three in the morning the door crashed open and two reporters burst in laden with bottles.

Terry O'Connor, the Olympic correspondent of the *Evening News*, and Laurie Pignon of the *Daily Sketch* were journalists who well understood the art of celebration. O'Connor wrote primarily about rugby and athletics. He was a close friend of Derek Ibbotson (who broke John Landy's world mile record, running 3:57.2 in 1957 in London) and ghost writer of Ibbotson's autobiography, *The Four-minute Smiler*. O'Connor regarded runners like the Ibbotsons and Bannisters of this world as gifted, the elite of athletics. He made no secret of the fact that he regarded Brasher as a 'hack', a journeyman runner, who had somehow shared the glory and glamour of Bannister and Chataway and was lucky to make the team for Melbourne.

O'Connor was incredulous that Brasher had broken through to win a gold medal, but nevertheless wanted to celebrate his victory and make sure he got the best quotes and copy on the story. Brasher remembered, 'We had a few drinks, in fact we had more than a few. They didn't leave until every bottle was empty.'

Next morning at around 11 a.m. Desmond Hackett, the celebrated *Daily Express* correspondent, called into the village to invite the new Olympic champion to lunch with the British press. 'Splendid affair,' Brasher remembered. 'Thirteen journalists all thirsty waiting for me at the Menzies Hotel. Hackett bought my first drink – a gin and tonic – and not a small one. Then everybody else bought a round. The next thing I knew, O'Connor was remarking that I was due to receive my medal at two forty-five, in three minutes' time. So we all stormed out of the hotel and rushed off to the stadium.

'I was rather the worse for wear. No, let's be honest, I was pissed beyond pain. I can't remember a thing about the presentation, not a thing. The word unique is overdone but I reckon I'm the only Olympic champion to be totally and absolutely slaughtered when he received a medal.'

Film of Brasher collecting his medal on the rostrum shows him beaming in his blazer and white slacks, swaying a little. He was given the medal by a little Frenchman and he was worried at the time that he was going to totter over and fall on top of him. He was reflecting that Laufer, the German in fourth place, had told him how he would throw the bronze medal back at them if they gave it to him.

The story of Brasher winning, then losing, then winning back again his Olympic track gold medal was seized upon by the press. It was very much the story of the Games but it was also taken up with anger by some of the reporters. Harry Carpenter in the *Daily Mail* wrote:

> Australia has the toughest outlook on athletics of any country in the world but even hard boiled officials here are appalled at what happened to Chris Brasher yesterday. The man in the street is downright ashamed at his country's part in one of the greatest Olympic fiascos of all time.
>
> Not ten minutes before he had been prostrate with exhaustion after magnificently winning the 3000 metre steeplechase for Britain but elation banished fatigue as he realised he had become the first British athlete in twenty-four years to gain an individual gold medal on the track.
>
> Then they heaped the ignominy of disqualification upon him. He was led to his dressing room like a fighter still coming around after a knock-out blow. His face was drained of every vestige of colour, his cheeks sunken and his eyes black spots behind his spectacles. He seemed to have aged ten years.
>
> Brasher has been a whipping boy for Britain's star runners for so long that he's automatically written off as an also-ran before he starts.

The charge that Brasher had been a whipping boy was true enough. Terry O'Connor was far from the only journalist to write him off as a 'hack' because of his sometimes indifferent performances, and there were many who labelled him as an awkward customer thanks

to his often outspoken comments. There were also those who saw
Brasher's attitude in haranguing, almost bullying the British team
management to launch an appeal against the decision of the judges
in a very un-British way as a hint of things to come, of the way that
Brasher might behave now that he'd won this gold medal.

It wasn't the first time that the British team management had
marked Brasher down as something of a rebel. When he left for
Australia in September, Brasher had been acutely aware of his
almost unreasonably privileged position by comparison with the
working-class infantry of British athletics, people like his team-
mate Eric Shirley. Accordingly he was very much a leading light in
a threatened strike against the Olympic team's management in the
days before the Games.

'It all centred round a good man, a miner named Fred Norris, a
10,000 metre runner who was employed by the National Coal
Board,' Brasher remembered. 'He had a wife and two children and
he wasn't getting paid while he was away competing for his country, and he was hard up, which meant it was a struggle for him to
buy a Coke or send a postcard home. So we and the British team demanded pocket money and threatened to strike if we didn't get it.'

The man at the centre of the athletes' hostility was Jack Crump,
secretary of the British Amateur Athletics Board and unbending
defender of the Corinthian amateur ideal. 'It would have been more
honourable to strike against British industry, but never mind,' said
Brasher to Pat Collins in 1996. 'Fred Norris got his allowance but
it didn't hide the fact that the whole thing was costing him money
he couldn't afford. That kind of thing occurs even to this day and
it's bloody wrong.'

At these summer Games in Melbourne Britain had won gold in
boxing, equestrianism, fencing and swimming. However, as the
only British track and field athlete to win gold at those Games –
indeed, as the first British athlete to win an individual gold medal
since the 1932 Olympics in Los Angeles – Brasher had broken the
drought that had starved Britain's track and field athletes for a gen-

eration. His future seemed assured and he basked in the admiration of friends, colleagues, even those who had written him off.

Even his fiercest critics were forced to acknowledge his victory. One of them was Terry O'Connor of the *Evening News*. O'Connor had leapt to his feet as Brasher crossed the finish line at Melbourne and cried out from the press box: 'No, no, no, not Brasher, no, no!'

8

The Golden Doors Open

'I always turn to the sports section first. The sports page records people's accomplishments; the front page has nothing but man's failures.'

Earl Warren

CHRIS BRASHER HAD returned to his old ways even before the Olympic gold medal had been hung around his neck. With his self-imposed abstinence and hard training over, he gleefully picked up where he had left off – smoking, climbing mountains and enjoying the pre-Christmas social whirl that was to meet him on his return to England in 1956.

Brasher was still a rising young oil company executive, and he went back to work with the consoling thought that after Melbourne he would be able to relax and enjoy the things that mattered to him. But when he returned he found that he had less free time, saw less of his friends and got even less sleep than before. He was showered with invitations; keeping the score, he reckoned he accepted one invitation from every ten he received. Even so, he was tempted into dinners and receptions five nights a week, often being called on to speak. Gilt-edged cards cascaded through Brasher's Kensington letter box, and while he found the adulation exciting and stimulating, all too often he found it more exhausting than his Olympic training.

'I hate to have to refuse invitations,' he said. 'The senders always have a hundred good reasons why I should accept. This especially applies where I have a direct interest such as in boys' clubs, charity events in general, and where the event involves the promotion of athletics. But it is physically impossible to be everywhere all the time.' Brasher enjoyed a huge range of interests – among them drama and ballet. One of the hangovers from Stampfl's enthusiasm was that he had come to worship ballet, an enthusiasm shared by his father Ken. But Brasher found in the helter-skelter days after Melbourne that he had just seen one play and not a single ballet.

Not only that, he had not visited the running track at all. The only exercise he took in the first two months of 1957 was one solitary game of squash, which left his right hand blistered and sore. A couple of times a week he would be interviewed by journalists. He enjoyed the attention. Arming himself with a drink and a cigarette (he had returned to smoking heavily), there always seemed to be the inevitable question about his future.

'Will that gold medal open the doors to other opportunities?' they asked. Brasher confided that he hoped to write a little on the subjects of climbing and athletics, but there were no plans for that just yet.

When Brasher arrived home bearing his gold medal, his mother Kitty told him that the mayor of Kensington planned a lunch in honour of his victory. Brasher protested that this was one of the invitations that he wanted to turn down. He said that Kensington had played no part in his winning of the medal, they had no athletics track and he had never used any of their facilities. He was extremely reluctant to go.

But Kitty had done much of her charity work in the Kensington area. That was where she'd set up home, that was where many of her friends and most influential contacts lived. She insisted that both she and her husband Ken and Brasher himself would attend the reception.

Reluctantly Brasher turned up. But when he gave a speech to the mayor, he issued a challenge that a fund should be set up to help other sportsmen and women who lived in Kensington. In order to get the fund under way he whipped out a cheque book and started the collection with his own donation for £25, then persuaded his father to make out a cheque for the same sum. Despite his gesture, the fund achieved nothing. Brasher was left with the inevitable conclusion that we in Britain 'are good at basking in the glory of sporting achievements but we were prepared to do little to make them possible'.

Shirley Brasher believes that this Kensington 'Olympic' lunch, and its failure to raise money, was a major influence on how the London Marathon was to be set up. 'Chris had failed to raise money for better sports facilities after that lunch,' she says, 'but in time the Marathon could help him to succeed.'

On 9 January 1957 Brasher had arrived at London Airport from New York and announced that he was to quit running. He told the press that the Olympic race was his last in competitive and international athletics. In future he would only run for recreation. He added that the race had imposed a big strain on him and was the climax of many months of hard work.

On his disqualification and reinstatement as the winner, Brasher said that all along he had been more than confident that the appeal would come out all right. When asked about his future plans for sport, he said that he enjoyed skiing and it might well be that he could get into the cross-country skiing team for the 1960 Olympics. But that would be the only competition he would be involved in again.

By February 1957, the attractions of a management career in Mobil Oil had faded. For a couple of years Brasher had flirted with newspapers, writing and submitting articles, and now he was given a real opportunity to write.

When, during the celebrations after his reinstatement as Olympic champion in Melbourne, Brasher had spent so much time drinking with colleagues from the press, one of the journalists on hand to buy him yet another gin and tonic was Michael Davie of the *Observer*. Described by fellow journalists as brilliant and unflappable, Davie was already a senior journalist on the paper owned and edited by David Astor. Born in London, the third child of the American-born 2nd Viscount Astor and the product of an immensely wealthy business dynasty, Astor joined the *Observer*, which his father owned, after working on the *Yorkshire Post*. By the mid-1950s, Astor had made the *Observer* a successful and influential paper. Despite his great wealth, he lived modestly, putting his money to good use through a network of trusts and charities. Astor was once described by Donald Trelford, the man who succeeded him as editor, as 'like a circus master given the wild and eccentric figures he collected. They usually weren't orthodox journalists. I was asked by a colleague in my early days on the *Observer*: "Are you a plumber or a journalist?" "What's the difference?" I asked. "Well, are you here to help David save the *Observer* or to help him save the world?"'

Having caught Astor's eye while an undergraduate at Oxford, Michael Davie joined the paper in 1950 and was rapidly appointed to his first executive post as sports editor. Davie had a rare knack for spotting and encouraging writing talent. Surprising names often found their way on to the sports pages during his tenure. The philosopher A.J. Ayer, the lawyer Louis Blom-Cooper and the academic John Sparrow of All Souls College, Oxford, wrote about football, and restaurateur Clement Freud had a brief innings giving his views on cricket. Davie nurtured the bon viveur Richard Baerlein and the former jockey Jack Leach on horse racing, while the award-winning writer Hugh McIlvanney, one of the finest all-round reporters of his generation, was another Davie appointment. Davie created a new literary style of sports journalism, treating sport with the same seriousness shown by newspapers to politics or theatre.

So 'Chris Brasher, Olympic Correspondent', hired as 'sports editor' of the *Observer* in March 1957 with no real experience as a

journalist – apart from a few freelance pieces written for the newspaper in the previous two years – was straight out of the Michael
Davie form book – inspired and revolutionary to some, amateur-
ish and incompetent to others.

Shortly after Brasher's appointment, an advertisement for a
deputy sports editor caught the eye of John Samuel, a former sports
editor of the *Daily Herald* with an experienced and professional
background in newspapers. 'Astor relished the amateur,' said
Samuel, 'but there was nothing amateur about Chris's drive and
ambition.'

The nuts and bolts of professional journalism, page make-up and
edition times were never Brasher's strongest suit. Samuel was
brought in to make sure that these areas were not neglected. He
understood how papers worked; he could cope with a deadline.
Samuel knew how to handle the printers, how to get the best out of
a picture desk and perhaps how to get the best out of Brasher. Ken
Obank, the paper's managing editor, saw that the job required a
professional editor's technique and authority, and Brasher, keen to
hang on to his writing and anxious to make a name in television,
agreed that the experienced Samuel could help him. Others were
also roped in to get the best out of Brasher.

Astor recruited Clifford Makins as a sub-editor from the *Eagle*,
a children's comic that told adventure stories, both fictional and
factual, of heroes of the Empire and the values they cherished. 'It
was a brilliant and inspired choice,' says Donald Trelford.
According to Shirley Brasher, Makins formed a great friendship
with her husband, who had tremendous respect for him: 'Cliff was
the only sub-editor that Chris would allow to touch his copy.'

Shirley believes that the friendship between Makins and her husband was somewhat puzzling. 'Clifford was not at all sporting or at
all athletic in any sense,' she says. 'That was one CB relationship on
the *Observer* that I never fathomed – but Clifford definitely had
Chris's measure and he rarely criticised Clifford to me. If Chris's
copy had been cut or altered I used to say it had been "subbed" by

Clifford – even when it might not have been. It made my Sunday life more harmonious.'

Overweight and shambling, Makins was a chain smoker and took no exercise – but he had Brasher's respect. He was extremely well read, cultured, loved classical music and cricket, relished talking about politics. And above all he had been editor of the *Eagle*. One of the things that endeared Makins to Brasher was that he had published *The Happy Warrior: The Life Story of Sir Winston Churchill, as told through Great Britain's* Eagle *comic of the 1950s*. Originally featured as a strip in the comic, it traces Churchill's life from his boyhood to his wartime leadership. In it Makins includes a history of the *Eagle* itself and a blow-by-blow description of what aspects of Sir Winston's life made it into the biography and what sections were omitted. This volume undoubtedly appealed to the boys who read the *Eagle* when it came out week by week.

Others at the *Observer* enjoyed a more tempestuous relationship with Brasher. The reverberations of a heavyweight row at the 1968 Olympics between Brasher and fellow writer Hugh McIlvanney, says Donald Trelford, could be heard all the way home from Mexico City, though in truth the two men admired each other.

'The problem with McIlvanney at the Mexico Olympics was that I asked them to write a big piece jointly for the front page about the shooting of students by the military. They argued fiercely over who should provide the opening paragraph. Their struggle to provide their own intro was apparently an epic wrestling match.

'Brasher and the executives around the newsroom would have the most violent rows,' said Trelford, 'but invariably they'd be seen sharing a drink in the bar that night. He was never a man to harbour a grudge.'

Shirley believes that the origins of this behaviour were to be found at school. 'When you go to a boarding school,' she says, 'you all learn how to have an argument at 4 p.m. and sit and eat supper together at 7 p.m. in comparative peace. I think it is very difficult for people who have not as children been to boarding school to understand this. They go home at 4 p.m. and probably still harbour resentment. Chris never really seemed to grasp the fact that not everyone could forgive and forget as quickly as he could.'

With Brasher's appetite for writing articles, breaking into television, his involvement with his hobbies of climbing and hill walking, to which orienteering and rally driving were later added, there never seemed to be enough time. He would desperately try, in his own words, to 'squeeze out what little talent I possessed', and it often led to him losing his temper.

Ron Atkin became sports editor of the *Observer* in 1972 some time after Brasher quit that position and moved on to become a freelance writer. This is Atkin writing over three decades later in the *Independent* about Brasher's style and problems he encountered dealing with him. The piece is headed 'I was The Editor, he was The Writer: But Who Was The Boss?'

I had been well briefed by my predecessor, the inimitable Clifford Makins, in the arts of conversation and confrontation with Chris Brasher when I became sports editor of the *Observer* in 1972. When Makins himself had replaced Brasher as sports editor in the early Sixties, days when the paper dwelt in an excessively cramped building in Tudor Street, he simply moved Brasher's desk into the corridor. It was the sort of gesture Chris understood and acknowledged – head-on, in-your-face.

Still, the first run-in with him shook me. It was the Munich Olympics, the year of Olga Korbut, and I rang to get him to do a piece on the gymnast British viewers were raving about. He refused. No interest, he said. When I persisted, he demanded to talk to the editor, David Astor. Brasher certainly had the ear, if not perhaps the heart and mind, of Astor and the gentle suggestion eventually wafted down from the top floor that perhaps another one of the paper's Olympic team might undertake the Korbut story.

At the 1972 Munich Olympics, known sadly as the Games of Death, the *Observer* was fortunate to have in Brasher and its chief sports writer, Hugh McIlvanney, two brilliant operators on the spot. Atkin continued:

> But as those Games came to an end we collided again. Why not, I ventured, head off to East Germany and undertake an investigation into whether all the gold medals they had won were down to skill or steroids? No can do, said Brasher. He was, he informed me, off to participate in one of his pet sports, orienteering, and intended to file a piece on it in due course. All this came as news to me.
>
> Such was working life with someone who was a maverick, even by the relaxed standards of the *Observer*. In this respect, Brasher had laid down an early marker, surviving an appeal alleging barging tactics to win the steeplechase gold at the 1956 Melbourne Olympics.

Atkin makes an interesting point here, that Brasher's initial disqualification for barging in the 1956 Olympic final was seen by him, and other colleagues at the *Observer*, as entirely part of his combative character.

Alan Hubbard, another of Brasher's successors as sports editor, was working as a young casual sub-editor when he first encountered Brasher. He knew Brasher well and admired him, but had grave reservations about some of Brasher's relationships: 'Ron Atkin had taken over from Chris as sports editor and it was about seven in the evening when this bearded, sweaty, bedraggled figure walked into the office demanding to know "Where is Shirley?"' At that point Brasher's wife was the paper's tennis correspondent.

'It was right on deadline. Brasher posed around in his climbing gear waiting for everyone to say "Well done Chris". I think he had just climbed Everest or something and then he disappeared down to the pub.

'Ron Atkin got on badly with Chris, whom he thought was un-manageable. Brasher somehow convinced Trelford that Atkin should go and that Atkin should be offered a different job as a sop. He should be given the choice of any writing job on the paper; he could take his pick. Ron Atkin told Trelford that his choice was "Tennis Correspondent" – with the result that Shirley Brasher was demoted to being a colour writer.

'Brasher,' says Hubbard, 'wrote brilliantly but always over-wrote and he was very obstinate and bloody minded to deal with. When Peter Corrigan was sports editor Brasher wrote a piece about Steve Ovett. Brasher suggested that some of the problems that Ovett had with his psyche and his attitude was because Ovett's mother was only fifteen when she had her son. This was of course subbed out. Trelford wanted it out, Corrigan wanted it out – and the lawyer took it out.

'It was all hot-metal in those days. Chris appeared on the stone (the composing room). "Where's my stuff?" Brasher demanded. "I've seen the proof." And he stormed back down to the stone. A tremendous row ensued. It was an indication of the obstinacy of Brasher. He ordered the printer to put the copy back in, but everybody told him it couldn't go back in because it was distasteful. Eventually it was taken out. Trelford, as the editor, was the man who had the last say, and he took it out.

'Chris sometimes went to Wimbledon and covered that as well,' said Hubbard of the period after Shirley Brasher's demotion. 'Chris was doing a piece on Jimmy Connors when Connors was involved romantically with Chris Evert. Someone in the crowd shouted, "Come on Jimmy." Connors replied, "I am trying for Christ's sake."

'Brasher reported that he had said "for Chris's sake". Nobody could talk him out of it. He was never wrong, you couldn't tell him anything. As a professional his depth of knowledge of athletics and the Olympics was formidable. But he was a bully, though I don't think that he ever realised that he was a bully.'

Whether or not that is so, Brasher was always up for a battle; he had a fine sense of justice and was prepared to pay for it. 'The thing I am most proud of when I was sports editor of the *Observer* was to bring some justice to footballers,' he said. In 1957, Jimmy Hill, who played for Fulham, became chairman of the Professional Footballers' Association and campaigned to have the Football League's £20 maximum wage scrapped.

'Jimmy Hill couldn't raise £150 for the lawyer's fee to challenge the legality of this maximum,' said Brasher. 'So I paid half and we went to Sir John Foster QC and he got the maximum wage declared illegal.' In 1961 Hill's Fulham team-mate, Johnny Haynes, became the first footballer in Britain to earn £100 a week.

Brasher the 'peacemaker' was a rare sight in the world of Fleet Street. But one who remembers it well is Stan Greenberg. A self-confessed sporting enthusiast, Greenberg is perhaps the best track and field statistician that Britain has produced and a former sports editor of *The Guinness Book of Records*.

'Perhaps my most intimate contact with Chris Brasher,' says Greenberg, 'came about at the 1966 European Championships in Budapest. Bob Sparks [a fellow statistician] and I had wangled press accreditations, easier than these days, so I was able to mix with the press.

'One particular individual whom I must admit that I probably hated was the writer billed as "The Man They Can't Gag", Desmond Hackett of the *Daily Express*, someone who knew nothing about sport. I doubt if he knew where a 400 metre race started or finished and anyway spent most of his time at the bar.

'There was no question that the week had been very disappointing from the British point of view but I was incensed to hear Hackett sounding off about the awful British athletes from his position at the press bar. I began to tell him just what I and others thought about him and his attitude. He replied in a most supercilious and offensive manner and myself, little weak placid me, readied myself to hit him.

'At that point Chris Brasher, who had obviously noted what was going on from the other side of the room, rushed over and put himself between us – ostensibly to ask my advice on something – and gradually pushed me away. Quite ludicrously I'd really lost it, and was still trying to punch Hackett over Chris's shoulder until eventually I calmed down. I suspect this might have been one of the biggest stories out of Budapest if it hadn't been for Brasher.

'But Brasher was quite extraordinary. One of the things he said had a long-lasting impression on me. He said that there is little doubt that an athlete in training ceases to be a normal human being. I think that may be true.'

For a long time on the *Observer* Michael Davie, whom Brasher much respected, was seen as the heir apparent to editor David Astor. But on 1 January 1976, Donald Trelford became editor and he kept the job for more than seventeen years until 1993. Brasher had commissioned Trelford's first sporting article for the paper in 1959, a report on a rugby match while Trelford was still at Cambridge. Brasher also got him to cover the first Oxford v Cambridge tiddlywinks match. During Trelford's editorship he and Brasher built up a good and long-lasting relationship. 'Although Chris did not always welcome Donald Trelford's advice or guidance for the *Observer* and the London Marathon,' says Shirley Brasher, 'I suspect that Donald made a lot of good decisions where Chris was concerned.'

Even Trelford had to admit that Brasher was not always the easiest person to work with. 'Brasher never found it easy to understand people who stood in his way,' he says, 'though Brasher's wife, Shirley, was often credited with tempering her husband's wilder ideas and smoothing out the jagged edges in his personality. Sometimes it worked.' Whether it was broadcasting or newspapers, Trelford says, Brasher often had difficulty in his relationships with colleagues: 'Cantankerous, obstreperous, cussed and abrasive were just some of the principal descriptions I recall from around the sports desk. He was not the most accommodating of colleagues.'

*

Brasher was to write regularly for the *Observer* until 1991, covering seven Olympic Games for the newspaper as 'Olympic Correspondent'. He left shortly before the Barcelona Olympics of 1992 to join the *Sunday Times*. Twice Brasher won the title of Sports Writer of the Year in the British Press Awards. Not long after he started at the *Observer*, however, Brasher – like other journalists who worked for the paper – had turned his attention to earning extra money from broadcasting and the BBC. Most of the paper's top names, Brasher included, employed the Bagenal Harvey organisation as agent. Although the writer's fees from the paper were not unreasonable, they did not easily support a mortgage or a family. And with his restless energy, Brasher soon found time for profitable and alternative career openings.

The growth of television in post-war Britain offered ground-breaking opportunities. So, from 1961 to 1965, Brasher was a reporter for *Tonight* – a daily programme which went on the air from 6.05 to 6.45 every weekday evening (the pop programme *Six Five Special* filled the space on Saturday).

Tonight was the equivalent of a daily newspaper's middle pages with a mixture of light and heavyweight topical items. It could often pull in seven million viewers. For a time Cliff Michelmore, the anchorman, was its best-known face but soon other reporters became almost as well known – Brasher among them. But perhaps the most familiar and immediately recognisable was Fyfe Robertson.

In 1943 Robertson joined *Picture Post* magazine. When that closed in 1957, he went to work in television. Robertson appeared on screen speaking in a slow and distinctive Scottish accent, his grey-bearded, weather-beaten face and 'uniform' of a checked tweed jacket and a tweed trilby hat making him unforgettable to the viewer. His filmed 'roving reports' would invariably be introduced with a close-up of his face and a drawling (and often parodied) 'Hellooo therrre . . . I'm Fyfe Robertson.' Like Brasher, he was a heavy smoker, but despite that, in his late sixties he took part in two exhausting televised expeditions, across the Scottish Highlands on horseback and paddling down the Severn in a canoe.

Robertson had picked up, in those early days of television, the importance of an image that could stamp his identity on the viewer, and it was a lesson not wasted on other *Tonight* reporters. These were directed by the urbane Ned Sherrin and included, alongside Brasher, Geoffrey Johnson-Smith, Kenneth Allsop, Alan Whicker and Brian Redhead, as well as Chris Chataway. In his *Tonight* appearances, Brasher was still the fit, fresh-faced, slim reporter with an Olympic gold medal to his name. He wore his steel-rimmed spectacles, a tie, a mac for outside broadcasts, and spoke in the clipped 1950s accent still remembered by audiences of the cinema's Pathé News.

Despite not yet having developed the colourful on-screen impact of Fyfe Robertson, Brasher soon made his mark as a BBC executive. In 1964 and 1965 he was editor of *Time Out* and *Man Alive* and was soon winning major awards.

As far back as 1953 the reception given to the conquerors of Everest had shown the public's appetite for stories of daring and adventure. George Band labelled the media circus that followed the climbers 'the other Everest'. These were men unaccustomed to hero worship. But television, as Brasher realised, had the power to change all this, transforming climbers into stars and mountaineering into a series of entertaining spectacles.

Televised climbing, which had begun in continental Europe, was picked up by the BBC in the 1960s. On 28 September 1963, the BBC broadcast a live programme of an ascent of Snowdon's Clogwyn du'r Arddu, 'the finest crag in Britain south of the Scottish border'. It starred the French climber Robert Paragot alongside the cream of British talent: Joe Brown, Don Whillans and Ian McNaught-Davis.

The programme, *4 Men, 1 Face*, had commentary by Chris Brasher. It was transmitted on *Grandstand* between Davis Cup tennis and horse racing from Newbury. *Grandstand* anchorman David Coleman introduced the climb as a TV first – the first ever live coverage of UK mountaineering. The audience would, he said, be treated to 'fireside mountaineering' and 'carpet-slippered climbing' by having dramatic pictures of a potentially deadly outdoor venture beamed into the comfort of their own homes.

However, it was not considered great television. Despite Brasher's enthusiastic commentary, the action was clouded by rain and mist. Many of the cameras failed on the day of the broadcast, leading one reviewer to comment that it was like watching 'several hours of dirty cotton wool twitching in a draught'.

In July 1965, there was a centenary climb of the Matterhorn, covered by a combined BBC/Swiss Television effort. This was originally planned by Brasher as a fifty-minute documentary re-enactment but it was decided that the programme should follow the precedent set by previous TV climbs in following the efforts of a group of elite climbers as they attempted the mountain live. A young David Dimbleby provided the commentary.

In 1967 *The Old Man of Hoy*, billed in the *Radio Times* as *The Great Climb*, was judged the Best Outside Broadcast of the Year. Fifteen million people were glued to their sets to watch one of the most audacious of the BBC's outside broadcasts. The Old Man of Hoy is a 450ft crumbling sea stack in the Orkneys separated from land by the erosive powers of the sea. The ascent featured six climbers in a broadcast that has been dubbed the first 'reality television' programme. It won much praise for the climbing and the camera-work, but some critics described Brasher's commentary as boring, like 'watching paint dry'.

By 1969 Brasher was promoted to head of general features at the BBC and in 1972 another documentary of his, *The Runners*, won yet another major international award. But Brasher's time as head of the department did not last long and in March 1972, despite the fact that some had tipped him as a rising executive bound right for the top at the BBC, he announced that he was resigning his post because he was 'bored with the job'.

'I find I have been getting so remote from programmes that it has become a bore,' Brasher explained to the press at the time. 'I spend three months getting a programme idea launched, accepted, financed, but when it comes to the real challenge of making the programme someone else takes over. My three-year contract doesn't run out until September but I asked yesterday to be relieved in July and the BBC has agreed.' Programmes made while Brasher was in charge included *Holiday 72*, *The World About Us*, *Ask the Family* and *The Sky at Night*. Brasher quit the post on 31 July and it was taken over by Desmond Wilcox.

There were rumours that Wilcox had queried some of Brasher's BBC expenses, but Donald Trelford says this was hardly surprising. He was known to be many months behind with his expenses, says Trelford, 'but he wasn't the only one.'

Still, Trelford considers that the *Observer* years were the ones that saw Brasher at the top of his journalistic game: 'His pioneering role in environmental journalism should particularly be recognised.' He points out that in the early 1970s, before any newspaper had appointed a specialist correspondent, Brasher wrote a column in the *Observer* called 'Breath of Air' that first raised many of the issues which were to appear on the political agenda in the following decades.

'He had an unquenchable appetite for stretching himself to the limit,' says Trelford. 'There was something of the great Victorian about Brasher. A manic energy and bustling singlemindedness that brooked no opposition in pursuit of diverse interests and campaigns that included the environment, mountaineering, fly fishing, racehorse breeding and the technology of running shoes.

'Brasher often quoted Browning, "Ah, but a man's reach should exceed his grasp or what's a heaven for." But he never found it easy to understand people who stood in his way.'

Trelford once asked Brasher, in the course of yet another row in the office, 'Are you so big-headed because you won an Olympic gold medal, or did you win the gold medal because you were so big-headed?'

Brasher looked at Trelford and growled; then he looked a little chastened. 'A rare occurrence,' Trelford notes.

'Brasher then chewed on his filthy pipe and said: "Good question. I don't know the answer."'

9

Love and Marriage

'The essence of sports is that while you're doing it, nothing else matters; but after you stop, there is a place, generally not very important, where you would put it.'

Sir Roger Bannister

UNLIKE THE KENSINGTON lunch held in his honour, there were some invitations that Brasher was very eager to accept. One of these was an invitation to visit the Wimbledon Championships in June 1957.

'I had been asked by a friend,' says the former Shirley Bloomer, 'a Queen's Club member, if I could give his friend from university, Chris Brasher, a ticket for Wimbledon '56. All I knew of Chris Brasher was his pacemaking in the four-minute mile two years previously. I left a competitor's guest pass on the Wimbledon gate.

'I didn't see Chris at the '56 Wimbledon or hear from him. I didn't mind. I was seeded in the singles with a world ranking in the top ten, and entertaining during the height of Wimbledon was not my idea of bliss.'

Shirley Bloomer was almost six years younger than Brasher. She learned her tennis at the Grimsby Town Tennis Club and afterwards at Sherborne School for Girls, and won three Grand Slam titles, including the French Open, during her career. High in the national rankings when Brasher met her, she was a member of the British Wightman Cup team between 1955 and 1960. She was in the winning team that included Christine Truman in 1958 – the first time that Britain had won the trophy since 1930.

By the time they met again, Chris was an Olympic gold medallist. 'I went to the *Express* 1956 Sportsman of the Year Awards. These came after the Melbourne Olympics. I think CB won the Sportsman of the Year, but he was surrounded by people and I didn't fancy the role of sporting groupie.'

They met properly at a party, soon afterwards, in January 1957. 'Chris remembered me,' said Shirley, 'and thanked me for his Wimbledon ticket. In return he asked me out to the theatre. We saw *La Plume de ma Tante*.'

It was a hot ticket, and Brasher was lucky to get a pair. *La Plume de ma Tante* was a French revue imported from London to the Garrick Theatre. There were songs and some dialogue and much of the evening was presented in pantomime. The production was rapturously received and the critics raved. It was rumoured that Princess Margaret came five times to see it. It was even said she invited the cast to act at a private showing in front of the Queen.

Brasher paid his 4d for the programme. 'After that,' says Shirley, 'we went out regularly when I was in London and not playing on the international tennis circuit. Chris was then beginning to work for the *Observer*. I was pretty useful as I had to leave a car in London quite often and he could use it while I was away. Chris's cars were never reliable.'

Shirley Bloomer at this time was not only one of the world's top ranking tennis players; she was also among the prettiest girls on the tennis circuit. A petite, short-haired brunette, agile, light on her feet, she played a hard baseline game, seeming to dance around the tennis court with a power that belied her size. She was a natural and gifted ball player and her frisky footwork and speed brought glamour to the tennis court.

Shirley was seemingly shy, but once she got to know people she loved to gossip. Feminine and flirty, she often appeared in outfits styled by the legendary fashion designer Ted Tinling, who gained a certain notoriety as the designer of the lace panties worn by Gussy Moran in 1949.

Many of Tinling's designs involved wearing a slip or petticoat under the tennis dress. These could sometimes be hazardous to a player's athleticism. Ranked number three in the world at the time, Shirley Bloomer had to deal with the Tinling problem while playing in a Wightman Cup match in 1958 when her light blue frilly slip fell down after the waistband snapped. According to press reports, 5000 male spectators shouted 'More, more' as she calmly stepped out of her slip. Despite plenty of wolf whistles she tossed it to the sidelines and ended the game with an ace.

Tinling said, 'It was her own fault. It was retribution for wearing last year's dress. I warned her something dreadful would happen.'

Shirley was able to reach the quarter-finals of Wimbledon in 1958 while holding down a job as a trainee at Simpson's department store in Piccadilly. In a world of strict 'amateurism' it was often necessary to maintain one's international ranking by taking a job that allowed plenty of time off to train and compete.

Shirley kept her figure and her looks in the decades that followed. She was top ranked as a veterans' player and worked as a coach trying to bring girls up to her own standard, producing a number of junior champions. Like her husband, she was never timid about going into battle with her sport's governing body, in her case the Lawn Tennis Association, whether over the selling of the Queen's Club or its failure to produce top ranking players.

Shirley Bloomer had grown up with tennis courts in the grounds of her Grimsby home, had ridden ponies since the age of five. Her father owned a high-class car dealership in Grimsby, specialising in Bentleys, Rolls-Royces and Daimlers, his clients often the wealthy potato farmers and racehorse owners of Lincolnshire. So Shirley was never short of a fine car. Driving fast cars, she says, was one of Chris's great enthusiasms. 'At first,' she jokes, 'I think he was only interested in me because of the fast cars.

'Before we were married Chris would often keep on to borrow a car from me, but I reckoned he was a fairly awful driver. And if my father had found out I would be in trouble. Eventually I gave in and let him borrow my car while I was abroad.

'This went quite well until Chris left one of my father's cars in some street and it was stolen. The police had been chasing a car right through High Wycombe and the car finished up in the ditch near Aylesbury. The thief filled up with petrol and drove off without paying at a local garage. The police rang my father and reported the car abandoned in the ditch, as it was in his ownership. "That can't be hers," said my father, "She's in Paris!" So what was my car doing in a Bucks ditch? Later I had to explain that it had been left in London in the care of Chris.

The incident of the stolen car in the ditch, reflected Shirley, 'was not a great recommendation for Chris. I had to pay the garage for the thief's petrol.' Nevertheless, her parents found the young Chris Brasher charming.

Soon after Shirley and Chris first met, Chris decided that they should go to Battersea Park funfair. 'Chris,' said Shirley, 'headed for the stall with prizes for shooting skill. He paid his money and took aim. I pretended to be enthusiastic, but privately knew it was quite hopeless – how could a bespectacled town boy shoot to win anything?

'I was quite an experienced funfair shooting spectator. This was because a number of my friends – whose parents owned farms and shoots – liked to go funfair shooting on the seafront at various Lincolnshire resorts. It was a regular holiday outing when we were all back from boarding school. The boys rarely, if ever, won anything; but were known to be excellent shots. When they didn't win the reason was always given, "the gun sights are fixed."'

To Shirley's utter amazement, Chris soon won a prize from one of the more difficult shelves. She chose a ginger ceramic cat, naming it Puzzle to reflect her incomprehension.

But Brasher's shooting skill, said Shirley, was to prove no fluke.

'On several later occasions he would win at seafront shooting. Finally, my unkind conclusion was that his eye must have been out just about the same amount as the funfair games were fixed. I shall never know – but Chris had talent at that sport for sure. And that cat's name remained appropriate.'

On 1 April 1957, Brasher appeared on *Desert Island Discs*. It was introduced by the programme's originator, Roy Plomley, on the Home Service of the BBC. Brasher was in good company. In the preceding months the spot had been occupied by Stirling Moss, Kenneth More (who had played Brasher's great hero Douglas Bader in the film *Reach for the Sky*), Peter Ustinov, Claire Bloom and Humphrey Lyttelton.

As the only track and field winner in the previous year's Olympics, Brasher was a natural for the desert island. His first choice of recording was Finnish composer Sibelius' Symphony No. 5, and for him it carried many memories. It reawakened the dreams that he had long carried of the Finns as a master race of distance runners. Finnish runners had dominated the sport in the years from 1912 to 1936. For Brasher, Sibelius filled the ears with stirring music and captured the Finnish spirit of *sisu*, a Finnish term loosely translated into English as strength of will, determination, perseverance, particularly in the face of adversity, but literally meaning 'having guts'.

The most famous Finn who ever lived for Brasher was Paavo Nurmi, known simply as 'The Flying Finn'; with stopwatch in hand, Nurmi trained harder than anyone before him, and it paid off. Nurmi was a shy introvert, obsessed with running, aloof from colleagues and rivals, dour and remote. One of only three athletes to collect nine Olympic gold medals, Nurmi once won the 5000 metres and 1500 metres in the space of ninety minutes. For decades Brasher would enthuse that Nurmi was the greatest runner who ever lived.

The other discs Brasher chose for his desert island included Beethoven and Prokofiev, with lighter items from Ava Gardner and

Eartha Kitt and a novelty hit from 1954 by Stan Freberg and the Toads. His luxury item was a sailing dinghy.

By June 1957 Brasher was partnering Shirley Bloomer at the Wimbledon Ball. Late that year he showed up at London Airport to see Shirley off to America to play tennis. He kissed a rather warm farewell, which prompted Bloomer's team-mates to tease her unmercifully about the 'possibility of wedding bells'. Her tennis coach, Fuz Dewhurst, who taught her from the age of twelve at boarding school and later became a great personal friend, proved very perceptive about Chris – 'and, for that matter, most of my boyfriends,' said Shirley. 'She was often interested and entertained to hear about them. She forecast that I would marry Chris long before I would ever have put any money on any likelihood of doing so.'

In December 1958 word got out that the two were indeed going to marry. Shirley's mother, Kathleen Bloomer, announced to the press when challenged about the news, 'It was a big surprise but a nice one. It came completely out of the blue.' Shirley and Brasher were out celebrating that same evening in London. Left at their respective Kensington flats were written instructions: 'Don't tell a soul'.

They were married on 28 April 1959, at Chelsea Old Church, with the reception at the Hyde Park Hotel, London. (Kate Brasher, their eldest daughter, was married at the same church and by the same vicar thirty-one years later.) 'The wedding date,' said Shirley, 'was carefully fixed so that I believe it came between the 1000 Guineas and the 2000 Guineas, so that my parents and racing friends were able to attend.'

It was a glittering wedding filmed by Pathé News for the cinema. Roger Bannister was there as best man, along with Chris Chataway as an usher, and many sporting stars of the 1950s attended. From Shirley's side there were plenty of Wimbledon icons, including tennis players Christine Truman, Anne Shilcock, Pat Ward and Angela Mortimer.

'We spent the first night of our honeymoon in comparative

luxury,' said Shirley, 'but the second night we spent camping in a field in France. It wasn't a proper camp site, just a farmer's field. It was wet, with cows that would come over and nose around our tent. I knew Chris would be blissfully sound asleep. I hardly slept at all. I have never been camping since.'

At the end of their three-week continental honeymoon, the bridegroom announced that he would be coming back to England alone. 'Shirley is staying on to play in the Swiss and French championships,' Brasher explained. 'Unlike me she hasn't retired from sport just yet and has to get in shape for Wimbledon.'

Chris and Shirley bought their first house in Chelsea as soon as they were married. They lived there until 1964, by which time they already had one child, Kate, and Shirley was pregnant with their second, Hugh. By the mid 1960s, the impetus of a growing family and the attraction of having a house on the fringes of Richmond Park where Brasher might practise his new found-enthusiasm for orienteering, sent him house-hunting. Brasher bought his new home, Navigator's House, by auction. But, says Shirley, 'Chris's family never owned a property — so he was not exactly practised at buying. He overpaid at auction when we bought Navigator's House, which turned out to be a very good buy in the long term. He would never be beaten at the auction, even though I had taken the precaution of having an agent with him. I'd hoped to prevent the competitive element overtaking him, but need not have bothered. The agent had no hope once Chris was into his bidding stride.'

Navigator's House is a fine detached property, a listed building, in Petersham near Richmond, set just a short jog away from the Thames towpath and the cross-country trails of Richmond Park. The houses that surround it, in a winding cul de sac that leads down to the river, are large and set in their own grounds and gardens — family homes, reeking of privacy and plenty. Round the corner was the Dysart Arms, the headquarters of the Ranelagh Harriers, of which both Brasher and John Disley were to become members.

In the late eighteenth century Navigator's House was owned by Captain George Vancouver, who sailed on two of Captain Cook's voyages and later himself surveyed the coasts of New Zealand, south-west Australia and the Pacific north-west of America. The island of Vancouver, the city of Vancouver in Canada and Fort Vancouver in Washington State, USA are all named after him. He settled in Glen Cottage (the former name of Navigator's House) on his return to England in 1795 and it was here in Petersham that he wrote his *Voyage of Discovery*. Vancouver is buried nearby in St Peter's churchyard, where his grave is tended by the Petersham and Ham Sea Scout Group. Vancouver shares the graveyard with the man who spent much of his life in Navigator's House, Chris Brasher.

For Brasher and Shirley it was a house with history. The memories it evoked of an explorer, an adventurer, must have tempted Brasher to bid well over the odds. But more important with a growing family, it was a spacious home within easy reach of central London and provided a base for the family's activities for decades to come.

Brasher's office, strewn with papers, books and running shoes, was a timber-framed building constructed over the garage. From there he would often take refuge in the snug bar at the Dysart Arms, often referred to by Shirley and the children as 'The Station' because of Brasher's habit of saying, 'I'm just off to meet someone at the station,' whereupon he would disappear for an hour or two to the Dysart. Proudly displayed in the pub's snug bar was a shield that recorded the record-breaking time achieved by the Ranelagh team – of which Brasher had been a member – in the Pennine Way Relay Race.

'Chris also bought a flat,' says Shirley, 'three floors up, with a beautiful view he said. But few people who could afford the asking price could climb three flights of stairs unless they were as fit as Chris. There was no lift. He must have been a developer's dream buyer. He lost there badly! Fortunately, when it came to buying property, I managed without his assistance. Property was not his forte.'

Quite soon after the wedding, Fuz Dewhurst – herself successful in business – asked Shirley to go and see her in her mews in Chelsea. 'She said, "Shirley, we all love Chris and I am sure he will be very successful in life – but I am also afraid that he could buy some remote area of land near a mountain and expect you to live in a shed at the foot.

'"So I am going to leave you in my will some of the property I own in London. Then, at least, you will have the option of not living in an isolated shed. I know you will be capable of managing and developing the properties until any time you may need to sell them."'

Until then, Shirley says, she had not really considered the likelihood of Chris expecting her to live the simple life: 'I have always liked the country but mountains, hills, sheds or bothies are another thing.

'Fuz remained true to her word. She left me two property companies which ensured I will never have to live in a mountain shed. She also made me wary, for the future, that investing with Chris might not be the best idea. In fact, I suppose, when I declined to back some of his business ventures it made it far more of a challenge for him to succeed – and succeed he did in business whether I invested or not.'

According to Shirley, Chris lacked patience with formalities and could not abide red tape. Following their marriage, she reckoned that there was little alternative but to join in and start working for him and with him. She came to the marriage with a wide knowledge of sport and she knew that she could help take some of the pressure off him.

She would often write drafts of articles and letters for Chris to amend and they spent a lot of time working together and swapping views on what made top sportsmen tick. Shirley was a journalist in her own right and had many articles published in a number of national dailies, mainly on tennis. In 1973 she was appointed lawn tennis correspondent for the *Observer* and in 1976 she was approached by the Mark McCormack organisation to work as a consultant on *Tennis World*.

Occasionally, Shirley would play tennis with Chris, and she remembers, 'I had to put the ball on his racket to get any sort of exercise. When he ran with me, he had no exercise either. It was too slow a pace. Also Chris liked to talk as he ran – I couldn't possibly spare the puff to answer. I could only nod, worried later what I might be agreeing to. I also feared I might get left on some remote part of Richmond Park or the Thames towpath on many of our joint runs, as Chris practised his sprints and was soon far out of sight.'

Domestic life went on, despite Brasher's frequent absences on journalistic jobs, business ventures, expeditions to the wilderness and skiing holidays. Shirley was left to bring up the children, Kate, Amanda and Hugh, with the help of their nanny, Glenys Telford, who moved in when Hugh was born and stayed with the family for years.

The first child, Kate, was born in August 1962. From an early age she showed potential as a first-class tennis player and so inevitably she spent much of her childhood being coached and escorted on the tennis circuit by her mother. By the end of her career Kate was British junior tennis champion at the under-14, under-16 and under-18 levels and played number one for Britain in the Junior Wightman Cup.

Kate competed in eight open Grand Slam tournaments and played on the women's professional tennis tour in the 1980s. In 1985, though only playing tennis on a part-time basis, she was still ranked tenth in Britain and played in the Wimbledon Championships.

Hugh was born three years later, in September 1964, and from the age of seven to seventeen he was educated at boarding school. He would come home when term was ended and fit in with the routine of family life, particularly the skiing and the holidays in Wales that he shared with his father and his younger sister. During his years at Eton he would often work in the holidays helping out his father at the Sweat Shop, the retail outlet in Teddington that Brasher had opened to sell orienteering and running shoes and equipment.

Amanda, their third child, was born in August 1967, and like her older sister Kate went to day school rather than boarding school. With Shirley shepherding Kate around the professional tennis circuit, as a child Amanda inevitably saw more of her father at home than the two older children. By the time Amanda was born, Glenys Telford had become her godmother, and had much influence on the growing family.

But the children all remember the family's closeness at home, with plenty of laughter which everyone shared. At least once a year Chris would carry off Hugh and Amanda to his cottage in Wales to share adventures in the sort of terrain that he loved most.

'It was a shabby cottage,' remembers Amanda, 'there were no inside loos, we had chemical loos that we had to bury, but it was beautiful. We loved it.' Amanda pulls out a picture taken on one of these 'adventures'. There she is, a little girl of six or seven, dwarfed by the enormous rucksack on her back, trudging up Snowdon. 'He took us fishing, walking, climbing, and for him everything was an adventure. We had fun.'

In the years that followed, Amanda recalls, her father used to send her postcards from his travels with little inspirational quotes on the back, 'but those holiday adventures gave us all the inspiration that we needed.'

Despite his reputation of being a man who aggressively got what he wanted, at home, Brasher, with two young daughters, appeared to be, in Amanda's phrase, 'a real softie'. 'I could sit on his lap, flutter my eyelashes and twist him round my little finger, but that's pretty normal for daughters.'

Hugh Brasher, too, speaks of the domestic closeness that existed between his mother and father. They never led 'separate lives', says Hugh, 'that would be to completely misunderstand their relationship.

They supported each other in their passions, which were often very different. But that meant they had a stronger relationship in the things they shared and did together. That might seem unconventional and it takes two very strong characters to make it work – but undoubtedly it did.

'The only person who could ever change my father's mind was my mother, and he relied on her an enormous amount.'

Shirley Brasher puts it simply. 'We had separate cars, separate bank accounts, separate racehorses, but we never had separate lives. There were many joint interests as well.' Don't forget, Shirley would say, that Chris was a steeplechaser. 'The way to control steeplechasers is to keep them on a loose rein. But my hands were always on the reins.'

When they tried to share their sporting pastimes and hobbies it often led to some amusement. Shirley recalls: 'When I used to drive around searching the streets of London, or some remote countryside wood, for CB and his broken-down vehicles, I was reminded of exactly why he had married me. Alas, not for my beauty, brains or sporting ability, but because of my family's business which could provide Chris with an excellent supply of spare cars. I could drive most vehicles from a Bentley to a Beetle, and above all I did not drink. I was readily available to be a chauffeur – even after the best of parties.'

However, says Shirley, Brasher had typically overlooked one detail. An inexpert map-reader, she would become infuriated by his habit of giving her map references when he either navigated or was letting her know where to find him in the countryside after training or competing.

'He did suggest once that I learned to orienteer – I would enjoy it, he said. I knew exactly why it suited him for me to learn to orienteer and understand maps and map references. My unladylike response to this suggestion was why this matter was never raised again – ever.'

Amanda Brasher says of her parents, 'They were together for

forty-four years and they really understood and supported each other. They were both aspirational and inspirational, but what came over was sharing the same sense of humour. There was always plenty of laughter in the house, and we often used to tease my father which would provoke gales of laughter.'

One of the nicknames by which Shirley and the family referred to Chris was 'Bellows'. It was always used in a teasing and jocular way. 'My father was given the name,' said Amanda, 'because of his constant way of bellowing "Where are my car keys?" or "Where is the Flora?"' Hopeless at finding things, his cry would echo round the house, but for all the family it was an amusing and endearing nickname.

In December 1976 the Brashers' domestic life was disturbed when thieves tiptoed away with many memories of their sporting lives together in broad daylight. Amanda and Shirley had gone to sweep snow from the communal tennis court that they shared with a handful of neighbours. Shirley said to Amanda that they should book the court to play later in the day, and Amanda went back to find a pen. She thinks she probably disturbed the thieves who were already hiding in the house. Witnesses say that they saw the men leaving Navigator's House carrying bags of loot.

The thieves made off with silver trophies which included a miniature replica of the *Daily Express* Sportsman of the Year Award in 1956 and Shirley's runner-up medal for the women's doubles at Wimbledon in 1955. Most valuable of all was a large silver trophy presented by the *Evening Standard* to Kate for winning the under-14 British junior tennis championship. There was also a club trophy of which Chris was particularly proud – the Ranelagh Page Cup for winning a five-mile handicap race, a trophy first awarded in 1883. One thing that the thieves missed was Brasher's Olympic gold medal – which, according to press reports, he had casually left on a bookshelf. 'There were other burglaries,' says Kate, 'mostly jewellery and other personal items. But the thieves knew exactly what they were looking for this time – they stole only valuable silver.'

A charming, crazy and romantic postscript from much later in their marriage tells much about the domestic life of the Brashers.

'At relatively simple jobs,' Shirley said, 'like letting the cat out of the back door from a distance of four feet, I was likely to be summoned to assist. I used to wonder as I raced from some distant part of the house how someone who could organise 25,000 pairs of legs to run twenty-six miles round the streets of London could not manage to get two pairs of paws to move a few feet outside of the back door.

'I was once given a Christmas present (among others from Chris) of a cat flap. On Boxing Day Chris decided to install it. Filled with trepidation, I watched silently as he sawed away. I knew soon enough that the cats would have to be tipsy to get through it – the flap wasn't straight. Worse still, the back door panel came apart – it was a listed building and had a heavy oak door. The new door which then had to be fitted meant that the cat flap was quite one of my most expensive Christmas presents ever.'

10

'How I Escaped Death'
by the Conqueror of Everest

*'Nobody climbs mountains for scientific reasons. Science is used
to raise money for the expeditions, but you really climb for the
hell of it.'*

Sir Edmund Hillary

IS COLUMNS FOR the *Observer* may have provided Brasher
with both an income and a favourite activity in which he
found some peace, but they were never going to keep
his restless mind happy for long. Brasher continued to pursue his
sporting passions with undiminished gusto, and as soon as the
Olympics in Melbourne were over he returned to two of his great
abiding passions – mountaineering and fast cars.

One of his friends at Cambridge was the climber George Band,
who followed Brasher two years later as president of the Cambridge
University Mountaineering Club. Having learned much of his
climbing in the Alps while a student at Cambridge, Band was the
youngest member of the 1953 Everest expedition where Edmund
Hillary and Tenzing Norgay made the first successful ascent of the
peak.

Brasher knew all about Everest. According to several obituaries,
he was a reserve for Sir John Hunt's successful Everest expedition,
although Hunt notes in his book *The Ascent of Everest* that the

reserves were 'J.H. Emlyn Jones, John Jackson, Anthony Rawlinson, Hamish Nicol, and at a later stage Jack Tucker'. Brasher himself never claimed to be a 'reserve' for the expedition; the truth was rather that if the 1953 Everest attempt had failed, Brasher was being considered for a backup climb in the Himalayas later in the season.

The team who, under the leadership of Sir John, later Lord Hunt, had conquered Everest were 'climber-gentlemen', models of British reserve, and gave the impression of being modest about even their greatest mountaineering feats. It was very much an image which clung to them on their return to London Airport on 3 July 1953. The *Daily Mail* reported that their account of their heroic exploits was simply 'a great adventure story told with understatement and shyness'.

Two years later, in 1955, Band and Joe Brown became the first climbers to ascend Kangchenjunga, though out of respect for the religious feelings of the people of Nepal and Sikkim, the pair stopped about ten feet below the actual summit.

Having been to Everest and Kangchenjunga, Band was a climber with an international reputation. In 1957 the Alpine Club planned a dinner in Switzerland to celebrate the club's centenary, and when Brasher and Band discovered that Swiss hoteliers were planning to add to the occasion with a generous offer of a free *raclette* party in Zermatt, the smell of melting cheese was enough to tempt them to the Alps. Brasher and Band were supposedly there only for the centenary dinner and the party – having recently been appointed sports editor for the *Observer*, Brasher had promised to file an article about the centenary – but Brasher had other ideas.

'We drove across France in Chris's green TR3,' said Band. 'I remember balancing a cardboard tray of fresh eggs across my knees in the cramped passenger seat. As usual we'd set off late. "Christ, George," Brasher would say, "I had to go back for my dispatch case." I had this theory that Chris only won his races because he was always trying to catch up, leaving others to tie up the loose ends – infuriating but endearing.'

They arrived in Chamonix, recalled Band, during a fierce storm. Frustrated in their intention to fit in some climbing before the dinner, they linked up with two other climbers, Peter Nelson and Mike Harris, in their Morris 1000 and drove east to St Moritz as if in a car rally, the storm clouds racing behind them.

'It was finer in the Bregalia, and we plumped to do some climbing on the North Ridge of the Badile. Mike and Peter shot ahead up the ridge. Chris and I soon passed an Italian with his attractive girlfriend from the hut. Around 2 p.m. we were close to the summit when the clouds closed in and it began snowing heavily. We beat it as fast as we could down the south ridge.'

'*A dicey descent into the unknown. It is bloody miserable and I feel wet through*', wrote Band in his diary.

'Both Chris and I had trouble with our spectacles misting up. In gathering darkness, Chris – rather reluctant to come on the rope earlier in the descent – no longer hesitated. "Have you got me, George?" Brasher asked uncertainly.'

They made their way down the ridge, slowly and hesitantly. One of the hut staff saw their torches and came to meet them, so they were able to avoid an uncomfortable bivouac on the mountainside. Of course, the climb had caused them to miss the Alpine Club dinner. 'John Peacock, the centenary dinner treasurer, was white with anger, we were told over the phone. We didn't get to the *raclette* party either, which had been the point of the exercise and trip to Switzerland!'

They had been lucky to get off the mountain safely. Five climbers on the south face of the Marmolada were to perish in the storm. But, said Band, Chris had plenty of material for his article.

Brasher and Band had to set off the next day, as they had to drive back to London overnight for Brasher to get to a meeting at the *Observer* office next morning. 'Back in Zermatt we drank a litre of milk between us,' said Band, 'retrieved the TR3, and took turns at the wheel across France, Chris chewing benzedrine tablets to keep himself awake. We breakfasted in Champagne country and reached his office only a few hours late! The trip had been a shambles, but great fun.'

The two climbers, Brasher and Band, were together again as members of a British expedition to the Russian Caucasus in 1958. In those days of the Cold War it took almost five years to get permission from the Soviet authorities. The group, nearly all of them Cambridge men who had been members of the university's climbing club, were the first foreign team to be admitted after the Second World War.

John Disley notes that in 1958 there had been 'four years of fruitless negotiations with the Russians by other climbing club members, but Brasher took over the job and within a year had engineered an agreement with the Russians to allow a party of British climbers to the Caucasus'. Not only that, Brasher had managed to persuade Sir John Hunt, leader of the expedition that conquered Everest in 1953, to join the party.

'It was a classic example of how Brasher networked a desired decision,' says Disley. 'He enlisted the president of his Achilles Club, Philip Noel-Baker, to approach Christopher Mayhew MP who was the chairman of the Soviet Relations Committee of the British Council who contacted the Russian ambassador in London, Mr Malik, who gave the go-ahead to the USSR Mountaineering Section to make arrangements for such a visit.'

In addition to Brasher, Band and expedition leader Hunt, the group which left England on 25 June 1958 consisted of Alan Blackshaw, Ralph Jones, David Thomas, Derek Bull, Michael Harris and John Neill. Their equipment was begged and borrowed, mainly by Brasher, who had cajoled the *Daily Express* into sponsoring the expedition with the promise of some press coverage. An account of the expedition was published in *The Red Snows*, a book jointly written by Hunt and Brasher.

The most dramatic incident on the expedition occurred during an ascent of the Bezingi Wall, a fearsome face of ice slopes and hanging glaciers, reckoned to contain the most challenging conditions in the Caucasus. Brasher was leading the climb when at around 16,500ft, with snow waist-deep, avalanches and appalling conditions, John Hunt vanished.

'Snow conditions had deteriorated,' said Band, 'and not very far from the summit on a dicey snow slope John disappeared into a concealed crevasse. He was successfully retrieved from the chasm using ropes, emerging like a snow-plastered Father Christmas.

'I don't know what Chris wrote, but the *Express* editors, tired of reporting depressing world news, decided to give it front page banner headlines: HOW I ESCAPED DEATH.

'After these epic ascents, I don't think Chris did much more roped climbing,' said Band, 'he preferred long ridge scrambles or journeys through mountains on foot or on skis.' But the pair kept in touch at mountaineering dinners and meetings, where Brasher would give Band an account of his latest epic: 'Christ, George, it was a hell of an experience!'

On or off the rope, Brasher's fascination with the mountains continued. He did much of his climbing in Snowdonia and the Lake District. Often climbers from London and the south-east would leap into fast cars and drive through the night to get to the mountains. So, as an added attraction to climbing, many rock climbers tried their hand at car rallying in the 1950s and 1960s.

Disley remembers that Brasher had a works-tuned Triumph TR3 in which he drove in the RAC and Tulip rallies, and recalls an incident after the 1957 Wimbledon Ball to which Brasher had partnered Shirley Bloomer. 'It was in this car,' says Disley, 'that he passed John Mawe in the Edgware Road at 4 a.m. Mawe in his Le Mans Frazer Nash was setting out to break the Marble Arch to Pen-y-Gwryd record. The two drivers considered racing together the next 240 miles but Brasher explained that he had caught John Mawe up to wish him good luck and Godspeed.' But for once Brasher found himself able to decline the challenge.

'On one wet and muddy two-day RAC Rally, deep in the wilds of Dyfed,' recalls Disley, 'Brasher showed his genius for organisation. Some dozen cars were stuck on a short, slippery hill with the only way up being achieved by a team of pushers. The problem was that the team kept shedding manpower as each car reached the top and disappeared into the night. Chris, seeing the danger of his car being left without pushers, ran ahead and confiscated the ignition keys until his car was up. Pat Moss, Stirling's rally driver sister, was not amused.'

Disley well remembers Brasher's repeated attempts at the RAC Rally. 'Our trouble was that Chris always insisted on doing the driving for most of the time, whereas he was a better map reader than me and I drove better than him. As it was his car he got his say on most of the two days.'

Others were not so generous in their assessment of Brasher's driving abilities. Graham Robson, former competitions manager of Standard Triumph, recalls: 'There wasn't much rallying Brasher could do in 1957 because of the original Suez crisis, and the cancellation of various events – there was no RAC Rally, nor any Monte Carlo Rally, in 1957, for instance. In January 1958, however, Brasher entered the Monte Carlo Rally in an MG Magnette with Gregor Grant [the editor of *Autosport*] but they didn't finish. They ran out of time.

'In March 1958 he entered the RAC Rally in a Triumph TR3A but retired once again. He was not with Gregor Grant, who wrote in *Autosport* that week that he was *hors de combat* with a back injury. In January 1959 Brasher entered the Monte in the TR3A, starting from Paris with Ted Wrangham as his co-driver. I don't think he finished. If he did finish, he was outside the top 120 cars. Memory tells me that he had an ex-press TR from the factory, and had Richardson's department prepare it for him, but he was never a works driver.'

Shirley Brasher agrees that Chris would never have claimed to be a 'works driver'. He was loaned the TR3A for purposes of publicity as the only man to bring back a gold medal from the 1956 Olympics.

Still, whether it was mountains, running or car rallying – whatever enthusiasm caught his eye – Brasher would be off and chasing his latest passion. He was very like Mr Toad in *The Wind in the Willows*, always up for a new craze, always ready to follow a new fashion, always searching for a new piece of heaven.

In Kenneth Grahame's 1908 children's classic, Toad is the ebullient extrovert, noisy and outspoken. Wherever he goes, drama follows him and he always finds it difficult to keep his tongue in check. Toad is the owner of Toad Hall, very rich and thus able to indulge his impulsive desires, such as punting, house boating, hot air ballooning, caravans and his love of Harris tweed suits. He has a boundless enthusiasm for travel and adventure, which some find enchanting, but also he has a tendency to be boastful, presumptuous, arrogant and self-centred.

Toad is always off on some adventure whenever something new catches his fancy and is always getting into trouble. Nevertheless, he is lovable and has his heart in the right place. The endearing rogue usually raises a chuckle.

When Roger Bannister read the original manuscript of this biography, he chuckled with pleasure and recognition at some of the characteristics of Brasher embodied in Mr Toad. There is the attitude to authority, the childlike energy, the grandiloquence of his aspirations that so often annoyed his critics. Like Mr Toad, Brasher lived by the river (in his case the Thames), and as age wrinkled his face even his countenance seemed to take on a toad-like grin. Brasher like Mr Toad could be utterly exasperating, but at the same time he was bewitching and disarming. Here is Toad (on seeing a motor car – the stirrings of his next craze): 'Poop-poop! . . . Glorious, stirring sight! The poetry of motion! The real way to travel! The only way to travel. Here today – in the middle of next week tomorrow! Villages skipped, towns and cities jumped – always somebody else's horizon. Oh bliss, oh rapture! Oh poop-poop!'

Brasher, like Toad, was the restless soul of adventure; all that was needed was the open road and the enthusiasm to make the best of it.

11

With a Map and Compass
We Can Take On the World

'If winning isn't everything, why do they keep score?'
Vince Lombardi

S HORTLY AFTER BRASHER was appointed sports editor of the *Observer* in 1957, he was invited to Norway to take part in a night orienteering competition. He wrote an article, published on 29 September 1957, which began: 'I have just taken part for the first time in one of the best sports in the world . . . It involves cross-country running with a map and compass. It is tremendously popular all over Scandinavia and the Norwegians have wondered why it is unknown in Britain.'

Orienteering was a sport that awakened many boyhood memories in Brasher. Having formed his obsession with cross-country running during his prep school days and wrestled with maps and compasses since he first tried hill walking in Wales while an apprentice, he took pride in his ability both as a runner and a navigator – and he was very competitive.

The week after Brasher's article was published, a letter followed in the *Observer* from Carl Hambro of the Norwegian Embassy saying that 'Orientation [*sic*] is not completely unknown in the United Kingdom.' But the formal foundation of the modern sport of orienteering in Britain dates from 1964 when John Disley, who

by this time had been appointed physical education officer for
Surrey County Council and a member of the Sports Council,
organised a series of fortnightly events in Surrey.

These attracted teachers and children and in order to gain media
interest, Disley invited well-known athletics friends including
Brasher, Roger Bannister and their fellow distance runners Gordon
Pirie and Martin Hyman to sample the sport.

The sport of orienteering had originally been practised in
Sweden, where it emerged at the end of the First World War. Major
Ernst Killander, a Swedish youth leader, decided to stage a series of
events using the Swedish countryside to tempt young people to take
up running. To add interest he issued maps and set out a number of
checkpoints that competitors had to visit.

The new sport spread quickly and in 1922 Sweden hosted the
first district orienteering championships. The next great
development came in the 1930s when the quality of the maps greatly
improved and the navigational aspect of orienteering became as
important as the purely physical running side. Up till then a good
cross-country skier or track athlete had been able to do very well at
orienteering; but once map-reading became as important as pure
fitness, navigators who could run a bit began to overtake runners
who could navigate a bit.

Orienteering was a democratic sport from the start – you needed
little or no specialist equipment. Competitors were told to come as
you like and they did, many of them in cast-off clothes and old
shoes. The first Swedish National Championships were held in 1937
and the following year the Swedish Orienteering Association was
formed. By 1964 the International Orienteering Federation had
eleven members.

Orienteering was imported to Scotland in 1961 and 1962 by an invited Swedish delegation including Baron 'Rak' Lagerfelt. The
Scots quickly saw the possibilities of the sport and offered enthusiastic co-operation to the Baron through the services of the Scottish
Council of Physical Recreation. The first Scottish championship

was held in May 1962 at Dunkeld in the Tay Valley and the early development of orienteering in Scotland was given credibility by an
influx of Norwegians who had arrived to take courses at Scottish
universities, in particular Heriot-Watt University in Edinburgh.

Soon enough, runners from the north of England began to travel
up to sample the sport in Scotland. One of the first was Gerry
Charnley, an athlete and mountaineer who was also a member of
Clayton-le-Moors Harriers and the South Ribble Search and Rescue
Team. Charnley was a police sergeant in charge of outdoor
activities for cadets, though he was rarely seen in uniform. His
'uniform' was habitually an anorak and climbing boots or an
orienteering suit and running shoes. His sports, like Brasher's, were
those in which the individual must be his own man – self-sufficient,
aware, and skilled in surviving in any conditions.

Charnley persuaded a team from Clayton-le-Moors to enter
the second Scottish Orienteering Championships in 1963 and to the
great astonishment of the Scots they took the team prize in
the men's race. This sowed the seeds for other events to be organised in England. The first, at Whitewell near Clitheroe in
Lancashire, took place over open moorland and used Ordnance
Survey 1:25,000 scale maps. Control flags were identified by grid
references and the wind was so strong that at one control, competitors had to jump to reach the marker punch which had been
hung from the branch of a low tree.

There were stirrings in the south too. Here the prime mover was
Disley. But Chris Brasher was never far behind and had started
writing a series of articles about the sport. Disley was the organiser,
and was able to use his position working for Surrey County Council
to get a course in orienteering run in Surrey schools in January
1965. Some of the international athletes roped in to try orienteering
by Disley and Brasher were very fit, but to the surprise and delight
of many of the teachers giving instruction on orienteering in
schools, they could be outpaced by pupils who had learned how to
read a map.

Disley published a book called *Orienteering* in 1967 in which he wrote:

> It was the fable of the hare and the tortoise in modern dress. Clutching at their maps, carrying their compasses like St Christopher charms around their necks, the trained athletes bounded off from the starting line down the first available path and hoped by sheer running ability to visit all the controls in the forest during their rapid if erratic progress.
>
> Interspersed among them, from the more academic world, were the professional geographers, youth hostellers, scouts and fell walkers. This group stepped confidently, if diffidently to the start. With the maps in their hands they quickly took good bearings, converted them to magnetic readings and set off through the trees. The pattern of success was fairly predictable and went like this in the early days of the races in Surrey.
>
> Initial success went first to the clever; and the first race was won by a schoolboy, fresh from GCE Geography at his Walton-on-Thames school.

Disley went on to describe the efforts of Gordon Pirie, one of Britain's leading athletes in the 1950s and a record-breaker in the 5000 metres, an event in which he won a silver medal at the 1956 Melbourne Olympics. Pirie had participated in three Olympics and set five official world records, along with perhaps a dozen more unofficial world bests, and had beaten most of the great athletes of the 1950s and 1960s. Yet, despite still being in good physical condition, he failed to finish the orienteering course: 'For nearly two hours he raced backwards and forwards across the Hurt Woods near Peaslake. After this time he had found only one control and that by chance . . . Eventually he had to knock on an old lady's door and ask his way back from her cottage to the village school where he had started from.'

But, wrote Disley, this was only half the story:

A month and two races later, the schoolboy Graham Westbrook was struggling to get into the first ten finishers while Gordon Pirie, homework done and manipulating his Silva compass with *élan*, had moved to second place in a field of sixty. This incident indicates the basic pattern that orienteering adopts when introduced into a community. First the tortoises win comfortably with the hares leaping all over the countryside from hill to hill, finding the red and white banners only by chance. Then the hares go away and do some studying and begin to run most of the time in the right direction to record better times than the tortoises.

Finally, deprived of the taste of honey that early success has given them, the tortoises shrug off their shells and start to go out running, training. Hence the cycle is complete and now the orienteering community allows success to go to those who are clever and fast; skilful with map and compass and fit in lungs and legs.

Disley's hard work gained immediate interest, not only from teachers but also from other veteran runners. As a result an invitation was issued to a team of orienteers from Lancashire to travel south and on 2 May 1965 a North versus South orienteering competition took place in the Surrey woods beneath Leith Hill.

It was the most competitive orienteering race held in England up to that time and was won by Bruce Tulloh – winner of the 5000 metres at the 1962 European Championships in Belgrade – with his team-mate Martin Hyman eight minutes behind in second place. The team event was won by the Southern Navigators Club and sparked an outbreak of activity among those wishing to try the new sport; races were held in north Wales, the Peak District and the west Midlands.

With orienteering fixtures popping up at random, the need for some sort of calendar of events and a structure became evident. At a meeting upstairs in the Dysart Arms in Petersham, the Southern Navigators Orienteering Club was formed on 2 May 1965. The

Southern Orienteering Association, whose committee was formed
of Brasher and Disley, Jeff Bull of Ranelagh and Martin Hyman
and Ralph Domican of the Occasional Orienteers, followed within
weeks. In October 1965 Brasher and Disley were the prime movers
in forming the English Orienteering Association. Its chairman was
Brasher and its first honorary treasurer was Disley, while Gerry
Charnley became its first secretary. It was an indication of how
small and cosy the world of orienteering was at this stage that John
Higginson, secretary of the Guildford Orienteers, remembers that
its meetings usually took place in the upstairs room of the Dysart
Arms, the headquarters of both the Ranelagh Harriers and the
Dysart Dashers, another running club.

As always in Britain, the sport was consumed with the rules that
covered amateurism and professionalism. Internationally, orienteering called all its adherents 'competitors' and made no distinction
between those who in other sports might be designated 'amateur' or
'professional'. Anyone could enter an orienteering race – the professional footballer, the fell runner for whom prizes might be
available in his chosen sport and the amateur athlete could all race
together. No money prizes were allowed in orienteering, so there
seemed little likelihood that any amateur association would object
to its members indulging in the sport.

Brasher made good use of his contacts with the Amateur Athletic
Association to smooth the way for orienteering to run its own
affairs, away from the problems that had haunted athletics for years.
Well aware of the bureaucracy that had kept the sport of athletics
locked in the past – particularly its hard line on 'amateurism' – he
adopted a more subtle approach rather than risk a confrontation.

He armed himself with a letter from Barry Willis, the honorary
secretary of the AAA, dated 16 July 1965, which quoted former
Cambridge athlete and member of the Achilles Club Harold
Abrahams, who was now AAA chairman. It made the position of
orienteering clear to Brasher as it affected amateur athletics.

Team player: The young Chris Brasher in his Oakley Hall days, 'small but plucky' his headmaster said, playing rugby (above left), soccer (above right) and perched before the cricket team (right). *Pictures courtesy of the Letts family*

Light Blue heaven: The Cambridge University cross-country team (below) from 1947 in the 57th annual Oxford v Cambridge held on Wimbledon Common. Oxford won the match by 17 points to 38. From left: J R Seale (Captain), J Anderson, P J G de Vos, Chris Brasher, T N C Wood and R M Jones. *PA Images*

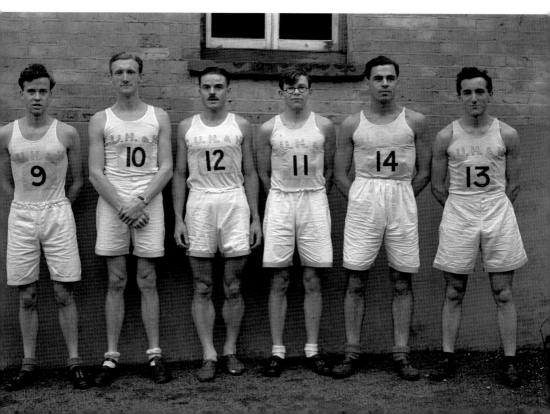

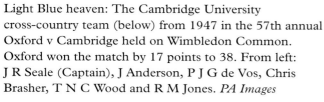

Winning smiles:
Brasher (above)
in the centre of
the picture, every
inch the 1950s
graduate. Shirley
Bloomer (right) at
Wimbledon with
Ted Tinling, the
fashion designer,
whose outfits in
the mid 1950s
revolutionized the
image of women
tennis players.
Mary Evans/
Michael Cole
Tennis Archives

Winning ways: The undergraduate Brasher (left) runs in the annual Oxford Cambridge Relays in 1948.

White City winner: Brasher (below) triumphs in the Three Miles in 14 minutes, 36 seconds when running for Oxford and Cambridge against Cornell and Princeton (USA) at a White City meeting on July 1, 1950. *PA Images*

Kings of the Common: Chris Chataway leads the way home in the 1950 Varsity Cross-Country match on Wimbledon Common. Chataway (Oxford) wears no. 6, D H Gilbert (Cambridge), in second place, wears no. 12, and Brasher, in third, wears no. 10. *PA Images*

Heroes in the making: Franz Stampfl, the legendary coach (above left), with the dark, curly hair, far right in the picture, with the Ronay family in Vienna in 1936. Abebe Bikila, (left) the great Ethiopian runner, who won the Olympic Marathon barefoot in Rome in 1960 and Emil Zatopek (above), the Czech running machine, who demonstrated to Brasher what training could achieve. *Courtesy of Nick Overhead; Gamma-Keystone via Getty Images; Time & Life Pictures/ Getty Images*

The Mighty Atom: Sydney Wooderson (left) is lofted shoulder high by his admirers after setting a new world mile record of 4:06.4 at Motspur Park in Surrey on August 28, 1937. *Getty Images*

Setting the pace: Chris Brasher (left) covers two laps of the first 4 minute mile in 1 minute, 58 seconds. And (below) Brasher, Bannister and Chataway savour the record that made them all famous. *Getty Images*

Their finest hour: Sir Winston Churchill (left) congratulates Brasher, Chataway and Bannister just four weeks after they had broken the 4 minute mile and had achieved 'The Holy Grail of foot racing.' *Getty Images*

Leaping to fame: Brasher shows great form leaping the water jump (above) in the final of the 1956 Olympic steeplechase. In the run-up to the Games he had been beaten regularly by John Disley (below). But (right) Brasher gallops to win the gold medal in Melbourne. *Popperfoto/Getty Images*

Golden dreams: Brasher proudly shows off his Olympic gold medal (below). It had taught him that anything was possible. *PA Images*

Cups and wedding bells: Brasher beams as he receives the Sportsman of the Year Trophy at London's Savoy Hotel on January 9, 1957. And (below) Shirley Bloomer weds Chris Brasher at Chelsea Old Church in 1959. Roger Bannister was Best Man. *PA Images; Wg Johnson/ Evening News/Rex Features*

Clock watching: Fred Lebow (above), founder of the New York Marathon, runs with Brasher through the streets of London in 1981. *PA Images*

Winners all: Hand in hand, Dick Beardsley and Inge Simonsen (left) share victory in the first London Marathon in 2:11:48, while Brasher smiles as he crosses the line in 2:56. *Getty Images*

New York's No.1: Fred Lebow (left) wearing no. 0001 lines up at the start of the inaugural London Marathon with Sir Horace Cutler of the Greater London Council. *PA Images*

Brasher presents a bottle of champagne to Joyce Smith (right), the first winner of the women's race in 1981. *Mark Shearman – Athletics Images*

Queen of Norway: Ingrid Kristiansen, four-time winner of the women's race, with husband Arve and Brasher in 1987. *Mark Shearman – Athletics Images*

Marathon Princesses: Princess Diana (above) was the official starter of the London Marathon in 1987. And Paula Radcliffe (below) shows her delight at breaking the world record with 2:15:25 in 2003 being presented with her trophy by Prince Andrew. *PA Images; London Marathon Ltd.*

In at the deep end: Jeffrey Archer (left) being shepherded around by John Bryant in 2004. The man in the diving suit (below), Lloyd Scott, completes the London Marathon course in 5 days, 8 hours, 29 minutes and 46 seconds. *London Marathon Ltd; Getty Images*

The fastest: Emmanuel Mutai of Kenya wins the Virgin London Marathon with a record time of 2:04:39 on April 17, 2011 in London, bringing the prospect of a two hour marathon ever closer. *Getty Images*

Good companions: Paddy Buckley and Brasher (left) taken at the start of the Karrimor Mountain Marathon, October 1990 at Kinloch Rannoch. Chris Chataway and Brasher (below) at the Thames Hare & Hounds water splash used for the Oxford-Cambridge annual fixture. *Pictures supplied by John Disley*

Messing about in boats: Brasher (above) with daughter Kate, Ed Sibiski, soon to be her husband, and Matthew Bryant aboard the Kestrel on the Thames in 1990.

Happiness in the wilderness: Brasher (below) with his ski poles, the snow and the wild Scottish landscape. He collects an honorary doctorate from the University of Stirling in 1989 (left).

At the wheel: Brasher (above) ran this boat aground in 1990 and had to be rescued. Shirley Brasher (right) at home in Chaddleworth. And (below) after winning the Lanzarote Hurdle at Kempton Park in 2000.
© *Racing Post*

The man with the Brasher Boot: The original logo (left) from the Brasher Boot Company. Chris Brasher had dreamed for a decade of a shoe that was waterproof, light and blister-free.

The Truth About WILSON

The real-life Wilson: Joss Naylor (left) running through the Lakeland fells. The fictional William Wilson who had fired Brasher's imagination with super-human feats (above). *Photo by Brian Duff, courtesy of River Greta Writer; Wilson ®© DC Thomson & Co. Ltd. 2012*

Three muddy men:
Chris Brasher with
John Bryant and
Dr Ronnie Williams
on an OBOE voyage
in 1996. Skippered
by Sir Robin
Knox-Johnston,
Brasher found the
running tough (left).

Picking up the baton: Chris's son, Hugh Brasher (right),
also an athlete, successfully extended the Sweatshop business
with now over 40 stores, and replaces Dave Bedford as race
director of the London Marathon in 2013. *Third Sector*

A meadow and a posy: As Petersham Trust Chairman,
Brasher (below) protected this land on the banks of
the Thames and in 2001 secured a 125-year lease from
Richmond Council with a posy of wild flowers. *PA Images*

Dear Mr Brasher,

You may recall you spoke to me at Windsor where we were gathered at the start of the Polytechnic Marathon on the subject of orienteering. I have had a word with Harold Abrahams in this connection and since he confirmed the view I can now say to you with confidence that amateur athletes can compete against who they choose in this sport without endangering their amateur status as far as we are concerned, provided always that there is no question of competing for money prizes.

This letter cleared the way for 'amateur athletes' to take part in the sport of orienteering, and to run against athletes who were professionals in other sports. Freed from such restrictions, over the next few months regional orienteering associations were formed, constitutions drawn up and membership of the international bodies sought and approved.

The first English championships were held around Hindhead, Surrey in May 1966 with Gordon Pirie emerging as champion. A team for the World Orienteering Championships in Finland was selected and Disley found sponsorship amounting to £850 to send an English team. Both Brasher and Disley were members of the team.

At these championships the International Orienteering Federation, the world governing body, told Brasher and Disley that they could only affiliate one organisation from the United Kingdom. The two immediately started negotiations with the Scottish Orienteering Association, and as a result the British Orienteering Federation was formed in 1967 at a meeting at Barnard Castle, County Durham. As soon as the proposal to form a British – as distinct from English – Orienteering Federation was formally accepted, Brasher began drafting the constitution with the assistance of others including Disley.

The constitution's clauses were specifically framed in order to avoid the problems which had beset athletics. For instance, every individual member of the Federation had one vote and had the power to elect officers. The chairman could not serve for more than three consecutive years: Brasher was elected chairman from 1967 to 1969 and when he stood down Disley was voted chairman for the next three years.

Back in the 1950s Brasher and Disley had set the pattern for opposing the entrenched amateurism and bureaucracy that had traditionally haunted British athletics. From his privileged position, public school and Cambridge educated, Brasher had been acutely aware that there were other athletes who trained without his advantages. He had been vociferous in leading the 'strike' against the athletics authorities to gain the 10,000 metre runner Fred Norris some pocket money and compensation for time off to compete in the Melbourne Olympics. Brasher believed that sport had to be run on a democratic and fair basis. Let the best man win, he would say, otherwise there is no point in the competition.

With orienteering, Brasher and Disley saw the opportunity to put these beliefs into action and to establish the sport on a democratic and efficient basis. To impose some structure on British orienteering, Brasher and Disley worked enthusiastically as volunteers, unpaid officials, freeing themselves from what they considered to be the stultifying hand of bureaucracy and the dominance of AAA committees. These bodies picked competitive teams and always insisted that team managers should be sent to shepherd athletes on any trip, often travelling first class while the competitors went steerage.

Soon the British Orienteering Federation was sending British teams to the world championships free from team managers. In the early 1970s these efforts were rewarded when Britain was awarded the right to hold the 1976 World Orienteering Championships. Brasher and Disley obtained sponsorship for the event from Scottish and Newcastle Brewery and set up an organisation to prepare for the championships, to be held at Aviemore on the Moray Estate near Inverness. Disley was made the director of the championships and

Brasher was the course controller. They met in secret at the farm-house of Dounduff in Darnaway Forest so as not to divulge the routes to the competitors. Gerry Charnley was also a prominent member of the team. During this period the only paid employees involved with the organisation of the World Orienteering Championships were the two full-time map-makers, Robin and Sue Harvey.

Thanks to the sponsorship that the British Orienteering Federation had arranged, the championships made a surplus of over £5000. This was partly down to the fact that Brasher, Disley and their team did all the paperwork from home, used their own cars and did not bother to charge for out-of-pocket expenses. The surplus was given over to the British Orienteering Federation in the hope that it might invest in premises which could be used to train young orienteers. It was a pattern that worked for Brasher and Disley – but, particularly in the case of the London Marathon – it was a model which was to provide a great deal of controversy in future.

As Brasher wrote ever more enthusiastically in the *Observer* about the new sport of orienteering, rival newspapers hit back. The *Observer*'s great rival as a heavyweight Sunday newspaper in the 1970s was the *Sunday Times*, whose editor at that time was the ever-enthusiastic Harry Evans. Evans, who had become editor of the paper in 1967, realised the potential of running for his middle-class readers. He was a 'jogger' himself, and had launched the Sunday Times National Fun Run in 1978. It was hugely popular. In 1979 15,000 people took part in the two and a half mile run in Hyde Park. Evans wanted to make sure that his writers, who included Cliff Temple and Norman Harris, were not scooped or outflanked by Brasher.

Chief among Brasher's rivals on the *Sunday Times* during this period was Harris, a New Zealander who in his home country had trained as a runner under the great coach Arthur Lydiard. Sent by the *Sunday Times* to the first World Orienteering Championships to be staged in Britain, Harris was immediately enthralled with the

challenge of running and navigating through the forest at
Aviemore.

'I was speaking to Stig Berge, four times the Norwegian champion, because, in writing about these championships, I wanted to
identify what it was that made an orienteering champion,' remembers Harris. 'Was it running strength over rough terrain? Brilliance
in map reading? Was it the ability to think under pressure? The vision to see a clever route to the next control point? Berg summed
it up in a single image. "The elite orienteer," he said, "is like a stag
in the forest. Its ears pricked. Alert."'

The day after the title races in the 1976 championships a race was
staged for the press. Harris, having bought some special 'O-shoes'
and a compass, fancied his chance. But he found it a humbling experience. 'I started by tearing straight through the forest like a
startled stag – not one with its ears pricked!' he recalls. 'The winner on that fairly short course did around forty minutes. I took over
three hours.' But it brought him into close contact for the first time
with Chris Brasher. 'It was as rival newspaper men that our relationship achieved a certain piquancy,' adds Harris.

There were endless circulation wars between the *Observer* and
the *Sunday Times*. Any time that the editors saw a chance to score
over their rivals, they would pour reporters and resources in to pick
up extra readers. Brasher had first brought orienteering to the
notice of the reading public, and it was natural that Harry Evans
wished to get in on the act. The *Sunday Times*, its adventurous
picture-led layouts inspired by Evans, knew that they couldn't be
left behind by this emerging sport.

'Chris, being a star writer for the *Observer*, always managed to get
some space for major orienteering events,' says Harris. 'The
Observer was the only national paper where anything in depth could
be read about orienteering, until the *Sunday Times* began to support
"participation" sport – and particularly jogging.'

In 1977 Harris was lined up to write a piece about orienteering
centred on the Jan Kjellstrom Festival, the big event staged over

the Easter weekend. Brasher was aware of what the opposition were doing and he knew that the *Sunday Times* would be reporting the event, which boasted two thousand competitors. His report in the *Observer* began with a reference to one or two veteran stalwarts before turning to details of the winners. The paper's report was a long single-column affair with no pictures. The *Sunday Times* had a far more impressive display; there were several pictures, headlines and text across the top of two facing broadsheet pages.

'Following Saturday's race we all travelled down to a Sussex wood for Sunday's relay day,' said Harris, 'and in the big parking field I was told that Brasher, who was being driven, had spent much of the journey counting words in my *Sunday Times* feature about this orienteering event – not reading, but *counting*.'

Harris soon came across a group including both Brasher and Roger Bannister. Before Brasher could speak, Harris demanded of him with mock seriousness, 'Chris, who can we speak to about getting more orienteering in the *Observer*?'

Bannister seemed amused but Brasher wasn't. He suddenly turned and barked: 'Five hundred words, that's all you have, same as me. And you didn't even have the winner.'

Off hand, Harris was not sure what his wordage had been, but he guessed that it was rather more than five hundred. He was mystified, too, by the allegation that they had missed the winner. 'We did have the winner,' protested Harris, who had used a picture of Geoff Peck and described how he had lost four minutes among the rhododendrons.

'Not in my edition,' growled Brasher. Harris walked away, puzzled, trying to understand how Brasher might not have seen this material. Back in his car he looked again at the *Sunday Times*'s double-page spread. The heading on the left-hand page said: 'A Day Out in the Woods with Two Thousand People'; the pictures and text on the right included details of the winner. Harris suddenly had a vision of Brasher being driven down to the event by John Disley – counting every single word.

'I folded the paper in half, so that only a single page showed – the left-hand page,' said Harris. 'I went back to the Brasher–Bannister group and held up the page.

"'Is that what you saw?"

"'Yes," said Brasher. "Your five hundred words."

"'So you didn't see this?" I opened out the double page spread.' For a moment Harris looked at Brasher in triumph. He understood the rivalry of the two great Sunday papers, and he was certain that Brasher would have to apologise.

'There was the briefest of pauses,' said Harris, 'as Chris glared at the two pages.

"'Bad layout," snapped Brasher. There was no way that Chris would allow a rival to get the better of him.'

12

Falling Out of Love with the Raddled Old Tart

'The Olympic Games are the quadrennial celebration of the springtime of humanity.'

Pierre de Coubertin

OR CHRIS BRASHER the iconic moment in the Olympics came on 10 September 1960, on a humid Rome night on the Appian Way. There, lit by flares held aloft by Italian soldiers, Abebe Bikila trotted down from the highlands of Ethiopia to astound the world of the marathon. The vision of a stick-thin, ebony-skinned runner whispering along the cobblestones of this great city, showing no signs of effort, was to haunt Brasher for decades, inspiring perhaps his finest achievement – the London Marathon.

Abebe Bikila, a member of Emperor Haile Selassie's bodyguard, glided silently through that race with all the nobility of a well-drilled soldier – tall, erect and impassive. Astonishingly he was barefoot, running with grace and dignity. The apparent ease with which Bikila won the race, the effortless superiority, aroused echoes of Brasher's great fictional hero Wilson of *The Wizard*. But this was no comic-book creation; this Ethiopian was real. The image of the man, virtually unknown to the press and public, who had put in the miles, barefoot, in the thin air of the Ethiopian highlands, immediately labelled him in Brasher's mind a hero; perhaps the greatest hero of these Olympic Games.

In 1960 Africa was just shrugging off the burden of colonial rule. Bikila's triumph was all the more stunning because it happened in Rome, the capital of Ethiopia's former military occupier. In the 1930s the Italian army had been responsible for killing thousands of Ethiopians by mustard gas. Legend has it that Bikila made his decisive move in the race just as he passed the Axum Obelisk, a towering stone slab that Mussolini had brought back from Ethiopia as war loot.

With less than a mile to go, panic set in among journalists in the press box. None of them had ever heard of this man who was speeding to victory. But there Bikila was, trotting rhythmically along the Appian Way, the route of the conquerors in a city to which his ancestors had once been carried off as slaves.

Bikila's triumph captured the new spirit of Africa, the 'winds of change' sweeping the continent. As he finished, officials rushed towards him but he pushed them aside; he stretched his arms to touch his toes and jog a little on the spot. What shocked onlookers was how calm Bikila appeared. He was completely undistressed. They brought him a blanket but he waved it away. His time was eight minutes faster than Emil Zatopek's 1952 Olympic triumph. Within minutes Bikila was hoisted aloft and laughing for joy.

This mysterious Abyssinian seemed to float out of the past – but his times belonged to the future. In two hours, fifteen minutes and sixteen seconds, the time he took to win the Olympic marathon, he changed African running and Brasher's view of the marathon for ever.

For track and field enthusiasts, the marathon was traditionally seen as the most punishing event in the Olympic calendar. Brasher wrote:

Peter Wilson of the *Daily Mirror*, one of the greatest sportswriters of the century, had taught me that the one event that had to be covered from start to finish was the marathon – an event which, he said, was always packed with human drama.

Obediently, I followed his guidance and will never forget the sight of the two African runners, Abebe Bikila, of Ethiopia, and Rhadi ben Abdesselam, of Morocco, their bare feet taking Rome by storm.

That was when I knew that if I was to understand this event which embodies courage and fortitude, I had to experience it myself.

It took Brasher nearly two decades before he tackled the marathon. The prospect of putting one foot in front of the other for 26 miles, 385 yards of road filled him with foreboding. 'I could run the distance on the glorious hills of Britain, but to do it on the roads, watched by three cows and a dog, was surely the height of masochism.' But courage and fortitude were marks for Brasher of a hero, and for him in 1960 the greatest of them all was Bikila. In Brasher's mind Bikila did indeed rank alongside that hero of his imagination, the fictional Wilson. And what made Bikila's triumph even more romantic were the details of the legend.

Bikila had been added to the Ethiopian Olympic marathon team only at the last moment. As the plane to Rome was about to leave, he was shipped in as a last-minute replacement for a team-mate, Wami Biratu, who had broken his ankle in a soccer match. Adidas, the official shoe sponsor at the Games, were running low on shoes and gave him a pair that did not fit comfortably. So he decided to run barefoot, as he had often done on the dusty, unmetalled roads of Ethiopia. After the race, when Bikila was challenged as to why he had run barefoot, he said: 'I wanted the world to know that my country, Ethiopia, has always won with determination and heroism.'

He was pointed out at the start, said Brasher, with amusement — a curiosity. Some runners joked that there was at least one person in the field they were sure to beat. But he was the first black African to win an Olympic gold, and the runners that followed in their thousands from the rift valleys and highlands of Ethiopia and Kenya broke new barriers and started a revolution in distance running.

From the 1950s, when Brasher first started to train for the Helsinki Games, to the end of his life, he had an enduring relationship with the Olympics, and nobody wrote with more feeling and often with more criticism of the Olympic ideal than he. The Rome Olympics in 1960 were the first Games that Brasher attended as Olympic correspondent rather than as a competitor. And although Bikila had made an indelible impression, Brasher voiced his reservations when it came to giving an evaluation on the Games themselves. Warning of the trend to include too many sporting events and the cost which inevitably spiralled as host cities strove to outbid each other, he expressed his fears for their future.

Brasher gave his verdict on those Games on 8 September 1960 – a judgement that beats a rhythm through all his Olympic coverage: 'The Games are getting too big and too expensive. The International Olympic Committee is seeking ways and means of cutting them down. In order to save the Olympic Games they had better do it quickly.'

Brasher was to author a series of books on the Olympics, usually at breakneck speed after they finished, and through those books it is possible to trace the changing nature of his affair with the Olympic ideal. On one such occasion Brasher wrote 45,000 words by dictating to two secretaries in relays for up to sixteen hours a day. Brasher completed the books in seven days. He had to; he had already promised delivery to the publisher, Stanley Paul. Shirley Brasher used to joke that she had to lock him in a room and take the key away to get him to hit his deadlines.

For the next Olympic Games in Tokyo in 1964, Brasher produced his *Diary of the XVIII Olympics* just six weeks after the closing ceremony. Despite his misgivings four years before about the cost and the size of the Games, Brasher's enthusiasm for these Olympics was undimmed: 'This is the greatest athletics team ever to leave Britain. There are no qualifications about this statement whatever,' he wrote. 'It is obviously important to find out what went right (a very unfamiliar sentence to any British sports writer of the last two decades).' This 1964 Olympic diary captured the spirit of elation that followed the Games and was able to contrast the number of medals that Britain won in 1964 with performances over the past three Olympics.

Brasher was delighted that his hero from the Rome Games of 1960, Abebe Bikila, was back in Tokyo. Bikila had travelled to Tokyo but, sadly, was not expected to compete. Six weeks before the start of the Olympics, Bikila started to experience stomach pain during a training run near Addis Ababa. He collapsed and was diagnosed with acute appendicitis. He was operated on and while convalescing he began secretly jogging in the hospital courtyard at night.

To the amazement of his doctors and coaches, Bikila declared that he was fit enough to run and entered the marathon, this time wearing lightweight Puma shoes. Brasher could scarcely believe it when Bikila entered the Olympic stadium alone to the cheers of 70,000 spectators. He lived up to his legendary billing, finishing the race in a new world record time of 2:12:11.2; four minutes eight seconds in front of the silver medallist, Basil Heatley of Great Britain. Kokichi Tsuburaya of Japan was third.

Bikila was the first athlete in history to win the Olympic marathon twice. After finishing he astonished the crowd by not appearing in the least exhausted. He lay on the infield on his back performing cycling exercises and other stretches. He declared to waiting journalists that he could have easily run another ten kilometres.

Later that day, in the press conference held beneath the concrete stands of the stadium, Brasher asked whether Bikila would compete in Mexico City and try for the hat-trick. 'Yes,' Bikila said, '*And I will win*. Mexico City is at the same height as Addis Ababa.' Mexico City stands at 2240 metres above sea level, Addis Ababa at 2300 metres. Bikila had been born at altitude and he knew at first hand the problems athletes would have attempting to compete in thin air comparable to that of his homeland. His answer highlighted for

Brasher an issue that was to consume him and to put him into conflict with many of the governing bodies of both British athletics and the Olympic movement.

Two days after Bikila's victory in Tokyo, Brasher visited the Ethiopian headquarters in the Olympic village and talked to Swede Onni Niskanin, Bikila's coach and a man who had spent eighteen years in Addis Ababa. Niskanin said quietly: 'An Olympic athlete will always do his utmost but few of them will have any idea what the lack of oxygen can do to those who are not used to altitude. Suddenly – blackout. There will be those who will die.'

Statistician Stan Greenberg recalls that Brasher contacted him just before the Mexico Games wanting him to provide 'some data to help him prove the contention that there will be those "who will die" in Mexico because of the altitude factor. I remember that I tried vigorously to argue him out of the idea as I thought his views were far too extreme.' But, says Greenberg, 'It seemed impossible to change his mind.' Niskanin's comment, the words 'There will be those who will die', provided the mantra that would haunt Brasher's Olympic coverage for years and led to some of his fiercest criticism of the Games.

Soon after the Tokyo Games had finished in October, Brasher returned to the issue of altitude and the plans to hold the next Games in Mexico City. In 1965 he produced a series of articles in the *Observer*, all of which betrayed his concern about the health of athletes competing at altitude. In one such piece he wrote:

> My opinion on such a matter may not carry much weight, but Dr Roger Bannister has said that he does not consider it justified to hold the endurance events in Mexico City. He does not go nearly as far as Niskanin. Bannister does not say there will be 'those that will die', but he does believe that there is the possibility that someone may be permanently affected. Surely the International Olympic Committee cannot take such a risk.
>
> A man who has lived all his life at over 7,000 feet will be far

better acclimatised than someone who has only spent a month at this altitude. It is on this question of the time taken to acclimatise that I base the weight of my argument. To hold the endurance events in Mexico City is to commit what I will call an offence against the spirit of the Olympic Games.

For years, argued Brasher, the International Olympic Committee had fought against professionalism in the Games. But, he pointed out, there were several aspects to professionalism; it wasn't just the money, it was Brasher's own sense of fair play, his desire for a level playing field:

> It is fairly easy to ensure no one who has competed for money is allowed to take part in the Olympics. It is much more difficult to eliminate what I call 'the time professionals', or in other words the people who have no job or career but are supported in some way that enable them to devote all their time and energy to their chosen sport.
>
> Up to now this has not been a serious problem. It has always been possible for a man who is prepared to devote two hours a day to his training to compete on equal terms with a time professional. In fact he often has an advantage in that he is mentally much fresher. But if the Olympic endurance events are to be held in Mexico City the time professional will have an immense advantage.

Taking teams of runners to high altitude training camps and keeping them there for many weeks would obviously cost money. But even the British athletic officials, so consumed with the amateur ideal, were prepared to contemplate it. In the last months of 1965 the British Olympic Association and the Sports Council set up a research team of six distance athletes, together with a coach and two doctors. Under the leadership of Dr Griffiths-Pugh, a noted skier and a mountaineer who was a member of the successful Everest expedition in 1953, research was carried out at the Mexico

City-based Reforma Athletic Club and the Human Physiology Laboratory in Hampstead. Tests and timed races were held in Acapulco and Mexico City.

One of the athletes who took part in these trials was Brasher's friend Martin Hyman, a one-time holder of the British six mile record. On his return to Britain, Hyman told Brasher: 'If I had my heart set on an Olympic medal I would give up my job one year before the Games and take another one at a similar altitude to Mexico City . . . Even with one year's acclimatisation at 7500 feet there is a possibility that you might be beaten by someone who had been acclimatised at a higher altitude.'

By 1968, the year of the Mexico Olympics, Brasher's optimism about the Games of 1964 had been superseded by thoughts of pessimism and failure. He began his next Games diary still convinced that, because of the altitude factor, the IOC had picked the wrong venue and that the Games were facing disaster. 'The first and most salient fact is that Mexico lies at an altitude of 7,347 feet above sea level,' wrote Brasher in his *Diary of the Mexico Olympics*:

> The higher you go above sea level the thinner becomes the air. Eventually when man reaches the summit of Everest just over 29,000 feet the air is so thin that he cannot walk even one step without taking two deep breaths.
>
> Bear with me if I go back to what I said about this problem when I first raised it in the *Observer* in 1965. I'm not trying to prove how clever we were to raise it at such an early date but I am trying to show that basic principles of the problem could easily be detected in 1965 and there was no reason why the International Olympic Committee could not have done a little homework in 1963 before awarding the Games to Mexico City.

But it wasn't just the altitude or the poverty of Mexico that appalled him:

It is hard to keep one's judgement, still harder to keep one's temper. One sees every facet of man's character and some of it is sickening. There are for instance two brothers here, Horst Dassler and Armin Dassler. They both run sports shoe firms making at least 6,000 pairs a day and they cannot sell that quantity unless every schoolboy, every Sunday footballer, every business man exercising in his health club wants to wear the same shoes that this or that Olympic champion wore. So they bribe these amateur athletes . . .

There is much irony here in Brasher's comments on the commercialisation of selling sports shoes and his attack on the Dassler brothers. Through his efforts to promote orienteering in the late 1960s, and later fell running and the marathon, he too was on the brink of putting branded training shoes on the feet of millions. The dichotomy between his belief that sport should be simple, democratic and unexploited and his commercial instinct to peddle sporting equipment was, in time, to give his critics a field day. Nevertheless, he continued:

Who do you blame, the athletes or the men who offer the money? Perhaps the root of this shoddy bargain lies in our own nature and we are prepared to pay £2 more to have some vicarious contact with a champion rather than buy an equally good football boot or training shoe whose symbol has never been planted in our minds.

Of course, it makes one wonder whether the whole Games have not reached such unruly proportions, that all that was good in their original conception has been lost.

But since he first spoke to Bikila's coach, Brasher had considered that the greatest threat to the Olympics was the issue of altitude. And when the world's finest distance runners stepped out on to the track he reckoned that his fears had been vindicated.

The first track final of the Mexico Games was the 10,000 metres

– an event in which altitude played a major role. Ron Clarke of
Australia was due to compete. Thirty-one years old at the time
of the Games, he was the world record holder, a man who had
brought new standards to the sport, a man who at sea level would
be an odds-on favourite to win any race.

On Sunday 13 October 1968, thirty-seven men lined up for the
start of the 10,000 metres. Among their number were seven who
were born and brought up at altitude and two or three who had
spent a considerable part of the last two years training at altitude.
The race was won by Naftali Temu, a 23-year-old private in the
Kenyan army. His time of 29:27.4 was nearly two minutes slower
than Clarke's world record.

After the race, in which an exhausted Clarke finished sixth,
Brasher observed:

> The stadium resembled a casualty clearing station with white
> coated attendants bending over prone athletes and administering
> oxygen. But the most pathetic sight of all was the almost lifeless
> figure of Clarke. He had given everything in pursuit of this gold
> medal that he so dearly wanted. Twenty minutes after the race
> had finished Clarke had recovered enough to get to his feet and
> with one arm around Brian Corrigan and the other arm around
> the Australian team manager he was virtually carried from the
> stadium.

Brasher's anger and disillusionment with the Olympics mounted.
'They call this sport,' he wrote in the *Diary*. 'I feel bitter and angry.
Altitude has now been proved to be the decisive factor. Altitude has
turned one of the great races of the Olympic Games into a handicap
event. The Olympic charter talks about assembling the amateurs
of all nations in a fair and equal competition. There is nothing fair
or equal about these Games.'

Brasher found his favourite event – the steeplechase – a
ridiculous farce. Maurice Herriott of Great Britain, who had won a

silver medal in Tokyo in 1964, was carried away on a stretcher after failing to qualify in his heat. Brasher wrote angrily that he 'felt like throttling the whole of the International Olympic Committee'.

But Brasher was excited that once again his old warhorse, his hero Abebe Bikila, had turned up to try for his third Olympic title. Once again Bikila and his fellow countryman Mamo Wolde were entered for the marathon, and symbolically, Bikila was issued with the starting number 1 for the race. This time, though, Bikila was nursing an injury. He had apparently broken a small bone in his foot a few days before the race while running barefoot. Bikila's right knee gave way under the pressure of the race and after just after ten miles he shook his head and pulled out. It is said that he turned to his friend and long-time running partner Wolde and told him: 'Go on, it's up to you. You must win.'

Wolde, the 36-year-old veteran, won the gold, but later stated that if Bikila had not been injured, he would surely have won.

By the end of the Games, Brasher's fury with the altitude question had ensured his complete disillusionment with the Olympics. On Saturday 26 October 1968 he wrote:

> This is the end of a love affair. Every four years since the beginning of the 1950s I have renewed a brief idealistic existence with this woman who transforms pure physical effort into an experience of spiritual beauty. Now she is a raddled old tart.
>
> It is not her fault. A sceptical world has courted her too fiercely and the world, being materialistic, nationalistic and mean, has made her parade her sex in front of a panel of doctors, urinate into a bottle to make sure she has not been taking drugs and breathe into a plastic tube to prove she is not drunk. To me and other romantics she is dying under this treatment.
>
> As Ron Pickering, Lynn Davies's coach and a man who has devoted his life to sport and recreation, says: 'I cannot see the Olympics surviving for more than another four Games, it is bloody tragic.'

In his own sport, Brasher could see two threats. He perceived the danger of the increasing use of artificial stimulants: 'Hormones . . . Now if you want to get anywhere in the heavy field events you must take Dianabol or its new improved version Maxibol. Your weight will increase, your performances will improve and your testicles will waste away. Those are the short term effects. The long term effects are unknown.' And, as predicted, he said, altitude had been decisive:

> These were, in the words of Jim Ryun (who broke the world record for the mile in 1966 and held it for eight years but failed to win an Olympic gold), the 'unfair Games'. Unfortunately altitude is a potent factor which will remain in athletics forever. We know now that if you train and live at altitude your performance in all events which take over two minutes will be improved. So the distance athlete of the future who aspires to a gold medal will have to uproot himself and take to the hills.

Without a doubt, he continued, the Mexico Games had damaged the amateur cause more profoundly than any amount of cash.

In his next Olympic Diary, Brasher noted more new threats. First to affect the 1972 Olympics, held in Munich, was the effect of boycotts. Even before the Games began, forty African nations lined up against the newly emerging Southern Rhodesia and Avery Brundage, the president of the IOC, found that at the age of eighty-four he was outvoted and had to give way to Rhodesia being thrown out of the Games.

Following this, Brasher wrote:

> I did not find many people in Munich who believed that the Olympics could survive much longer, after all it was politics and commercialism that killed the ancient Olympic Games in Greece and the same thing is happening to the modern Games.
>
> I do not like it, but then I do not like many of the things that are happening in sport these days . . . I know that it is ridiculous to

expect politics to be kept out of the Olympics, to expect the International Olympic Committee can cut down on the size of the Games so that they are not restricted to the richest cities of the world and because it is ridiculous to expect these things I do not know how much longer the Olympic movement can continue.

Indeed, the Olympic movement is a strange anachronism trying to stand loftily above the materialism and politics of the world standing for truth and honesty, but for how much longer?

But worse was to come, as terrorism made its impact on international sport. The 1972 Games were overshadowed by what has come to be known as the Munich massacre. On 5 September a group of eight Palestinian terrorists belonging to the Black September organisation broke into the Olympic village and took eleven Israeli athletes, coaches and officials hostage. By the end of the ordeal, the terrorists had killed all eleven hostages, as well as one West German policeman. Brasher wrote:

> I hate fanaticisms. I hate fanatics who would deprive others of life because they are convinced that their cause is the right cause. I hate fanatics who will pursue one objective so relentlessly that they lose all sense of the completeness, the roundness of life . . . We know what the fanaticism that grew up in the Munich beer cellars did to Europe and the world in the 1930s and 40s. We know what Arab and Israeli fanaticism has done for the Middle East, the airlines of the world and now to some competitors in the Olympic village. But are we quite certain that we know what fanaticism has done to sport.

Brasher was also turning his thoughts to how much the human body could take in preparing for the four-yearly contest of the Olympics. He wrote of the British distance champion David Bedford, who was later to work closely with Brasher on the London Marathon:

Bedford, before Munich, was training up to 200 miles a week,
which is more than twenty-eight miles a day. Others followed his
example . . . But there are limits. And I confess that I have been
extremely slow in coming to this conclusion. The reason for that
is that people, especially journalists, have always talked about the
impossibilities like the four minute mile, climbing Everest and yet
others. Besides, there is something magnificent about the man who
refuses to acknowledge the impossible . . .

I was mulling these thoughts over with Hugh McIlvanney, once
a colleague on the *Observer*, as we sat sipping a drink in the press
bar of the stadium. I had pointed out there was little difference that
I could see between the dedication of the modern sportsman and
that of a classical pianist or a ballet dancer or a poet in a garret.
He made the wise reply that the difference was that the pianist, for
instance, did not just practise scales but was being constantly
subjected to the minds and emotions of the great composers. Of
course he is right. What distresses me is that utter fanaticism about
the human body leads to utter neglect of the mind.

So what is to be done about it? First of all we can change
completely the showpiece of sport, the Olympic Games. We must
stop them being a gladiatorial nationalistic fight, a sort of a
substitute for war between nations.

Brasher advocated getting rid of all nationalistic symbols, national
anthems and flags at the victory ceremony. He advocated, too,
getting rid of team sports, including the relays in athletics and
swimming. But he believed that you had to go further, and make it
possible for hundreds of cities to stage the Games instead of just a
handful. That would mean, he thought, a maximum of about ten
sports. He worked out that there were five sports which should
retain a permanent place. Two would represent speed on land in
the water – athletics and swimming; two individual combat –
boxing and judo; and one skill allied with art – gymnastics. Then
you would allow another five sports on a rota basis. Finally, you

should hold these Games every two years so that a young man did not have to devote such a long period of his youth to preparation.

'Of course,' he concluded, 'it will not solve all the problems of the Olympics or of sport but who could do that? All one can do is to trust human nature and instinct, provided that you believe that man is basically good rather than basically evil.'

Brasher's old hero Abele Bikila was invited as a special guest to the 1972 Olympics. This time, however, he appeared in a wheelchair. In 1969, during a spell of civil unrest in Addis Ababa, Bikila had been driving his Volkswagen Beetle when he had to swerve to avoid a group of protesting students. His car landed in a ditch, trapping him. They fought to free him but the accident left the two-time marathon champion quadriplegic.

The Emperor, Haile Selassie, flew Bikila to Stoke Mandeville Hospital in England where his condition improved somewhat to paraplegic. His coach, Niskanen, persuaded him to compete in archery competitions for athletes in wheelchairs and Bikila joked that he would win the next Olympic marathon in a wheelchair. But it was from his wheelchair that he witnessed his countryman Mamo Wolde (now forty years old) finish third in the marathon behind American Frank Shorter. After Shorter received his medal he went to Bikila to shake his hand.

On 25 October 1973, Bikila died in Addis Ababa at the age of forty-one from a cerebral haemorrhage, a complication related to the accident he had suffered four years earlier. He left behind his wife and four children. His funeral in Addis Ababa was attended by 75,000 people and Emperor Haile Selassie proclaimed a national day of mourning for Ethiopia's national hero. Brasher produced no great writing to mark Bikila's death; his reaction was simply one of great sadness. The shock had been seeing Bikila reduced to a wheelchair after being the finest athlete in the world; for Brasher it was as if his life had ended after the accident.

Brasher was in Montreal for the 1976 Olympics, but this time did not publish a Diary. Because of the Munich massacre, security at these Games was highly visible, which Brasher believed ruined their atmosphere. But what disturbed him more was the growing influence of politicians and the dangers of a boycott. If nations were to stay away, he believed, it was futile to pretend that the Olympics could produce a true champion.

The effect of boycotts on the Montreal Games was devastating. In protest at a tour of South Africa by the New Zealand All Blacks rugby team, Congo's Jean Claude Ganga, head of Africa's National Olympic Committee, led a boycott of twenty-eight African nations as the IOC refused to bar the New Zealand team.

In a close echo of what Brasher had seen from Emil Zatopek in 1952, Finland's Lasse Viren achieved a double in the 5000 and 10,000 metres, but finished fifth in the marathon, thereby failing to equal Zatopek's Helsinki achievement. But with the Kenyans and the Ethiopians absent, Brasher feared the boycott had produced some hollow victories.

Boycotts were still in the air, and greatly angering Brasher, before the 1980 Olympics in Moscow. The 1979 Soviet invasion of Afghanistan had led the United States to threaten a boycott of the Games. President Jimmy Carter issued an ultimatum in January 1980 that the USA would not send a team to the Olympics if Soviet troops did not withdraw from Afghanistan within a month. Their athletes pulled out, as did those of other leading countries including Japan, West Germany, China and Canada.

Margaret Thatcher was keen that Britain should join the boycott. Brasher hated her stance on this, and it was rumoured that he had turned down any chance of an honour because she urged athletes to join the boycott. The sportsmen were not so keen either, but in the event Great Britain and France sent smaller delegations of athletes than usual.

But Brasher was not so disillusioned that he could ignore events on the track in Moscow. Among the 170 British athletes who competed were the two leading middle-distance athletes in the world that year – Sebastian Coe and Steve Ovett. Their clashes in the 800 and 1500 metres were eagerly anticipated as the highlight of the Games for track and field enthusiasts. Brasher, with his own track background, was fascinated by their rivalry.

The 800 metres final was first to take place. Favourite to win the event, Coe was beaten to the gold by his arch-rival Ovett. Gutted and despondent to take only the silver medal, Coe himself wrote of Brasher's involvement in what happened immediately after his defeat:

> 'I can't believe how badly you ran,' Brasher said shaking his head in the way a father might wearily admonish a teenager for writing off the family car for the second time in a few weeks. 'I'm going to have to go away and think about this. You just can't run like that again in the 1500,' he told me.
>
> Brasher was right and I had three days to do something about it. A few hours later I returned to my room. On the bed in the sparse accommodation that passed for the Moscow Olympic village in 1980 was an envelope. Brasher had gone away and 'thought about it' and in four sides of handwriting had identified how he thought I could win or lose the 1500 metres. Win it I did.
>
> Its contents were targeted at the tactics of middle distance running, but it inevitably, in classic Brasher-esque style, roamed into the great history of track and field, of Nurmi and Zatopek, of Landy and Elliott. There was even a paragraph about Sibelius and about a breathtaking view in his beloved Lake District. Over twenty years later it is still a letter I re-read, one that probably says more about Chris Brasher than any biographer or tribute could ever say.

Before the Barcelona Olympics of 1992, Brasher was still putting forward his views about what had gone wrong with the Games. In the *Sunday Times* of 9 May 1992 he identified the issues that had dogged his life as an Olympic correspondent:

Should everybody be here at the Olympics, poor and rich, amateur and professional? Are the ideals of Olympia sullied beyond redemption by the drugs scandals? Are the Games too big and is there too much flag waving, too much nationalism?

The first can be dismissed quickly. The division between amateur and professional is a relic of England's Victorian class structure, a means of preventing the working classes from competing against the aristocracy and its time has long since passed.

Brasher believed, too, that with the right medical backup the battle against drugs could eventually be won. He continued:

And so to nationalism. When I was an Olympic athlete I believed, and so did most of my contemporaries, that we were not competing for our country but for ourselves and there were those of us who preached that national flags and national anthems should be replaced by the Olympic flag and the Olympic hymn.

Brasher's conclusion on the Olympics was brutally simple and chimed with his view that sport should always be played on a level playing field. 'Every competitor in the Olympics wants only one thing,' wrote Brasher, 'to compete against the best in the world.'

13

Shopping for Shoes

'I learned that the only way you are going to get anywhere in life is to work hard at it. Whether you're a musician, a writer, an athlete or a businessman, there is no getting around it. If you do, you'll win — if you don't, you won't.'

Bruce Jenner

WHEN CHRIS BRASHER set out for that first hill-walking expedition in the hills of Snowdonia back in 1946, he had shown his obsession with equipment. He carried with him his father's prismatic compass, a relic of the First World War. He took an anorak in a rucksack which contained a whistle, and his boots with do-it-yourself hammered-in nails which would give them purchase on the ice, rock and snow of the mountains.

Right from the beginning he had been prepared to experiment and tinker with the stuff that made him faster and enabled him to do more efficiently what he wanted to do. He showed the same obsession when he was training for the Melbourne Olympics. He had been to his cobbler in Wimbledon and begged him to take more and more leather off his shoes in order to produce the lightest pair possible. He had engaged his optician to make those rather hideous contact lenses — big as bottle tops, Brasher said. But he took no chances with his equipment when winning mattered to him.

Brasher's preoccupation with getting the right equipment and his obsession with the tools of the trade for running, walking or climbing had been there from the start. In the 1950s he had his running shoes hand made by Sandy Law of G.T. Law and Sons, Wimbledon. The usual situation at that time was that northern athletes had their shoes made by J.W. Foster and Son of Bolton and runners in the south had theirs made by Law. When Brasher returned to running in the mid-1960s, he found that Law had retired and he had to buy off-the-shelf Adidas shoes, which he considered never fitted his feet properly as Law's hand-made shoes had done.

When Brasher was challenged, as he often was, about what had given him more satisfaction, his business or his sporting successes, he affirmed that sport had been the highlight of his career because that came at the right age. 'But really,' he said, 'the things that apply to sport also apply to business. There is a lot of hard work that is more important than talent and you need common sense not to get hauled off by the latest piece of gimmickry or fashion. Over-riding all this though must be that extra and often insatiable desire to succeed. I have a very competitive temperament. God knows where it comes from.

'If you are competitive you are also a perfectionist and that can be quite uncomfortable sometimes. It means you will not accept anything but the best. Therefore anybody who doesn't quite produce the best gets the thin end of my tongue.'

It was in the context of the years that he had spent developing, expanding and codifying the sport of orienteering and his obsession with equipment that Brasher and his close friend and colleague John Disley began to explore commercial interests.

For orienteering, you need two items of equipment. One is studded shoes; the other is a good compass. The Scandinavians, who had devised the sport, were naturally the leading producers of specialist orienteering compasses – a Silva protractor magnetic compass was developed in Sweden in the 1930s by the Kjellstrom brothers, Alvar and Bjorn.

Alvar Kjellstrom had been one of the three top Swedish

orienteers in the 1930s and with Bjorn ran Silva Compasses. In the mid-1950s Brasher discovered that his friend Disley had already become involved with the small British company that had the franchise from the Kjellstroms for the sale of Silva compasses in the United Kingdom. The company was called B.J. Ward Ltd and was owned and run by Elsy and Bertie Ward from a tiny Victorian office building in Westminster Bridge Road.

Disley began acting, unpaid, as a consultant for Silva compasses, but was reimbursed for his out-of-pocket expenses and given a bottle of whisky at Christmas. During the early 1970s Bertie Ward's health declined and at the request of his wife a new company was formed called Silva Compasses (London) Ltd. Disley asked Brasher if he would become involved in the project and he readily agreed. During July, August and September 1973 the details of the new company were hammered out and on 14 September 1973, Silva Compasses (London) started trading from an address in Teddington, Surrey.

The shares of the new company were split, 50 per cent to the Kjellstroms and 25 per cent each to Disley and Brasher. The Kjellstroms contributed £1750 and a four-month credit facility while Disley and Brasher put up cash of £3750 each. In return the Wards received cash for their stock plus a life consultancy fee of £1800 a year.

For Brasher and Disley, eager to promote the infant sport of orienteering, this move into the commercial world seemed a natural progression. In 1974 Disley was appointed vice-chairman of the Sports Council; he was already chairman and secretary of the newly formed British Orienteering Federation. He now also became chairman and managing director of the British branch of Silva Compasses and Brasher a director.

Brasher, Disley and Alvar Kjellstrom had become firm friends and Kjellstrom's only son, Jan, was being groomed to succeed him as the boss of the company. By Swedish standards Jan was a modest orienteer, but by British standards in the 1960s he was magnificent and a good teacher. The pioneers of orienteering in Britain learned from him much of what they new about the principles of course setting and navigation. But in his late twenties he went back to Sweden, where he was killed in a road accident in January 1967.

Kjellstrom and his wife Yvonne were devastated. Since Jan had done so much to give British orienteers a vision of what they themselves could achieve, Brasher and Disley wanted to commemorate his contribution to orienteering and it was Brasher's idea that they should start an event to be run every Easter between Swedish and British clubs.

It was called the Jan Kjellstrom Trophy. Brasher managed to persuade his wife Shirley to part with a valuable silver salver which she had won in a tennis match, and had it engraved. He asked Alvar and his wife to visit Britain to present the trophy themselves. Their closeness at this time was such that Brasher could recall Easter weekends when Brasher's own son, Hugh, still at primary school, came to the Anglo-Swedish contest and Alvar played chess with him, seated in the open air on the ground in a Scottish forest. The salver is still competed for annually and the J.K. Trophy is now established as a premier international event.

A fellow orienteer named Tony Wale, a former business associate of Gordon Pirie, joined Brasher and Disley's company as a manager. For a couple of years the company struggled and then in the mid-1970s, with the growing popularity of orienteering, the cash flow improved.

More capital was introduced by Brasher but at this time a dispute broke out between Kjellstrom and Disley. There had been a disagreement because Alvar did not believe that any part of the company's money should be put into furthering the 'promotion of orienteering as a sport'. Brasher said in the 1990s that the atmosphere became unpleasant, with allegations being made about Disley being dishonest.

The fallout was that Kjellstrom sold his interest in the company to the owner of the factory in Sweden which made the compasses. Shares were valued at £50,000 each, so that Disley and Brasher each got £12,500 for their 25 per cent stakes plus a bonus of £5000 each and a consultancy fee of £7500. Disley remained as a director of the new company and was paid an annual consultancy fee for promotional activity.

Brasher's next venture was into supplying orienteering shoes. His fellow athlete, Gordon Pirie, showed him the way. Having taken to orienteering after his great career as a track athlete – he won the English Orienteering Championship in 1966 and followed this with a victory in the British Championship in 1967 – Pirie realised that even basic orienteers needed some equipment. So, operating as Gordon Pirie Ltd, he began importing and supplying specialist equipment.

When he suddenly emigrated to New Zealand Pirie left his stock with Tony Wale. In 1969 Brasher telephoned Wale to order a new pair of Swedish orienteering shoes and was told that Wale was not happy with Pirie's departure for New Zealand, since bills had not been paid and he was not in a position to get fresh stock. Brasher was struck by the conundrum of how to get the shoes he needed and asked Wale if he would be prepared to continue selling them if finance could be found. Seizing this opportunity, Brasher founded Brasher and Wale Ltd, making a contribution of £1000. Wale and Brasher each had a 50 per cent share in the business.

In July 1977 Wale wanted to pull out of the company. Again there had been a dispute about expenses, and he asked for his share to be bought out. Brasher purchased the shares and the company then became Brasher Leisure Ltd, the shareholders of which were Brasher himself and, initially, his wife Shirley. Expanding what was essentially an orienteering business, Brasher began trading from premises in Teddington which was set up as the Sweatshop (the name was later changed to 'Sweat Shop').

In a further, bizarre change of name in 1978 the Sweatshop had a bright new frontage painted. Runners turning up to buy shoes or compasses were confronted by a sign which read: Christopher Brasher's Sporting Emporium. Hugh Brasher said that all the family had sat round at home poring over a short list of new names. Nobody, says Hugh, liked the new name – except his father. But the name went up. Nothing, it seemed, could change Brasher's mind once he was enthusiastic about an idea. But he often lost that enthusiasm, reconsidered and changed his mind rapidly. 'It didn't last long,' said Hugh. 'It was soon back to the Sweat Shop and Christopher Brasher's Sporting Emporium was no more.'

It reflected that in 1978 this was just one very small retail outfit catering to the specialised needs of orienteers and runners. It had moved on from selling compasses and studded shoes from car boots and mail order – but not very far.

The same year, Brasher saw an advertisement in an American magazine called *Runner's World* for width-fitting running shoes manufactured by New Balance Athletic Shoes. These were rated as being the best shoes on the market and Brasher sent off for a pair. To his delight he found them to be the most comfortable running shoes he had ever worn.

Many more people were running by then. They weren't just athletes. They were doing it for their health and the jogging boom that had swept America was catching on in Britain. Brasher ordered 300 pairs of New Balance Model 320 shoes from the company's factory in Boston, Massachusetts for the Sweat Shop. The shoes sold well and Brasher increased his orders.

In November 1978 the president of New Balance Shoes, Jim Davis, contacted Brasher and said that he wanted to expand his operation into Europe. He visited Brasher at his home and Brasher advised him to set up a factory in Britain. Always a man to follow up an idea with action, Brasher contacted the Board of Trade, who placed an advertisement in *Shoe and Leather News* to the effect that an American manufacturer wanted to buy a factory or have shoes made under licence in Britain. The response was overwhelming. Brasher helped an official of the Invest in Britain department of the Board of Trade sort out the potential candidates and then Davis and Brasher toured the country looking for a factory.

But in the late 1970s the UK shoe manufacturing trade was in a bad way. Many companies were going bankrupt; employment in the industry fell from around 120,000 in the mid-1970s to around 60,000 in the early 1980s. Davis also visited Ireland, where the Industrial Development Agency was offering great incentives to potential manufacturers, and when he saw the inducements on offer, he took on a former shoe factory in Tralee. At the same time he offered Brasher the UK distributorship. The shoes would be made by Davis's company in Tralee and distributed under licence by Brasher in Lancashire.

Brasher decided to take up Davis's offer and invited Disley to join him in forming a company to handle the distributorship. This new company, called Fleetfoot Ltd, was formed in December 1978. Brasher needed someone to manage Fleetfoot, and as so often he turned to one of his fell-running, mountain-walking companions, a man who shared his thirst for adventure and was prepared to put up with his mercurial approach to such expeditions – Paddy Buckley.

Buckley had been made redundant in his mid-forties in July 1975 from his job as librarian with Bakelite Xylonite, when its research station in Essex, where the young Margaret Thatcher had worked as a chemist, was closed down by its American owners Union Carbide. That year he spent a month working on the restoration of Bearnais, a ruined bothy south of Strathcarron. Brasher was then the editor of *Mountain Life*, in which he invited his readers to the official opening of 'Beardie's Bothy' (Brasher's private name for Bearnais, after fell runner Eric Beard, who had died in a motor accident in 1969) at New Year. Brasher and three friends made the journey to the opening of Beardie's Bothy and on New Year's Day 1976, Buckley poured out Brasher's finest Glenmorangie whisky to open the Bothy.

As controller for the 1976 World Orienteering Championships, Brasher invited Buckley to join the team of orienteers planning the courses and building the controls. Later that year Brasher bought

Pant Lleni, a traditional Welsh cottage on a hillside above Llyn
Gwynant, an ideal place for Buckley to demonstrate his all-round
DIY skills. It was not all hard graft. Each day there was time to run
over the hills of Snowdonia. It was also a time for the two
contrasting personalities to learn how to work together.

On New Year's Eve 1976 Brasher and Buckley had talked of
crossing Scotland on skis. 'Chris had once made an attempt on skis,'
said Buckley, 'which had failed in the hills around Ben Alder. He
was keen to try again. I had offered to guide him through the
territory I knew best.

'On 14 January 1977 Chris and I set off from London Airport
for Glasgow where Chris had a meeting with the BBC. Beyond
Grantown the road had been closed by the police because of
snowdrifts. Undeterred, Chris drove on, drawing on his car rallying
expertise.

'Next day we set off on our attempt to be the first to make a
coast-to-coast crossing of Scotland on skis.' Brasher wrote his
account of the trip in the *Observer*. Buckley wrote his own account,
the 'Ross Crossing' in the *SMC Journal*. 'I sent a copy to Chris,'
Buckley said, 'and over three years later, he wrote a short note to
thank me, after finding my article buried in a pile of papers.'

'You write well,' Brasher said.

On 21 December 1978 Brasher had offered Buckley the job of
manager of Fleetfoot Ltd. The two of them spent three days in mid
January 1979 visiting Burnley, Blackburn, Accrington, Preston and
Whalley, looking at derelict cotton mills, a former Co-op, a nightclub, a weavers' institute and an old shoe factory, most of them quite
depressing. The best premises they had seen, a former nightclub in
Whalley, proved to have dry rot. They spent another four days in
February looking at more buildings. None was suitable. Brasher
remembered that a pub had been recommended to him if he was
ever in the area.

'It had been pretty wet and pretty cold,' said Brasher, 'and I
remember someone had said, "If you are ever up in that area, go to

the Barbon Inn, between the Lake District and the Yorkshire Dales, opposite the Lune.'" It had been recommended to Brasher and Buckley by Egon Ronay and Ashley Courtenay. 'I thought we needed a decent meal and a decent night,' said Brasher.

'The next morning it was one of those marvellous winter days when there's a covering of frost on the ground. Paddy and I went for a run on the Barbon fells and then looked at the map and thought we'd not been to Lancaster – we've only driven through it on the A6 up to the Lakes.'

Lancaster was pleasant enough and they visited a number of estate agents, but still with no luck. Still mixing business and pleasure, the next day, 10 February, they drove up to the northern Howgills for the start of the first British ski orienteering event, one of Gerry Charnley's visionary ideas for creating challenges on the fells. The competitors were faced with a ferociously cold head wind.

'I was first away,' Buckley said, 'carrying my skis up to the snow line. At the first control I found that I had forgotten my ski poles. I continued without them. An hour or so later a rosy-cheeked Carol McNeill caught up with me and asked to look at my map as hers had blown away in the gale.' A champion orienteer and fell runner, McNeill like Buckley often used to join Brasher on his expeditions. 'She won the event. I was second; two hours thirty-three minutes for 12 km; Chris, who had lost his compass, was third in two hours forty-three.'

On 20 February Brasher, Buckley and John Disley met in London for a New Balance product meeting. Next day the three of them went up by train to Lancaster hoping to make a final decision on a warehouse for Fleetfoot. Not only was the town on the doorstep of the fells, but Paddy Buckley lived close by, and Tralee, where Davis manufactured New Balance shoes, was easily accessible.

They went to the town hall to meet David Taylor, who managed the council's properties. He took them down to St George's Quay where the council owned some derelict eighteenth-century warehouses, next to what later became the Maritime Museum. The side door needed a hefty push to open it. They had to strike matches to see into the gloom.

'It was absolutely shambolic, full of pigeon droppings and rags, every cat in the neighbourhood had used it as a litter tray. But it obviously had potential,' was Buckley's verdict. 'Then we went to the pub next door and ordered three pints. There was no fire. I handed over £2, standard in the south, and got £1 back and twelve pence. Prospects had quickly improved.

'Here in Lancaster you could live within half an hour of the office and choose between beaches and town. You had the Lune Valley and the Lake District. We drew a circle on the map of places that were within forty-five minutes and the Langdale Valley was just on the limit, yet right in the heart of the Lakes.'

So the decision was made to rent 26 St George's Quay. Buckley spent the next few months transforming the derelict warehouse, with no water or electricity, into a place ready for business. The first delivery of New Balance shoes arrived from Tralee on 30 April.

It was obvious that quality control at the Tralee factory was very lax – some 30 per cent of the shoes were faulty. The quality of the shoes was not the only problem. Brasher kept tight control on the finances, which occasionally led to New Balance refusing to send an order until their bills had been settled; that led to all kinds of delays and misunderstandings, both in Lancaster and Tralee.

For most of that first year Brasher and Disley kept away from Lancaster. When they did visit, Brasher had the habit of working late in the office. The next morning the room was stale with cigarette smoke and the ashtray would be overflowing.

Communications between Brasher and Buckley were often tetchy. Both were obstinate, and overnight Brasher would often leave long, hectoring messages on the Fleetfoot answer phone. 'On 31 January 1980 Chris left a rambling message,' says Buckley, 'that he was at the end of his tether and was thinking of winding up the company. He asked me to meet him on 3 February at a café on the M6 near Stafford where he told me about Fleetfoot's financial difficulties. As I had invested a huge amount of effort in establishing my part of the business, I didn't want to see this wasted and me out of a job. So I offered Chris £9000 to keep Fleetfoot going. He accepted. The crisis was over – for the moment, but the arguments over managerial style rumbled on.'

The first few years of Fleetfoot were extremely difficult but by the beginning of 1982 it looked as if the company was beginning to make a profit. For the first three years of the company's life Brasher and Disley had been living in bed and breakfast accommodation whenever they visited Lancaster. That was far from ideal and prevented them from working in the evening. Accordingly they decided it was time to find a house, preferably within an hour of the town. The two decided to establish a directors' pension scheme, paying £99,500 into it. The pension scheme bought them a house – Silver How near Skelwith Bridge, for £56,500 – and it was leased back to Fleetfoot.

In May 1982 Brasher accepted the invitation to become a director of a subsidiary of New Balance. At the same time he learned that Jim Davis wanted to open another New Balance factory. The Tralee factory was giving trouble both with low productivity and low standards, and Brasher's hope was that the new factory would be opened in Britain. Davis and Brasher resumed their tour, looking for suitable premises. Davis's decision was to open a factory in Workington, Cumbria, in a factory where K Shoes had recently been made. Hundreds of unemployed shoe workers applied for the forty or fifty jobs in the New Balance factory.

But then, in the last few months of 1982, the global economy was to play a part in Fleetfoot's future. The dollar exchange rate turned against the company. New Balance had factories in the USA and Canada, in Ireland and the Far East, but wherever they were made, Fleetfoot had to pay for the shoes in dollars.

During 1983 Disley and Brasher fought to keep the company

alive as the pound declined gradually. By December 1983 the two of them had decided that the company could not be saved. Fleetfoot was effectively losing money on every pair of New Balance they sold and its directors met Davis to tell him so. Brasher and Disley offered him the distribution contract back and Davis suggested a fifty-fifty joint venture 'in recognition of your achievement for establishing this brand in Britain'.

Disley and Brasher were uncertain. 'John and I had put in five years' hard work,' said Brasher. 'Most of that time we had been on half of what were pretty small salaries. We had ended up with about £6000. We could chuck it in or we could try again. One of the things that was important was that we had a staff of ten who had really worked so hard throughout the good times and the bad. We thought, right, with that staff, let's have another go.

'I had heard that Reebok who were based in Bolton were looking for a new distributor, so I rang them up. We became their new distributor in July 1984, knowing that if we didn't make a go of it we would be bust within six months.'

Hugh Brasher says that it was not just coincidence that prompted his father's phone call: 'I heard while working at the Sweatshop that Carter Pocock, the existing distributors of Reebok, were no longer going to be distributing them in the future. I had seen two very good shoes from Reebok that were coming out shortly – the Phase One tennis shoe and the Phase One running shoe.

'I told my father he should look into distributing them. He rang one of the Fosters, who had owned the brand, and negotiated the deal. The huge risk he took was that Fleetfoot with New Balance at the time had a turnover of £2 million – Carter Pocock with Reebok had a turnover of just £0.75 million.' By pulling out of New Balance to take on Reebok, Brasher was gambling on Reebok vastly increasing their turnover.

'We hit the targets and ended the year about £100 in profit,' said Brasher. 'If it had been £100 loss we were so near the edge the company would have gone bankrupt.'

Brasher and Disley were very fortunate. After the initial cautious performance their company made a great breakthrough with Reebok in the following years. This followed an international upturn in Reebok's fortunes in 1985. Reebok's UK turnover rose from £3 million in 1985 to £34.5 million in 1988. The company's success, both in Britain and abroad, was not principally derived from the running shoe market but from the expanding world of fitness, fashion and aerobics. Late in 1982, Reebok launched in America the world's first shoe designed specifically for aerobic exercise. The shoes' bright colours and fashionable styling took the footwear market by storm.

At the end of 1984, before this explosion of profits, there was a change in Fleetfoot's management. Disley had an operation on his hip, having been in considerable pain for over a year, and wished to take some months to recuperate. Accordingly Brasher took on more of the responsibility for running the company and an arrangement was made whereby he bought some of Disley's shares year by year. At the same time Fleetfoot was refinanced and Pentland Industries, of which Reebok International was a subsidiary, took 50.01 per cent of the shares.

Given the enormous profits that were coming out of Reebok and Pentland Industries during the course of 1988 and 1989, Brasher disposed of a number of shares to his wife and children and to the newly formed Chris Brasher Trust. The end of the Reebok distribution contract came in December 1989. Both Disley and Brasher wanted to continue the relationship but Reebok wanted to do its own distribution. So at the end of 1989, Reebok UK bought out all of Reebok's Fleetfoot assets for a net figure of £2,478,244. Brasher found himself a millionaire as a result of the deal.

Brasher was given a three-year contract as non-executive chairman of Reebok UK, but when that expired at the end of 1992 he decided not to renew it. However, he had turned his love of equipment, for finding the most comfortable and lightweight shoes, for experimenting on himself and his friends, into a very big business; a business that was to make him rich for the rest of his life. But it was also a business that was to lead him and his colleague, John Disley, into trouble – trouble that might see many of his hopes hobbled on the roadside.

14

The Brasher Boot

*'Flaming enthusiasm, backed by horse sense and persistence, is
the quality that most frequently makes for success.'*

Dale Carnegie

ONE WEDNESDAY EVENING in March 1982, a bunch of
Ranelagh runners were in the bar at the Dysart Arms in
Petersham. They were enjoying themselves and
knocking back pints to combat the dehydration brought about by
their run in Richmond Park. Among them was Rex Lofts, a past
president of the Ranelagh Harriers and one of those who had
featured back in 1965 in the first orienteering event to be held in
the south of England in Richmond Park.

'Chris Brasher came in,' Lofts remembers, 'a crutch under each
arm and one foot heavily bandaged. We were naturally very
sympathetic and anxious to know what had happened. He told us
that he had been walking in north Wales and field-testing a new
walking boot which he had designed. Brasher explained that he had
tripped over his own feet and this was the result. I'm sorry to say
that amidst gales of laughter we were all of the opinion that the
Brasher Boot would never be a success.'

Brasher had been walking in north Wales with Paddy Buckley,
and Buckley's diary for 22 March 1982 records that he, Brasher and
Ken Ledward, who ran an equipment testing service based in

Cumbria, were testing prototype lightweight boots in Rhinogs
when Brasher stepped into a hole and wrenched a knee. He limped
a bit but seemed OK the next day.

Brasher had spent much of the late 1970s and 1980s returning to
his roots as an avid hill walker and mountaineer. In 1978, while
walking a 180-mile route in Wales, he reported, 'After three days of
walking in the conventional walking shoe of the late 1970s my feet
were killing me and I was wondering why I couldn't experience the
comfort of a good running shoe.'

The story, often repeated in the Dysart Arms, was that Brasher,
suffering from serious blisters in his tough mountaineering boots,
had posted the boots home and completed the walk in a pair of
trainers. That was possibly an apocryphal story. But, realising that
there could be a market for comfortable walking boots, Brasher
decided to design his own, just in time to catch the outdoor leisure
boom.

The concept of a lightweight walking boot had begun to
germinate in Brasher's mind early in 1978. On 3 January that year
long-distance walker John Merrill had set off on a walk around the
entire coastline of Britain. Brasher, looking for a story for his
column in the *Observer*, arranged to meet him in north Devon for a
couple of days' walking. Brasher had brought with him three pairs
of boots to try out. But Merrill didn't believe in lightweight boots.
He wore an all-round mountaineering boot of a type that was too
heavy for Brasher.

Not easily put off, in March 1978 Brasher and Buckley began to
plan a long walk through the mountains of Wales, using the line of
the yet-to-be-opened Cambrian Way, which runs for some 275
miles from Conwy to Cardiff. They took along with them to test a
range of boots that included the Everest and Pennine models made
by Hawkins and a pair of Romika, as well as a couple of pairs of
trainers from Brasher's sports outlet, the Sweatshop.

They set off from Margam on 15 May 1978, having dropped off
spare boots at the Castle Hotel, Llandovery. By the time they

reached the ruins of Strata Florida Abbey, Brasher was in need of his chiropodist. He made a long phone call to her in London. The traditional walking boot of that period needed a lot of breaking in. John Merrill reckoned you had to cover 500 miles before the boots became comfortable. There had, thought Brasher, to be a better way.

For the next two years Brasher concentrated on selling training shoes for New Balance. But the idea of using running-shoe technology to produce a lightweight walking boot had not gone away. On 16 March 1981 Brasher went to see John Hall, who ran a workshop from a disused chapel in Llanfrothen in which he made rock-climbing boots. Within a month the first prototype of the new, very lightweight boot was ready.

It had a narrow wrinkled rubber sole, a rand (a strip of rubber to protect the heel and sides, which can help in rock climbing) made from a lorry inner tube and a soft leather upper much wider than the sole. The boots looked crude and ugly but were surprisingly comfortable once you had struggled to get your feet inside them.

A second prototype was constructed in late August at Hall's workshop and in November 1981 Brasher took Hall to K Shoes in Kendal to explore factory production. In a marketing report to New Balance during the first six months of 1981, Brasher wrote: 'In May I produced a prototype of the Brasher boot and this has proved to be exceptionally good . . . There is a good market for the taking in 1982 and there will be several competitors, but the Brasher Boot could take the major share if we can get a good quality boot produced to sell at £29.95. A conservative estimate of volume is 10,000 pairs.' However, the management at New Balance were, said Brasher, lukewarm about the proposal. They were already producing a lightweight walking boot of their own and saw no need for a rival.

But testing of the boot went on throughout 1982. Brasher, Buckley and Ken Ledward used the boots for climbs and walks, continually tinkering with them and offering improvements. On 21

March Brasher and Buckley tried out the Kendal prototype in snow in Cwm Merch, north Wales and found it had an excellent grip on wet rock. The new, lightweight Klets sole had been designed by Ledward, who arrived next day and gave the boot rugged testing in the Rhinogs range; and Buckley climbed the Great Slab at Cwm Silyn in what he called the 'bendy boots'. In July 1982 Brasher turned up at the Saunders Mountain Marathon wearing a prototype.

At the end of July Buckley took a week in the Cuillin mountains in Skye, testing the new boot sole for grip and wear. Brasher's local shoemaker at Petersham, John Ellis, nicknamed 'John the Boot', knocked up a useful modification by gluing the Klets sole on to a pair of New Balance trainers – smart enough to wear in the pub, said Brasher.

But still there was no one around to market Brasher's dream boot. It was not only New Balance who were lukewarm about the boot. When he transferred his running shoe distribution service to Reebok, he got very much the same reaction. For all the effort he and his friends had put into it for the best part of a decade, the Brasher Boot appeared to be another of those Brasher-inspired mutations that would be overtaken by time.

But Brasher wouldn't let it die. One of the reasons that he had decided not to renew his contract as non-executive chairman with Reebok at the end of 1992, some ten years after he had first toyed with the concept of a lightweight boot, was that Reebok like New Balance before them had gone cold on his concept. Brasher had great faith in his pet project and he now took steps to remove it from the Reebok stable.

'We can produce the best lightweight boot ourselves,' Brasher had said to Ken Ledward. It was obvious to Ledward that Brasher meant that they should form their own company to both manufacture and market the boot to their own specifications.

Brasher was aware of the marketing possibilities. He was aware, too, of the consumer, because he had tested the boot on himself and friends like Ledward. He reckoned that a lightweight boot, which would support your foot, be waterproof and not slip in the great outdoors, not give you blisters and was stylish enough to wear in a bar, was the Holy Grail for manufacturers.

Many were seeking it. Some were already more than halfway there. But Brasher was sure that it would be better to market the Brasher Boot himself.

In December 1992 he asked his old sparring partner Paddy Buckley to come out of retirement to set up the Brasher Boot Company at White Cross in Lancaster. Buckley and his wife Sally worked during the Christmas holiday to get the office ready for the first working day of January 1993, bringing in four of the staff who had worked for Brasher at Reebok. Buckley became office manager and Sally was made accounts manager.

In the years since he had been a fresh-faced reporter on *Tonight*, Brasher's image had evolved as his business and his reputation grew. Gone was the slim, tie-wearing reporter who faced the BBC cameras in the 1950s. Brasher was now characteristically seen sporting a polka-dot cravat, a waterproof jacket and a storm-proof cap, accompanied by a pipe, a grin and an ever-changing array of footwear. Other boots might hope to rival the Brasher Boot, but Brasher himself was determined to stamp his identity and image all over it. It was a triumph of marketing and bound up intimately with the Great Outdoor Man himself.

An early promotional card promoting the Brasher Boot carries a full colour picture of him clambering among the rocks, grass and heather. There on his waterproof jacket is the logo, proclaiming that the leggings, the blue cap and boots have all been produced by the Brasher Boot Company. On the logo is a facsimile of Brasher's signature. On the other side of the card is a statement of the Brasher Boot Company's — and Brasher's own — philosophy. 'Happiness,' quotes Brasher, 'is being able to enjoy the moors, hills and mountains of this Sceptred Isle while remaining warm, dry and comfortable.

'That was my objective when I set out to design gear that would keep me happy in the hills. It is gear designed for hill walkers – not those who want to put on a rope and climb steep rock or those who need crampons for steep ice.

'It is gear designed to keep you and me warm, dry and comfortable in all sorts of conditions that we experience in the mountains – even in a Scottish blizzard.' The card bears the identical signature that appeared on every pair of Brasher Boots.

The Brasher brand soared to success. It was quickly embraced by walking enthusiasts around the world with an especially fanatical following in Britain. The brand eventually produced all manner of hiking boots, walking shoes, trail running shoes and even comfortable walking sandals.

In February 1993 Brasher and Buckley went running and walking on the fells for five hours. At the end of the run they stopped at a café on the M6, where Brasher needed to use the phone. The good news was that Stephen Rubin, chairman of the former Pentland Industries, now renamed the Pentland Group, had agreed to buy 75 per cent of the Brasher Boot Company shares. Buckley stayed on as manager for a year until he reached the retirement age of sixty-five. With his own retirement Brasher, together with members of his family, sold their 25 per cent shareholding in the company to Pentland's parent company, Robert Steven Holdings, making the latter company the sole shareholder.

Shirley Brasher believes that any thought of real profit was far from Brasher's mind when he first started toying with the idea of the Brasher Boot: 'To my mind, at the start, he was absorbed by the prospect of proving that a comfortable, waterproof, light, walking boot could be manufactured and would sell. Financial gain was an outsider compared to all the interest of testing, proving such a boot could exist and succeed. Once designed and marketed, then the next challenge – or standard for success – had to be the profit and the sales figures.

'I believe CB's reasoning was that the Brasher Boots would walk across many miles of British countryside, and that a small percentage of each pair of Brasher Boots sold would go back to the environment.'

Brasher himself always said he had done it to get rid of blisters rather than to make a fortune. But by following the unlikely dream of the Brasher Boot, the boot that had his running club mates chuckling with derision in the Dysart Arms, Brasher had become a millionaire all over again.

15

The Dream of the Marathon

'The future belongs to those who believe in the beauty of their dreams.'

Eleanor Roosevelt

LIKE SO MANY of Chris Brasher's crazy ideas, the London Marathon was hatched in a pub. But unlike the dreams that vanish when the last pint has been downed, this one survived and grew into one of Britain's greatest sporting events. Here are Brasher's own words recounting the genesis of the London Marathon one Wednesday evening:

'It all started in a pub, the Dysart Arms hard by that great running territory known as Richmond Park – the home of Ranelagh Harriers which, at the time, was 98 years old. Men (no women were allowed to join until the club was 100 years old) drifted in from our Wednesday night run and talked, over their pints of bitter, of this marathon where the spectators never allowed you to falter – much less drop out.'

Brasher had taken much of the inspiration for running the marathon from Abebe Bikila, one of his greatest heroes. He had never forgotten the image of the man, bare feet whispering on the ancient cobbles of the Via Appia, taking Rome by storm in the 1960 Olympic marathon. He had dreamed of experiencing the marathon for himself. And now, in 1979, with stories of the

New York Marathon whirling in his head, he could live that dream.

One crazy runner who was always up for a new challenge was a man called Steve Rowland. A member of Ranelagh Harriers, in the 1970s Rowland was manager of the Sweat Shop, Brasher's tiny running store. Rowland had read an article about the 1977 New York Marathon, with its thousands of runners in crowd-lined streets through the heart of the city, and he wanted to go and see the race for himself.

Rowland had always been a bit of a wanderer. He had hitch-hiked to the Munich Olympics in 1972 with another Ranelagh man, Ivan Boggis, and spent the Olympic fortnight living in Brasher's VW camper van in the press village. Keen to get to New York to see for himself what this marathon had to offer, he talked to Brasher and the two of them decided that it would be a good idea for the Sweat Shop to organise a trip to the race.

Rowland advertised in the *Observer* and *Athletics Weekly* and some thirty or forty people joined the group – including around half a dozen from Ranelagh Harriers. Rowland does not remember Brasher being particularly interested in joining the trip himself that year, 1978, but Rowland travelled out with the group and they stayed in a low-budget YMCA hostel in what seemed a very dangerous and run-down part of New York.

The race, though, was a wonderful experience for them all. The runners, particularly the Ranelagh Harriers, couldn't wait to get back to tell people of their experience. Their enthusiasm for this iconic event was infectious. Brasher's ears caught the excitement and he reckoned it would make a good story for the *Observer*, and in 1979 he and Disley decided to go out and try the event for themselves in another party organised by Rowland and the Sweat Shop.

Brasher and Disley came back stiff and sore but bubbling with enthusiasm for this wonderful city spectacle. Disley had run round in under three hours and won himself a prize. Brasher ran accompanied by a photographer so that he could get some good shots for the race, because his trip had been paid for by the *Observer*.

In the *Observer* on 28 October 1979 Brasher wrote an excited and emotional account of his visit to New York:

> To believe this story you must believe that the human race can be one joyous family, working together, laughing together, achieving the impossible. I believe it because I saw it happen. Last Sunday in one of the most trouble-stricken cities of the world, 11,532 men, women and children from 40 countries of the world, assisted by one million black, white and yellow people, Protestants and Catholics, Jews and Muslims, Buddhists and Confucians, laughed, cheered and suffered during the greatest folk festival the world has seen.
>
> And at the end of it all the story was written in their faces — faces of contentment and happiness. I'm sure that it was written in my face because I was one of those thousands who won the New York Marathon. For more than 10,000 of us who finished, it was a great personal victory over doubt and fear, body and mind. And for most of us, we won only because one million New Yorkers came out of their homes and holes to feed and water us, to make music and brotherly love and to be Good Samaritans to all who felt like dropping by the wayside.
>
> I have heard the crowd shouting Sir Gordon Richards home in the Derby; the roar of the winning goal at Wembley; Olympic chants in four continents; but I have never heard such fervour as came from the crowd who cheer you as you approach the finish of the New York City Marathon. Nearly 2,000 years ago, Paul saw a vision on the road to Damascus. Last Sunday millions of us saw a vision of the human race, happy and united, willing their fellow human beings to a pointless but wonderful victory over mental doubt and bodily frailty.
>
> I wonder whether London could stage such a festival? We have the course, magnificent course, but do we have the heart and hospitality to welcome the world?

Shirley Brasher reckoned the piece was a bit too emotional and excited. Brasher read it aloud to her in the early hours of the night before publication. 'I don't remember taking the New York Marathon very seriously,' she said. 'However, when Chris announced on his return that he was writing an article on the London Marathon and I had to listen to it at some unearthly hour of the night, I knew it was serious.

'My initial feeling about the marathon article in the *Observer* was to pray for no reaction. I did not see how Chris could fit one more thing, either paid or unpaid, into his life. I was afraid he would finish himself with exhaustion, me with exasperation and our marriage with sheer pressure.'

In the days that followed, Chris's enthusiasm for the challenge knew no bounds. 'I can remember standing in the hall at home one evening,' said Shirley, 'as Chris rushed out of the front door leaving all of his supper after coming back hours late and saying to him: "If only you could have some sane and simple ideas for a change, this one is going to finish us all off, I know it is."'

But Brasher was eager to keep the momentum going. The Wednesday after the *Observer* column appeared, a small group were huddled together in a corner of the Dysart Arms as Brasher, full of preposterous pipe-dreams worthy of Mr Toad, attempted to support his fantasy with a few flimsy foundations. With Brasher were Disley, Rowland, John Hanscomb and Dave Wright. It was clear to the others in the group that Brasher was getting carried away, especially as the beer flowed and his mind started racing. The detail was daunting, particularly in relation to a possible route and the breaking down of bureaucratic officialdom.

Disley, who had worked so closely with Brasher when they organised the 1976 World Orienteering Championship in Aviemore, believed it could be done if they could make use of the experience they had picked up along the way with orienteering. 'We weren't exactly innocents to the slaughter,' he says. Those championships had thrown up loads of problems for

Brasher and Disley – everything from getting the Royal
Engineers in to build a bridge across the spectacular gorge of the
Findhorn river, capable of rising twelve feet after heavy rain, to
the conundrum of mobilising enough voluntary unpaid labour
to run the event smoothly.

They had picked up the tricks of promoting the orienteering
event as they went along, recovering quickly from their mistakes
and doing what they could to free themselves from the bureaucracy
that dragged so heavily on athletics at the time. 'We wanted nothing
to do with committees, governing bodies and officials,' said Disley.
'We wanted to get on with it and sweep aside any problems.
Orienteering was new, and we could get away with doing it our
way.'

Disley had been the overall director of the Aviemore event, with
Brasher in charge of the course, and over a pint in the Dysart they
decided that if their marathon was to go ahead they would swap
roles. Brasher would be the overall director and Disley would take
charge of the course arrangements.

Once the idea of a marathon took root, Brasher lobbied the
editor of the *Observer*, Donald Trelford, to organise a lunch to see
if they could get the concept moving. At this and subsequent
lunches Brasher and Disley were to meet many of the authorities
who would be involved in organising such an event. Among them
were the Greater London Council, the City of London Police, the
Metropolitan Police, the Royal Parks Police, the Amateur Athletics
Association and the London Tourist Board.

As the man in charge of the course, Disley reckoned that the
route would have to show off the historic parts of London, would
have to be reasonably fast with no big hills and shouldn't stop the
city of London in its tracks. New York's huge straight avenues
could easily accommodate masses of runners. But the city of
London was full of twisting, narrow streets. Brasher was adamant;
he wanted a race in the heart of London. He knew it could be done
and he was determined to steamroller through his vision.

The obvious way to move the project forward was to pick the brains of the New York organisers. So Brasher and Disley spent a lot of time talking to Fred Lebow and Allan Steinfeld, the kingpins of the New York race, and became heavily reliant on tapping in to their experience. Lebow even came across to London and ran with Brasher in Richmond Park just before one of the big decision-making meetings in June 1980 with Sir Horace Cutler, leader of the Greater London Council, and Squire Yarrow, chairman of the AAA.

The New York Marathon was the first of a new generation of big city marathons. The Boston Marathon had existed for the best part of a century, but the New York Marathon was designed to cater for the 1970s jogging boom. With American evangelists of the new fitness cult urging their converts to jog their way to health and happiness, this was a race that encapsulated a sporting revolution – it was open to runners of all shapes and ages, no matter what their sporting ability. In this, their proudest pilgrimage, legions of runners took to the streets for a 26-mile procession which was half race, half carnival.

Lebow's first New York Marathon attracted just 126 starters, only 55 of whom finished the four-lap course. But when, to coincide with the American bicentennial celebrations in 1976, the event changed its course through Central Park to take in all the New York boroughs, the race changed its character and took off.

Press and television turned its also-rans into celebrities and stars. Suddenly the New York Marathon was like being in a Broadway show – one with a 26.2 mile standing ovation. Lebow well under - stood the revolution that had changed his event from being a domestic low-key race for specialist runners into a carnival for all. It became trendy to run it. Celebrities flocked to be part of the story, getting their pictures and stories into newspapers and television, and sales of running kit and training shoes boomed as never before.

But by the end of the first lunch in the *Observer* offices it was perfectly obvious to both Disley and Brasher that the problem of stopping London in its tracks was going to be a sticking point as far as the police were concerned. Never a man to be daunted by a refusal, Brasher demanded to see the Commissioner of the Metropolitan Police. Previously the AAA had tried to persuade the police to shut the roads for a race, but had met with no success. Brasher simply went over the heads of what he called 'the Chief Inspector class'. He charmed the Commissioner and his team and they told Brasher and Disley that if the course was reasonable, and that not too many bridges had to be closed, they could shut down the necessary streets for around six hours.

At the second lunch organised by the *Observer*, however, Sir Horace Cutler, the chairman of the GLC, struck a sobering note. He told Brasher and Disley, 'You should never ask the rate payers to bail you out. Not a penny from the GLC.'

Brasher and Disley were privately very concerned by this warning. There was no money coming in, no sponsorship. They were relying on volunteers as they had done with orienteering and clinging obstinately on to their dream. Undaunted, they visited New York again. By this stage the concept of the London Marathon was becoming a reality and they took with them a number of key personnel from the GLC and the media to look at logistics. Brasher's penchant for publicity came to the fore on the flight. He fitted out all of the tour group, which numbered over one hundred, with gaudy red London Marathon sweatshirts and had publicity shots taken in the airport in New York in front of a British Airways plane. Brasher always recognised the need for good public relations and he saw the Sweat Shop group as ambassadors for the race. They hired a large suite in a New York hotel, plied the tour group with champagne and entertained anyone who wanted to come in and listen to Brasher's dream.

Brasher and Disley considered that the goodwill of the police was crucial to their success. They flew senior officers with them to New York to ensure that the police were 'on side'. Commander Barker and other senior officers were entertained royally by the

New York Police Department. They were driven around in fast cars at four in the morning. They were taken to picnics which, as far as Disley could see, were 'extended drinking bouts on beaches'.

For Brasher one prime objective was to reassure the London police that a large crowd was not necessarily hostile. For the police, in the late 1970s and early 1980s, a mass of people meeting meant trouble. Following the marches by striking miners organised by Arthur Scargill and his colleagues, the general police attitude was that any crowd that assembled had to be dispersed. When they went to New York they saw what a friendly atmosphere the Marathon engendered – everyone was having a great day and the police began to realise that this experience could be shared in London.

Brasher was now devoting all his energies to making the London Marathon a reality. He always went to great lengths to press into service every media contact he had. On one occasion he contrived to get free seats on Concorde and flew Sir Horace Cutler over to New York. During the flight he had arranged that they would run from one end of the plane to the other. Someone had calculated by the time they had done this the plane would have travelled twenty-six miles, the distance of the marathon on the ground. The whole trip was predicated around the stunt but it seems that Brasher and Cutler forgot to carry it out. They drank too much champagne and kept putting off the run. By the time they remembered that this was the purpose of their visit they were already strapped into their seats for landing.

One of the real problems for Brasher and Disley was that they still had no sponsorship. Disley remembers, 'Everything was financed by Chris and me apart from some of the accommodation, which was paid for by the *Observer*.' They badly needed a backer and an old friend, BBC sports commentator and agent Peter West of West-Nally, a public relations company, found one. Gillette, the razor manufacturers, had just ended a sponsorship deal with cricket and were looking out for other events to get involved with. They had heard about the running boom in New York and were shrewd enough to wonder if the London Marathon might catch on and be worth sponsoring.

'West told them that he had two young friends who were going to put on a London Marathon,' says Disley, 'and would they be interested in sponsoring that. In the end we got £50,000. The alternative would have been to mortgage our homes. We had no money until the entry fees started coming in.'

Another big issue was whether the London Marathon could achieve charitable status. The matter dated back to the luncheon in Kensington given to Brasher on his return from the Melbourne Olympics. Brasher felt strongly that any profits should be ploughed into improving sports facilities in London. The Marathon was not to be run like a business; it was to be answerable to no shareholders and it could not be taken over. This was an unusual route to adopt, but Brasher was determined to get the Marathon established as a charity and spent tens of thousands of pounds in legal fees in order to win charitable status.

Disley and Brasher enlisted volunteer help from athletes and orienteers to handle the entries that were flooding in. With computerisation in its infancy, most of the work was done manually. Effectively the whole event was created on the back of a cigarette packet; apt, perhaps, because Brasher, feeling the pressure, had returned to his habit of chain smoking.

The night before the race, Ranelagh member Dave Wright was mobilised to help to paint the blue line along the road. 'We met at a pub near the start in Greenwich and at closing time set off,' says Wright. 'My job was to jog slowly some 100 metres ahead of the guys laying the line down so I could show them the runners' best route. Jogging through Surrey Docks alone at 3 a.m. was not an experience to be repeated.'

Brasher and Disley busied themselves with every detail. To tow round the timing clock, they borrowed an idea given to them by the cobbler who made Brasher's shoes; they simply used a milk float, which did not emit fumes.

In the days leading up to the race, Brasher's publicity stunts hit new highs. In Britain, celebrities like the disc jockey Jimmy Savile and the gossip columnist Nigel Dempster were eagerly signing up. Appearing in his trademark gold lamé tracksuit – waving an outsize cigar and surrounded by a pack of minders – Savile raised £50,000. The following year his sponsorship was up to £200,000 and he went on to run well over 200 marathons or fun runs, raising millions for charity. He would trundle around the London course yelling, 'Come on, all you wonderful guys and gals, give us a cheer and give us your money. This London Marathon is a marvellous idea.'

MPs clamoured to get on the marathon bandwagon. Gary Waller, at the time the member for Brighouse and Spenborough, helped Brasher to launch the race. Brasher had come to speak to a party committee, of which Waller was secretary, about the forthcoming event. 'It was in the Strangers' Bar that the idea of my taking part was hatched,' says Waller. 'No one knew whether the Marathon would take off in London. When I was very hesitant, pointing out that I was not a regular runner, Chris was quick to explain that I need only complete two or three miles. I ran carrying a voucher from London Transport entitling me to travel back to the start.'

Matthew Parris (in 1981 the MP for Derbyshire West and subsequently a columnist with *The Times*) also ran in that first London Marathon and is fiercely proud of his 2:32:57 triumph as the fastest MP in 1985. The raft of MPs were joined by an unlikely superstar, pensioner Madge Sharples – 'Marathon Madge' – and she was followed by 'Supergran' Jenny Wood Allen, who completed subsequent London Marathons and hung up her racing shoes at the age of ninety-one.

Like the Pied Piper, Brasher and his team lured an ever-increasing cast of celebrities into his race. Out they came, the singers, the sportsmen, the princesses, the television stars; over the years Frank Bruno, Graham Gooch, Steve Redgrave, Clive Woodward, Seb Coe, Charlie Dimmock, Ronan Keating, Nell McAndrew, Gordon Ramsay all added their magic to the London Marathons.

Emerging from the chaos, the dream of the first London Marathon came true when just over 7000 runners (in those far-off days only 300 of them were women) set out to run from Greenwich on 29 March 1981. Brasher had been on the radio the night before pleading for Londoners to get out and feed drinks to the runners, but when the race day dawned conditions were wet and windy, though warm. Some 20,000 people had applied to run; 7747 were accepted. They were led home by the American Dick Beardsley and Norwegian Inge Simonsen. The two men staged a spectacular dead heat at the rain-swept finish on Constitution Hill, holding hands in 2:11:48. The race referee, Squire Yarrow, disapproved of this collusion, and threatened to disqualify both runners if it happened again. British Olympian Trevor Wright was more than a minute behind in third place. The elite athletes were joined by a small number of runners who have reached the finish line each and every year since the event began. These men are known as 'The Ever Presents'.

Joyce Smith, forty-three years old and the mother of two children, broke the British record in 2:29:57 to win the women's race, some nine minutes ahead of her nearest rival, Gillian Drake. Behind them came many thousands, delighting the crowds as the slow were cheered as enthusiastically as the fast. There were 6255 finishers; seven hours after the start Marie Dominque de Groot, thirty, from Paris and David Gaiman, forty-seven, from East Grinstead ran past the tape holding hands – they were the last to complete the course.

Gary Waller recalled of his Marathon: 'A day or two before the run, Chris sent me a new pair of running shoes, which I wore on the day. To my surprise I completed the race although I suffered afterwards from abrasions to my thighs as well as runner's nipple – a fate which I was able to avoid in later years with lashings of Vaseline.' Waller claimed that he did no training whatsoever. 'The only exercise I get is the occasional game of squash.' Many who had witnessed the race from the pavement or through television thought to themselves: 'If these people can do a marathon, so can I.'

The event was a huge hit with the runners, the thousands of spectators who lined the course, and viewers who followed the race on the BBC. A thousand volunteers marked the route, joined by 500 special constables, 26 first-aid stations and 300 St John Ambulance helpers, with a cardiac unit on standby at Constitution Hill. Out of the Gillette budget came 2000 foil blankets, 75 portable lavatories, 400 gallons of coffee and 50,000 plastic cups.

Despite the hassle Brasher was still planning to join in with everyone else. 'I got up for that first London in 1981 still determined to run the Marathon myself,' he said. 'I had wanted to savour the meal we had prepared just as a chef wants to sample what he has cooked. I wasn't aiming for any particular time but as I crossed the line in 2:56 there was a huge sense of relief. Afterwards I had a few drinks and dozens of people came up to me and said that the experience of taking part made it one of the great days of their life. What they said to me then made it one of the greatest days of my life too.'

Not everyone shared Brasher's enthusiasm. One athletics writer haughtily declined an invitation to cover the race on the grounds that 'I am employed to cover marathons, not circuses.' But when the carnival was over and the last weary stride had been completed, it was clear that the marathon was no longer the exclusive preserve of supermen and superwomen. It had become an event for ordinary, fallible, weary, footsore but sublimely determined people. Those who had taken part limped to their offices and factories the next day proudly displaying their blisters and medals. 'The success of the Marathon,' said Brasher, 'is that when it's all over all the painful stuff will be forgotten and the competitor will say, "Christ that was good."'

Indeed, most reviews were ecstatic, and Brasher and Disley wondered just what they had started. The sales of shoes, vests, tracksuits and running magazines all soared to unprecedented heights. Running was suddenly revealed as a healthy, sensible, socially acceptable, even chic pastime.

In 1981 Brasher and Disley had been surprised and delighted to receive so many requests for a place in their race, but in the following year the applications exceeded 90,000, of which 18,059 were successful. Gillette responded by doubling their sponsorship to £100,000, while the GLC allocated an office which was rather larger than the desk and two chairs they had initially made available to the organisers. The early Marathons finished on Westminster Bridge, with Parliament as the backdrop. As Gary Waller explains, 'When this later became impossible because of the impending redevelopment of County Hall, Chris Brasher enlisted my support at a meeting with the Permanent Secretary at the then Department of National Heritage to reach a new agreement. Chris was so committed to the Marathon by then that he found it difficult to believe that anyone could not immediately accede to what he regarded as his very reasonable requests.

'Despite his notoriously abrasive approach, including a threat to terminate the Marathon altogether if his proposals were not accepted, I was delighted that good sense prevailed and the current arrangements whereby the Marathon finishes in the Mall were agreed.'

The foot-racers were soon joined by wheelchair participants. Brasher had originally fiercely opposed the introduction of wheelchair athletes, decreeing: 'Wheelchairs will not be allowed in the London Marathon. Let's be quite clear about that, it would be far too dangerous. The first rule of the marathon is that it should be a foot-race – but it's really the danger to everyone, including those in the chairs, that worries me.'

By 1983, the Labour-controlled GLC, and particularly its deputy leader Illtyd Harrington, were having none of it, and threaten to withdraw their support and backing. There were three wheelchair accidents in 1983, but once the wheelchair race was started fifteen minutes ahead of the field the problems were soon resolved. And soon, Tanni Grey-Thompson, born with spina bifida, became as a big a London Marathon celebrity as any of them.

The race has also been completed by courageous entrants such as the brain-damaged boxer Michael Watson, who walked the twenty-six miles in 6 days, 2 hours, 27 minutes and 6 seconds. He was joined by forty-year-old Lloyd Scott, a leukaemia sufferer who, wearing a 120lb antique diving suit, struggled round the course in just over five days.

Scott was the most prominent of an ever-increasing army of participants who run in fancy dress to raise millions for charity. One study by researchers who measured the heart rate of a 24-year-old woman as she ran the London Marathon in a rhino costume revealed a peak heart rate of 191 beats per minute and an average of 181 beats per minute after completing the course in three hours twenty minutes. The unlikely world records that pantomime horses and fairies broke often appeared in the *Guinness Book of World Records*.

The first London Marathon had been arranged in a helter-skelter manner with virtually no offices, and most of the work was being done by Brasher and Disley from their desks at home and in manic phone calls. They had almost lost sight of the six rather grand-sounding aims that they had scribbled out after a drink in the *Observer* offices in 1980. These were:

> To improve the overall standard and status of British marathon running by providing a fast course and strong international competition.
>
> To show to mankind that, on occasions, the family of man can be united.
>
> To raise money for the provision of recreational facilities in London.
>
> To help London tourism.
>
> To prove that when it comes to organising major events, 'Britain is Best'.
>
> To have fun and provide some happiness and sense of achievement in a troubled world.

One of these aims, to improve the overall standard of British marathon running, was to cause Brasher much heartache. The statistics of the race bore out his feeling that the standard had been higher during those early days of the London Marathon. As a 52-year-old man running two hours fifty-six minutes Brasher was good, but not that unusual. No fewer than 144 runners had completed the course in less than two and a half hours, 1294 in less than three hours, and 4881 in under four hours. More than 80 per cent of the accepted entries had managed to complete the distance.

The year after her initial triumph, Joyce Smith set a new British record of 2:29:43, which put her third in the world rankings. She was joined in victory in 1982 by fellow Briton Hugh Jones, a member of the same running club as Brasher and Disley, the Ranelagh Harriers. Brasher had arranged a sponsorship deal for Jones with New Balance. In the hour before the race, according to Jones's coach Allan Storey, the runner agonised over whether to race in the colours of Ranelagh Harriers or New Balance. In the end he pulled on the New Balance vest, won the race in 2:09:24 and collected his $4000 for doing so.

There seemed not to be much wrong with the standard of British marathon running in these early years as Mike Gratton, a physical education teacher from Kent, won in 1983 in 2:09:43. By 1984, an Olympic year, Gateshead's Charlie Spedding won the Marathon and selection for the Games in 2:09:57. The following year again saw the British up front with an epic duel between Spedding and Steve Jones, which Jones won in 2:08:16.

It was a triumph for British marathon running, but in the years that followed British winners were to become an endangered species. In the women's race there had not been a British victory since Smith in 1982. Then in 1989 there was a win for 33-year-old Veronique Marot, a Leeds solicitor with a charming French accent and the enchanting habit, shared with Brasher, of lighting the odd cigarette to round off a tough race. In the men's race, Allister

Hutton from Edinburgh cruised to victory in 1990 in 2:10:10. Britain's last victory in the men's race came in 1993, when Basildon's Eamonn Martin triumphed in 2:10:50. So bad did things get that in 2003 one of the fastest Britons lining up in Greenwich on marathon morning was a woman. The great champion, Paula Radcliffe, shattered the women's world record by running 2:15:25, but it served to embarrass many of the British men.

The years that passed without a win in the men's event were a sad reminder to Brasher and Disley that while they may have created a great mass marathon, they had failed to achieve the goal of raising the standard of British marathon running. The year before his death, Brasher said that the failure of the top British men runners was his greatest disappointment. He accused them of being defeatist. 'They've got discouraged by the success of the Africans and think they can't compete. If you think you can't compete then forget it and do something else. To be a world or Olympic champion at marathon running you have really got to graft. You've got to be mentally and physically tough so that nothing can put you off.'

Brasher's enthusiasm, from that first article in the *Observer* to the starting cannon in just seventeen months, was very much his style. Impatient, impulsive, abrasive, he met all the problems head on. Peter Corrigan, one of his sports editors at the *Observer*, said, 'He takes some living with but what he has you want to have. You want him on your side.' Just as the executives in Fleet Street still wince at the memory of the ear-bashings they received over the telephone when anything went wrong, so many of the volunteers who helped stage that first marathon received equal ear-bashings.

When it came to people at the top, the decision makers, Brasher was not quite so cavalier. 'Our policy was never risk the answer "No",' he recalled. 'If you looked like getting a refusal you backed off. Manoeuvre your way to the top man and persuade him to say "Yes".'

In subsequent years Brasher was still incredibly hands-on. He was concerned with every detail of the race, and that included his own experience of running the Marathon. 'If you want to know the highs and lows then you've got to get in it and run yourself,' he said. 'That's how you'll discover something new about yourself, about who you are and how you perform when your body and soul are challenged. That's why I had to run it myself. It made me realise that ordinary people are really extraordinary.

'Apart from helping to bring up my family, the Marathon is the most satisfying thing I have ever been involved with. I remember when my daughter Kate ran to raise money for Great Ormond Street Children's Hospital. She had been working very hard with her job, around 110 hours a week, and I knew she hadn't trained properly. I was very worried about her. At the end of the race I went out on to Westminster Bridge looking for her but there wasn't a sign. I wandered down through Parliament Square towards Birdcage Walk and there were all these people staggering home in the last stages of total exhaustion.

'They had pain written all over their faces but they came storming across the road to shake my hand. "Thank you," they said. "Thanks for giving us the chance to do this." To tell the truth I was in floods of tears. Then at last I found Kate and she was fit and fine. You'd give a lot for a memory like that.'

Brasher was unwilling to relax his grip as the London Marathon grew to rival and then overtake the New York race. As its field grew to more than 30,000 and the budgets grew accordingly, Brasher would still be in the driving seat. One minute he'd be firing off an angry letter to the BBC because he didn't like their coverage, the next he would be ordering some bemused spectator to unblock a drain that had created a large puddle on the course. This was his creation and he was going to hang on to it.

Brasher's style was such that perhaps no other man could have fulfilled his unlikely dream of creating the London Marathon in such a short time. But in so doing he had made a few enemies. He had trodden on too many people's toes. He had brought people to tears of frustration once too often. Some of these critics were to step in and attack Brasher, Disley and the London Marathon in the years to come in a way that would challenge Brasher's whole identity and make him wonder what he had done with his life.

16

Happiness is a Walk in the Wilderness

*'A person is a success if he gets up in the morning and gets to bed
at night and in between does what he wants to do.'*

Bob Dylan

CHRIS BRASHER OFTEN made enemies as easily as he made
friends. His shortness of temper was legendary. Some
found his aggressiveness, his will to get his way endearing, amusing: 'That's just Chris,' they would say. Others found
his behaviour more than difficult. Ron Atkin became sports editor
of the *Observer* in 1972 after Brasher quit that position and moved
on to become a freelance writer. Atkin was later to comment in the
Independent, 'The best occasions for peace on the desk were
Brasher's periodic departures to some remote part of the
Highlands to do one of his "Breath of Air" columns, filed by
candlelight from a bothy or snowhole, too far away to cavil about
cuts in copy.'

Brasher's 'Breath of Air' columns, appearing in the paper on the
first Sunday of every month, were to become legendary. It is in
these pieces that he forged his view of the world, his love of the
open air and feats of daring and endurance. Brasher became an
evangelist for the wilderness, for that patch of wonderland he had
first come across at his prep school, Oakley Hall.

Why, Brasher was asked in the *Observer* in August 1977, do you call your column 'Breath of Air'?

Because, he said, the newspapers were full of stories about death and destruction, trouble and disorder. 'It is as if the visitor to Britain who did nothing but read the newspapers got a view of our country from Spaghetti Junction on the M6 – soulless and ugly. Whereas the truth is that Britain is peopled with incredible characters who are as diverse as the sea lochs of Scotland and the rolling downs of Sussex. These people are the soul and beauty of Britain and they vastly outnumber the rioters of Lewisham and Ladywood. Out there you get a breath of air through your mind as well as through your lungs.'

Brasher's vision of a perfect day on the fells was to work, walk, take in a pub and a bath. Here's a typically acerbic yet romantic piece he wrote in the *Observer* in February 1978. Its headline is 'Mad as the Mist and Snow':

Paddy Buckley had already telephoned me about the full moon on January 24th suggesting that it might be a good opportunity to indulge in an aesthetic experience – a skyline walk over the mountains of Snowdonia some twenty miles in moonlight in winter.

I had agreed and we drove northwest and came to the Inn that sits on the watershed and stopped for a pint and there by chance in a smoke room were eight of the finest, fittest mountain men that you will find in the land. They sat there, bellies full, and told us of how they had been lifted off the high ridge of the Carneddau in a screaming gale that very afternoon.

Paddy and I said we were going to enjoy an aesthetic experience on crisp snow on a calm night in the moonlight. They bought us a drink and wished us well and you could hear in their voices the memory of their day.

On we went into the clag over the boulder field on the summit of Drosgyl, setting our compass course for Bera Bach, white snow blending into white mist so that we could not tell what was up and what was down. Besides, the cloud had got between our faces and our spectacles doubling the misting – and mystification – which is probably why we missed the summit of Yr Aryg, which in turn put us in danger of crossing the spine of the Carneddau and sliding down to the other side.

So we stopped and thought and that is very difficult when the wind is needle sharp, whipping the map and coating the compass with ice. Paddy said we were on the spine, I said we had already crossed it, but I knew it was not much use arguing because Paddy is as stubborn as I am and has a far more developed instinct for the mountains.

Paddy said the refuge was forty yards away to the north under the lee of some rocks. We went north peering under every rock until I started to make asinine remarks like 'You don't know where you bloody well are Paddy.'

After twenty minutes we arrived back on the summit, got the map out and couldn't read it. I took off my glasses and all was clear. They were two lenses of ice and the torch was dimmed because the light could not penetrate an inch of ice on its glass. So we scraped the ice off the compass and set off east . . . We retraced our steps, thinking as we ticked the summits off that this night was a good illustration of the dangers of high mountain refuges. Didn't six children die in the Cairngorms while trying to find the Curran bothy at 3,700 feet and hadn't four boys started off one of the biggest searches ever undertaken in Wales when they were heading on a Duke of Edinburgh's Award expedition for that very same refuge on Foel Grach?

Three hours later we emerged below the crag and saw the stars and the moon above Bethesda.

Brasher reports on another trek in 1978 – again with Buckley – inspired by the legendary Welsh journalist and broadcaster Wynford Vaughan-Thomas, author of numerous books on Wales and the Welsh countryside; he sets out this time, not in snow but in May.

I thought we would try a more gentle perambulation when the days were long and the weather kind. I remembered a series of radio talks given many years ago by Wynford Vaughan-Thomas, that great raconteur, who had walked across the Roof of Wales route. What a lovely way, I thought, to spend nine days in May.

And so it was that close on midnight on Sunday we found ourselves looking at the sea off Margam Beach, the moon reflecting off the top of the waves. A few yards away we found some close cropped turf and pitched our tent amidst the small white flowers of the wild strawberry plant.

As we cooked a delicious meal of *langue de boeuf, sauce madere*, the moon illuminated a towering man made mushroom cloud red flecked at the bottom as it belched out of Margam steelworks and I thought that before we pitched our tent again, British Steel would have lost another million pounds or so of our money.

That first contrast turned out to be typical. When you walk, snail like, through the land with all you need to sustain life on your back you are regarded as slightly mad – 'touched' would be a better word – and yet it is you who observes the madness of the world. And can there be any greater madness than to produce goods of which there is already a surfeit and lose hundreds of millions of pounds doing so and produce something which ruins a man's health? But my thoughts are already ahead of my feet . . .

Wynford Vaughan-Thomas, the man who put the idea into my head, would be taking a holiday soon. Now past his 70th year he is shortly to repeat his walk of twenty years ago and he would be talking about it on the radio. I shall be listening because I know that he can tell us of the changes that are transforming the wilder parts of Britain, changes that are happening faster now than at any time since the ice retreated.

In June that year, at the age of seventy, Vaughan-Thomas set out to repeat the solo walk that he'd first undertaken at the age of fifty. Brasher and Buckley listened to his mellifluous voice on the car radio at a pub in mid-Wales. Vaughan-Thomas had had a hard day, getting lost and wondering whether he had taken on too big a challenge. Brasher decided he needed help. Having changed course to track him down at a nearby village, they found him soaking in a hot bath.

Buckley was volunteered by Brasher to guide Vaughan-Thomas the next day. When they reached Bwlch y Groes, the highest pass in Wales, Vaughan-Thomas made his daily broadcast to BBC Radio Wales. Buckley was encouraged to sing on air in Welsh, while Brasher, said Vaughan-Thomas to the listeners, was quite simply 'a life enhancer', enriching every walk and every experience.

In that same year, 1978, Brasher caught up with a long-distance walker he much admired, and whose story would echo some of Brasher's preoccupations. 'John Merrill has gone for a walk lasting nine months,' wrote Brasher in his column in March, describing the expedition which was also incidentally to provide him with the chance to test some of the forerunners of the Brasher Boot. 'So when I heard news of the blizzard that had devastated the West Country two weeks ago I thought of him, a man alone, facing the worst blizzard in memory. By various devious means I made a rendezvous to meet him the next evening. He planned to walk 25 miles along the Devon coast, I to drive 200 miles from London to pitch tent with him beside the River Heddon.'

Buckley recalls that Brasher was late for the rendezvous. 'The road was blocked by snowdrifts on Countisbury Hill. We retreated to the Culbone Stables, a pub on the northern edge of Exmoor. It was bright and welcoming, its customers Exmoor farmers in wellington boots and outdoor clothing. We booked a room for the night and ordered a meal. Chris was now in his element; a pub and good company. We were late to bed. Next morning we caught up with Merrill at the Valley of the Rocks and over the next two days we took it in turns to walk with the pilgrim.'

Merrill was obsessed with walking and Brasher found his lifestyle seductive:

> As Merrill loosened and our strides built a rhythm, I realised that he was a man who had turned the activity he most enjoyed into a profession, and I remembered someone telling me in my youth that the secret of a happy life is to make sure that your work – the way by which you earned your livelihood – was also the activity that held your compelling interest.
>
> Originally Merrill wanted to be a mountain guide and at school in Yorkshire he kept meticulous records of all the mountain ranges of the world. But there were family expectations and a living to earn so he went into the family business – a chemical works and a chemical pump factory in Sheffield learning accountancy. After six years of hard work and no pay, he negotiated with his father to take three months off and he spent them walking in the Hebrides. The day he returned he walked into his father's office and said he wanted to leave because he had discovered what he really wanted to do with the rest of his life.
>
> It took him a few years more to get free but now at the age of 34 he has worked out his new way of life, based in a cottage in Derbyshire which he converted and restored. In winter he writes and lectures building up finance for his plans, plans not made for the coming spring but for years ahead.
>
> As I watched him I too began to wonder whether it was he who was so strange and unusual or was it instead the way that most of us live, herded into rush hours trying to beat the rate for the job or wangle some material advantage over our fellow men. I did know that I had never met a man so at peace with himself.

But, above all, Brasher used many of his *Observer* pieces to write about a challenge that both inspired and defeated him – the Bob Graham Round. This was a legendary 24-hour run over peaks in the Lake District.

The man who devised it, Bob Graham, set off from Keswick at 1 a.m. on a June night in 1932 to see how many mountains he could climb in twenty-four hours. That day Graham scaled forty-two peaks, including all the highest fells like Skiddaw, Helvellyn, Scafell and Great Gable – a distance then claimed to be seventy-five miles and including 30,000 feet of climbing. It was reckoned to be the equivalent of climbing Everest two and a half times from base camp to summit.

For twenty-eight years it proved impossible for anyone else to repeat the Bob Graham Round inside twenty-four hours. Then in 1960 two members of Clayton-le-Moors Harriers succeeded. They were Alan Heaton, a stocky 32-year-old, and Stan Bradshaw, a 48-year-old tripe butcher from Padiham.

Most of their successors were content to run the traditional forty-two peaks, but a few set out to increase the number of tops that could be traversed in under twenty-four hours. Leading this elite group was Joss Naylor, a sheep farmer from Wasdale, a hero to rank for Brasher alongside Abebe Bikila and Wilson of *The Wizard*. Of Naylor, Brasher wrote, 'I saw Joss come down off the Langdale Fells in a rainstorm at three in the morning. He had already been running for 17 hours . . . it is still a memory equal to any of the greatest Olympic races that I have ever seen.' In 1975 Naylor set the record at seventy-two peaks.

Many were to try this challenge, but as Brasher found, it was only for the tough. In the *Observer* on 5 June 1977 Brasher wrote about an attempt on the Bob Graham Round made by his friend, equipment tester Ken Ledward. An accomplished climber, fell runner and skier, Ledward was no mean performer in caving and canoeing and had been an Outward Bound instructor both in Britain and East Africa. Brasher decided to accompany Ledward on part of the route:

So there I was last Sunday night ensconced in a warm sleeping bag, with the alarm set at 5.20 waiting for Ken Ledward, an unlikely applicant for this exclusive club. He is the very antithesis of the lean, lanky, strong sinewed image of a great fell runner. Indeed, his legs are so short that they disappear in deep heather. But after a breakfast of bacon butties, hot sweet tea and some tinned pears, we were off up Steel Fell into the early morning sunlight.

Now I knew why I had driven 250 miles through the night and slept under the stars. Here we were, three friends on the fells. The sun warming our backs as it burned away the mist of the night, chattering about the distant views and the solitude, thinking of the tourists down in the valleys below, sleepily starting towards breakfast, and we up high moving freely over the most beautiful land on earth.

'Soon,' Brasher continued, 'I had had enough.' He had managed to keep up with Ledward for nearly six hours and fifteen peaks, including the highest in England. But Ledward kept going. 'Later,' wrote Brasher, 'the regulars at his local pub in the Duddon Valley welcomed Ken home with cheers and the landlord broke open a bottle of champagne and a mighty tired 43-year-old settled himself into the corner of the bar with a cigar in one hand and a champagne glass in the other.'

The concept of the Bob Graham Round excited Brasher. You couldn't buy your way into the exclusive club that had climbed these peaks. You couldn't just join. You could become a member only by accepting the challenge of the forty-two peaks. A few weeks later, on Sunday 21 August 1977, Brasher wrote about his first abortive attempt to complete the Bob Graham Round himself:

Ten days ago three of us decided to join this select band. Paddy Buckley, 48, redundant but now working in the bowels of a concrete yacht, George Rhodes, 49, a garage proprietor from Biddulph, Staffordshire and myself 49 today. None of us was really fit enough. Paddy says 12 hours' work inside a concrete yacht doesn't leave him with any energy to train. George had returned from fishing in Ireland in June with such a painful skin complaint on his backside that he had to kneel at the table to eat and I had fallen down the south side of the North Downs while training one Sunday.

We took it easy, George and I, coming down Scafell because it is downhill sections that stiffen the thighs and buckle the knees. At Wasdale I lay on a camp bed and luxuriated in the ministrations of a small army of helpers. Stan Bradshaw's beautiful wife, Ida, made me soup.

A police sergeant and one of his cadets removed my shoes and massaged my legs, helped by a small girl who said: 'You will do it now won't you.'

Yewbarrow, they say, breaks men's hearts. It is a beautiful mountain, a long ridge springing up from Joss Naylor's farm. At the south side it is ugly and savage, huge boulders, heather and high bracken. Just before I joined battle with it I was sick. Three times my stomach came all the way out to the path and I had nothing left inside me and no strength in my legs.

'Finally,' wrote Brasher, 'I've had it. I'm going to Joss's farm to get a glass of milk from Mary. So ended my first attempt on the Bob Graham Round.'

The next day Brasher went to see fell runner Jean Dawes, the first lady to complete the Round, to get some tips on how to tackle the forty-two peaks. 'Once you start,' said Jean to Brasher, 'you are hooked and you've just got to keep going.' She looked at Brasher and said, 'You'll do it next time.'

Brasher concludes this piece by asking himself, why attempt the forty-two peaks? 'There are really many reasons,' he writes, 'from the pleasure of being on the tops at sunrise and sunset, the satisfaction of being fitter than most, the joy of running, the company of friends for a whole day in the mountains and perhaps the perverse pleasure of stepping out of line occasionally and extending one's own range of achievement.'

Brasher would have dearly loved to have completed the Bob Graham Round himself. But despite having the very best pace-makers and encouragement, each time he gave up. The challenge eluded him three times, but he believed that no challenge could defeat his greatest hero, Joss Naylor.

17

Death by Television

'Chris Brasher has done more for the corporate spirit of London than anyone since Adolf Hitler.'

Sir Christopher Chataway

O N 21 JANUARY 1981, just two months before the first London Marathon, a report appeared in the *Daily Express* by Tony Barnes, himself an experienced marathon runner. It read:

> Angry athletes are accusing Chris Brasher, organiser of the Gillette London Marathon, of sharp practice and there is widespread criticism from club runners all over the country. They and leading sports companies allege that Brasher has taken unfair advantage of his position to promote the brand of running shoes he imports. It is also said that the limited number of British entries allowed in the field of 7,500 for the race on March 29th is being unfairly calculated.
>
> Brasher is the Athletics Correspondent with the *Observer*, owns a retail sports shop and is chairman of a company that imports and distributes New Balance running shoes.

Everyone who applied for an entry form for the London Marathon had received a leaflet recommending only New Balance as 'The shoes for the Marathon'. Mike Tagg, a former international runner and managing director of Reliance Sportswear, told the *Express* that he was angry. 'I would love to have been given the chance to send a leaflet about our Nike running shoes to London Marathon competitors but we were not told about it.' A spokesman for Reebok said: 'As a London company and the only major British manufacturer of running shoes we are disappointed that the official supplier of footwear at the London Marathon is an American company whose distributing company in the UK has a director who is a member of the race organising committee.' And Adidas spokesman Graham Smith added, 'It seems strange practice to me to exploit something like the London Marathon in this way for commercial gain.'

Brasher protested and put his case to the *Express*: 'I took my hat off and did not participate in the decision. Two AAA officials, Ray Stroud and Andy Norman, made the decision and came down in favour of Fleetfoot.'

On the one hand Brasher presented the image of an eccentric old buffer. Pictured in his crumpled anorak and polka-dot cravat, he appeared something of a folk hero to the public. But on the other hand his personal style often left people thinking that the Brasher feet had ridden over them roughshod. He was notorious for reducing staff to tears with his verbal hectoring and there were legendary tales about employees he had forced out of the London Marathon.

In April 1984 Tony Ward, a former media spokesman for British Athletics, a coach and the author of many running books, interviewed Chris Brasher at the Dysart Arms in Petersham. Brasher had arrived for the interview an hour and a quarter late and entered the bar, Ward said, 'The usual picture of cultivated inelegance – wild Wast Water rather than sophisticated Surrey.' Brasher had apparently been held up by wheelchairs – not some sort of convoy in Richmond Park, but a meeting on the subject at County Hall.

After a few beers, Ward moved the conversation around to the criticism that had been meted out to Brasher over the London Marathon. There were the inevitable gripes about non-acceptance of entries: 'Each year,' said Ward, 'a plethora of letters appears in *Running* and *Athletics Weekly* from those that have not been accepted for the marathon about the convoluted methods of entry, created in the belief that if a thing is worth obtaining it was worth working for.' Or, as Ward put it, 'In this case worth queuing for.'

'The point had come home most pertinently,' wrote Ward, 'when Brasher walked into a pub in Ambleside and some locals had said, "Well Chris, what do we have to do this year, leap twelve feet or swim the English Channel?"' Ward believed that Brasher over-reacted to such criticisms. It was impossible, he said, to please all the people all the time and to answer those petty gripes was to give them a gloss of importance they did not deserve.

However, continued Ward, in an echo of the criticisms detailed by Tony Barnes before the inaugural event, a much more serious criticism had now emerged concerning 'a conflict of personal interest':

> In 1983, there had been a storm over the race being used to exploit Brasher and Disley's commercial interests. Towards the end of the 1970s they had formed a company, Fleetfoot, to distribute New Balance shoes in Britain and Brasher's name in particular became synonymous with the brand. In the envelope that went out to all race applicants were two leaflets. One gave details of entry, the other advertised New Balance shoes.

Both leaflets were signed by Brasher and Disley. 'Many, many runners,' observed Ward, 'had been deeply offended. It was a disaster in public relations terms, and tarnished them with a grasping commercial image.'

John Disley has admitted since that with hindsight they should not have signed the commercial leaflet. Brasher agreed but told Ward: 'It doesn't occur to me that anyone else had lower standards.'

Among Brasher's critics was Duncan Campbell, an investigative journalist and a marathon runner himself. Campbell had taken up running in 1976 at the age of twenty-four, caught up in the jogging boom that swept Britain and the United States in the 1970s. His first attempt at a race was a fun run held in October 1980 on Hampstead Heath. Campbell trained regularly in London with a runner who was an avid reader of *Athletics Weekly*, and who kept him up to date on the news, gossip and controversy that surrounded Brasher and Disley's initiative of a big mass marathon in the capital. In 1982 Campbell became a co-opted member of the Greater London Council, where he served on the Public Safety and Fire Brigade Committee in his capacity as an expert in civil defence.

Prompted by the reports he read and criticism that he had heard about, Campbell began to ask questions about the London Marathon. In April 1982, he rang Ray Stroud, a fellow councillor on the GLC, to ask how much Brasher was paid for his work at the Marathon. The upshot was that Brasher rang the *New Statesman*, where Campbell worked, three times, and allegedly threatened to sue.

The following month, on 12 May, Campbell wrote a memo to Ken Livingstone, leader of the GLC, asking 'What happens to the Marathon money?' Again Brasher was back in touch and threatening to sue. Campbell's regular training partner wrote to Brasher asking what Brasher got out of the London Marathon. Brasher took the letter seriously enough to reply:

I am sure you will appreciate we do get thoroughly fed up with carping criticism . . . you want to know what I get personally out of the London Marathon? Other than a lot of trial and tribulations from a small minority, I and my colleagues get a lot of satisfaction from the enjoyment of the vast majority.

As far as finances are concerned, we organised the 1981 event
without paying anybody anything except their bare, out-of-pocket
expenses.

Campbell himself ran in the London Marathons of 1982 and 1983
and says he had his first direct contact with Brasher by phone on 20
April 1983, asking him about the financial allegations that had been
made. Two days later, on 22 April, the *New Statesman* published an
investigation, headlined 'Money-makers', alleging that there was a
conflict between Brasher's business interests and the interests of the
Marathon itself. Brasher and Disley made it clear that they believed
that these allegations were totally untrue. 'However, although the
article is defamatory,' said Brasher, 'the London Marathon
organisation, John Disley and I were at that point so short of funds
that we were not able to sue.'

Ward said that on re-reading the article he had been struck by
the fact that Brasher had been his own worst enemy, going on the
defensive against those who had attacked him for using voluntary
helpers to make the Marathon a possibility while he, Disley and
others had been paid. 'The vast majority of those who entered for
the race would be totally surprised if either Brasher or Disley did
not receive proper recompense for the 1½–2 days per week per year
that they worked for the London Marathon.' Ward observed:

> Brasher's personality induces a love-hate relationship with many
> people that he comes into contact with. Campbell called him
> abrasive but this is too simple and too crude a term. Disley, who
> works closest with him both at the Marathon and Fleetfoot,
> admitted that some days are better than others and another worker
> said that Brasher could be read like the seasons of the year in
> relation to the race.
>
> 'In the morning he'll be bawling you out for some alleged
> mistake or something he feels is not quite right, and by lunchtime
> he'll be buying you a pint in a nearby pub.'

'Quite right,' said Brasher, when this point was put to him. 'Life is too short to harbour a grudge.'

'Brasher clearly does not suffer fools gladly,' said Ward. 'And he does not like being crossed, which many people can vouch for. One of the problems lies in sequential thought.'

'Chris will often jump from point A to point C and F,' said John Disley, 'while the rest of us are still cogitating point B — and he'll get a bit impatient with that.'

In the years that followed these criticisms increased and by June 1990 Brasher was called before a special meeting of the Marathon's Board of Governors to explain why he wanted to sack his closest assistant, David Griffiths. The board was not satisfied with the reasons Brasher gave for his letter of dismissal to Griffiths, who had been the assistant race director for only a year. Griffiths, a friend of Brasher's from when they competed on the British orienteering team, and formerly chief executive of Wembley Stadium, was the latest in a series of officials to quarrel with Brasher over what they considered Brasher's autocratic style of management.

Griffiths appealed to the governors to overturn the dismissal and was invited to answer Brasher's charges. He was the fourth senior member of staff to leave suddenly in the past year and Brasher's autocratic style appeared to be of increasing concern to some of the governors. People who had chosen to leave included Griffiths' predecessor David Bedford, who had resigned after recruiting the best field in the race's history in 1989. Bedford, who had worked for the London Marathon since 1985, was himself a headstrong and combative personality who shared much of Brasher's self-belief; a major clash had therefore seemed almost inevitable. (Having left in 1989, he rejoined two years later and subsequently rose to the position of race director.)

With the dispute over Griffiths brewing, Duncan Campbell's name cropped up again. On 5 July 1990, at a Marathon general purposes meeting, several of those attending mentioned that

Campbell had spoken to them on the telephone. He had said he was writing another article for the *New Statesman* and was investigating improper behaviour and practices at the London Marathon.

Brasher said that this action prompted him and the Marathon to contact the *New Statesman* and offer to meet Campbell the following day to answer any of his questions. Campbell, according to Brasher, was not able to make this meeting but made a second arrangement to meet Brasher at Euston Station. Brasher explained that he had just ten minutes to catch a train and alleged that Campbell's attitude on that occasion was both 'aggressive and accusatory'.

'That weekend Campbell met with Peter Nicholls, who had worked for the Marathon first as a press officer and then as International Race Director,' said Brasher in a statement later. 'There appeared to be no way at such short notice that the Marathon could look up the sort of information which Campbell was demanding.' The treasurer of the Marathon had gone abroad and Brasher himself was about to go on holiday on the Thames.

The *Statesman* article was published on 13 July 1990. Headed 'Going for Gold', it made serious allegations about the conduct of both Brasher and Disley. It began:

> On Monday the governors of London Marathon Limited, a registered charity founded by the GLC in 1980 to provide recreation and sports facilities in London, meet to give their verdict on the leadership struggle at the top of the race organisation. The growing row has helped bring to light allegations of deliberate concealment of profits, improper financial payments, lavish hand-outs to athletes and their agents and reticence about 'honoraria' paid to officials like the ex-Olympic runner, Chris Brasher, now 62, founder and Race Director of the Marathon.
>
> For British athletics the battle is of great significance, especially since next year the 1991 London Marathon will incorporate the

World Marathon Cup. The row is the culmination of a ten year long history of dissatisfaction with Brasher's stewardship.

Pointing out that Brasher's business and sporting interests had made both him and his partner John Disley extremely wealthy, Campbell went on to lay out the purpose of the Marathon governors' meeting – to review Brasher's decision the previous May to sack David Griffiths, the assistant race director. He explained:

> Griffiths is the latest in a series of officials to choose to leave or be told to go. In the last year alone Brasher has parted company with Griffiths's predecessor, former athletics star David Bedford, and three other officials. The former press officer Mike Butcher who left in January after a row with Brasher says that he is a truculent and abrasive man. Brasher and Disley, a yes-man says Butcher, sacked Griffiths after only seven months on the grounds that the relationship between 'yourself and the London Marathon team is not working.' Griffiths, in an unparalleled challenge to Brasher's dominance of the Marathon, has exercised the right of appeal to the governors.

The allegations were long and detailed. Chief among them, the *New Statesman* reported, was that

> Athletics correspondents have long noted how hard it is for Brasher and Disley to keep their marathon activities and business interests at arm's length from each other. Most years from 1981 to '91 the kind of shoes promoted by the London Marathon to journalists, and to its unique mailing list of hundreds of thousands of eager applicants, has been the brand of shoes sold by Brasher and Disley's own company, Fleetfoot.

As a result of the turnover of Fleetfoot, said the *Statesman* article, Brasher and Disley had become 'millionaires many times over'.

'The fundamental issue before the governors next Monday is not simply Griffiths's dismissal nor any allegation or counter-allegation of mismanagement, incompetence or impropriety,' the article continued, it was the question 'whether after ten years of buccaneering management the London Marathon can now convince the public that it is being run in the interests of sport in London and not largely for the benefit of a growing band of wealthy athletics business people.'

Campbell's article had, according to Brasher, been passed to the *Daily Mirror*. He also believed that ITV had been approached with the material that Campbell was preparing, although ITV decided not to pursue the matter after Brasher had spoken to their researcher. Eventually Campbell did have an article published in the 22 July 1990 issue of the *Independent on Sunday*, co-authored with Neil Wilson, for many years the athletics correspondent of the *Daily Mail*. They reiterated many of the points raised in the *New Statesman* and followed this up with speculation about Brasher's future control of the Marathon.

'Will Mr Brasher really relinquish all responsibility for the race he has managed since its inception?' said the article. Its authors speculated about the possible candidates to succeed Brasher:

> The first is Mr Griffiths, 49. For four years he was a Chief Executive of Wembley Stadium before moving to a similar post in Hong Kong. He plans to take his blueprint for the London Marathon of the 1990s back to the Governors in December. He hopes to make the race's finances more flexible by introducing more modern marketing techniques by widening the organisation's sponsor and manage other races.
>
> A second candidate is Mr Bedford; much of the British athletics world regards him as a natural successor for Mr Brasher. Peter Nicholls, the *Observer*'s Athletics Correspondent, is a third aspirant.

The outcome of the stormy and long-anticipated meeting was that the governors of the Marathon backed the decision to terminate Griffiths' contract. They refused to reinstate him as an assistant director and Brasher's heir apparent.

Brasher and Disley said they took the view that this article was defamatory but that the libels already published in the *New Statesman* article were more serious. After consulting with the London Marathon's solicitors, Max Bitel Greene Emanuel, it was decided to bring a libel action against both the Statesman and the Nation Publishing Company Limited, the publishers of the *New Statesman*, and Duncan Campbell. They may have been short of funds in April 1983 but, with Fleetfoot's turnover having grown from £1.7 million in 1983 to £34.5 million in 1988, Brasher and Disley were indeed now very wealthy men.

But for Brasher and Disley there was worse to come. On 4 December 1990 the London Marathon received a call from the manager at the Strand Palace Hotel, who said that a man called John Mair had telephoned to ask permission for a film unit from Channel 4 to film inside the hotel where the Council of Management of the London Marathon was due to hold its annual December meeting.

Brasher telephoned Mair and learned that he was working for the production company IPTV Limited, which was making a programme about the Marathon for Channel 4. Brasher subsequently found that the research address for IPTV Limited was also the editorial address of the *New Statesman*.

During the week beginning 14 January 1991, Mair and a film crew went to the Lake District to take some footage of fell runners. The filming had been arranged with Elaine Wright, the wife of the secretary of the Fell Runners Association, Seldon Wright. In a sworn affidavit produced during the libel hearing about Mair's programme, Elaine Wright said that she knew Brasher well through his membership of the Ambleside Athletic Club, of which she was president. John Mair, she continued, told her that he wanted to film some runners on the fell to show Brasher's association with the Lake District. He gave no indication at that stage that the programme had any particular slant. One or two volunteers, Keith Anderson and Roger Bowl, had arranged to meet the film crew, including Mair, at 9 a.m. on Tuesday 15 January at Ambleside Rugby Club.

'I was surprised when a little later he said it was to do with the financial side of the London Marathon,' said Wright in her affidavit. 'I asked him what he meant by it. He said it (the programme) is to show that Chris Brasher has made money out of the London Marathon. Those were his exact words. I was not very happy with this idea as John Mair had never given any indication that the programme was to have this slant. I told John Mair I was not sure whether I wanted to go ahead and make the programme. At one stage John Mair said: "Chris Brasher has made £3.5 million out of The London Marathon."

'We continued the filming and although we were all enjoying it as it was a beautiful morning and the film crew were saying they were getting some great pictures. I clearly recall John Mair saying to me that "The programme will break Chris Brasher and that will be the end of Chris Brasher. Chris Brasher will be no more."'

There were certainly problems with the way Brasher characteristically operated. Keith Dovkants, a well-respected and long-serving reporter on the *Evening Standard*, noted in his curtain raiser to the programme, published in his newspaper on 19 March 1991 and headlined 'Money and the Marathon Man', that 'today the demon that drove Brasher to victory in the Melbourne Olympics is driving him harder than ever . . .' He pointed out that in Melbourne Brasher had been disqualified for allegedly jostling a fellow competitor but then reinstated on appeal. Although, he said, the disqualification had been unjust, people still muttered complainingly about Brasher's 'jostling style'. The piece continued:

Tomorrow, Channel 4's *Dispatches* series takes an investigative scalpel to Brasher and his partner and friend John Disley. Business dealings and controversial management methods are laid bare. Claims are made that the Marathon's unique appeal has helped bolster sales of the sports footwear company in which they have an interest.

What emerges is truly disturbing. For an investigation into Chris Brasher is a conflict between the perception of him as a hero of his time and some people's view of him as a tyrant, carefully protecting his marathon power. That is how his critics see him. They say that his insistence on dominating every facet of the Marathon with an imperious, irascible style is now sapping the organisation's strength.

The Marathon's governors, continued Dovkants, had been concerned for some time with the high numbers of resignations and sackings that had punctuated the race's history. Attention had also been focused on the Marathon's role as a charity and Brasher's charitable intentions. Dovkants then returned to the theme of Brasher's personal style:

A former marathon official told me how he left the organisation: 'Part of Chris's technique for getting rid of people is to treat them totally as non-persons. Chris would walk into the office and ignore me as if I simply were not there. Then he would make a point of picking up the phone and start giving instructions to someone or another about something that was my responsibility. As far as he was concerned I had ceased to exist, I had no alternative but to leave.'

When former athlete Dave Bedford quit he told a friend, 'I just couldn't take any more members of staff sobbing on my shoulder after Chris had finished with them.'

Citing the response of David Griffiths to being sacked, Dovkants continued: 'He lays down a challenge to Brasher's leadership and the Griffiths affair may yet become the hurdle Brasher could not clear.'

One athletics insider confided to Dovkants that 'Chris wants a knighthood, he won't let go of the marathon until he gets one.' (This was despite Brasher's apparent refusal of an honour – saying: 'That bloody woman did nothing for sport' – after Margaret Thatcher called for a boycott of the Moscow Olympics in 1980.)

'Two things,' added Dovkants, 'must be said in conclusion. Only a man with Brasher's awesome will and domineering character could have made the Marathon the global success it is today and secondly such men often make bitter enemies.'

Lawyers tried to stop the Channel 4 documentary from going out. Brasher and Disley decided on legal advice that if an undertaking not to broadcast the programme was not received by 1 February, an application should be made for an injunction.

There was a delay in showing the programme before 27 February, but on the assurance of Campbell, Mair and Channel 4 that nothing would be broadcast which they could not prove to be true, Mr Justice Moreland decided to give it the go-ahead. The documentary was given a press preview on 18 March 1991 and broadcast to the general public on 20 March.

On the following Sunday, 24 March, Nick Pitt wrote in the *Sunday Times*:

> The London Marathon, the race, the phenomenon, the charity is in crisis. One governor is resigning, another, Peter Yarranton, the chairman of the Sports Council no less, is threatening to do the same unless he receives the necessary answers . . .
>
> Brasher and Disley attempted and failed to get a High Court injunction preventing the screening of the programme and the accusations against Brasher and Disley that are related to the London Marathon could be summarised as follows:
>
> One, that Disley and Brasher used their position in the London

Marathon to promote their business distributing running shoes; two, that moneys which should have been paid directly to charity were retained by the London Marathon Company; three, that consultancy payments were made by London Marathon to a company controlled by the wives of Brasher and Disley.

Brasher, for his part, was said to have explained: 'John and I have been paid a nominal sum each year for our services to the Marathon . . . The way in which these moneys were paid to us was the subject of detailed professional advice.' Pitt concluded his article:

> Brasher and Disley have done a great deal for the running boom in Britain and the running boom has done a great deal for Brasher and Disley. The London Marathon was a brilliant idea, realised with remarkable persistence and energy. The credit for that belongs to Brasher and Disley. If it had been set up primarily as a business no one would have begrudged them a good share of the proceeds as well. But it was established not as a commercial vehicle but as a charity and as such a different set of standards apply.
>
> Conflicts of interest are unacceptable. Unexplained payments, unless in full accounting, are not good enough. Brasher and Disley have made a triumph of the London Marathon but they still have much to explain.

Following the programme's broadcast, Brasher and Disley issued proceedings for libel in respect of both the press releases and the programme itself.

18

Meet Wilson of The Wizard

'These high wild hills and rough uneven ways
Draws out our miles and makes them wearisome'
William Shakespeare, *Richard II*

IN JUNE 1986 BRASHER wrote in the *Observer*: 'The greatest athlete I have ever known has now embarked on an enterprise which boggles my mind. In the past I have said that there is only one man in history to whom he can be compared: Wilson of the *Wizard*.'

Describing, for those unfamiliar with the name, Wilson as 'a Maradona of all sports . . . single handed he could win the World Cup; take the Ashes from the Aussies; win all the premier events in the Olympics and climb Everest alone', Brasher continued:

Joss Naylor is a real-life Wilson. Yesterday he set out on a six-day run which will take him over 214 Lakeland fells, all the fells that appear in Wainwright's classic series of guidebooks. The distance as measured on the map is 391 miles and the total height that Joss will climb is 121,000 feet. That is the equivalent of thirty-four ascents of Snowdon from sea level, or four attempts at Everest plus one Ben Nevis.

Joss is now 50 and as lean and as fit as I have ever seen him. He

still farms in Wasdale and holds down a full time job at Windscale
which is now called Sellafield. His greatest feat in the past has been
to set records for the Bob Graham Round which nobody has been
able to approach.

Brasher wrote a postscript for a booklet entitled *Fifty Years
Running, a History of the Mountain Trial* in which he gave this
colourful description of Naylor's abilities:

> The moon was full behind us but it still seemed very dark at half
> past one in the morning as we climbed out of Honister Pass
> towards the summit of Dale Head. The pace was fast enough to
> keep me silent, but out of the dark came the voice of Eric Roberts,
> a good athlete and a great man of the mountains: 'I was thinking,'
> he said, 'of how to equate this effort of Joss's with any known
> performance. I thought of Ron Clarke when he first ran under
> thirteen minutes for the three miles – great performance but not
> great enough. I thought of Emil Zatopek and his three gold medals
> in one Olympic Games – still not good enough; and then I decided
> that there was only one man in athletic history who is in this league
> – Wilson of *The Wizard*.' And then he laughed: 'A man of fantasy
> for a fantastic performance.'

Brasher continually referred to Naylor as the greatest of them all.
'Joss,' he wrote, 'has sinews stronger than any man made substance
and his will is harder than a diamond. There is nothing to him
except bone and gristle. He stands 5ft 11in tall and yet weighs only
9 stone. There does not seem to be any muscle included and yet he
can climb faster, descend more recklessly for far longer than any
man of his time.'

When, in 2010, I set out to spend a day walking, running and
chatting with Joss Naylor it became easy to see what all the fuss
was about. I visited Naylor in his home in the Wasdale Valley,
where he lives with his dogs and his wife Mary. It is a small,

secluded corner of Cumbria circled all around by the fells, their peaks clouded in mist though this was high summer.

Even by Lakeland standards, Wasdale seems well off the map. It's tucked away – a little hamlet, rain-sodden. There is a chilly meadow, a scattering of climbers' tents, and it's enclosed by a glowering horseshoe of mountains and fells – Yewbarrow, Kirk Fell, Great Gable, Scafell Pike. Its own lake, Wastwater, only four miles long, has a sinister scowl of gloom. It is the deepest of the Lakeland lakes. In the shadow of the massive fells is the Naylor farmhouse – many back-breaking climbs away from the cosy world of cream teas and tourist shopping of Ambleside and Grasmere.

Joss met me at the gate, a tall beanpole of a figure, slightly stooped with tacky tracksuit bottoms, his eyes alert and intense. They reminded me of a sheepdog. He walked stiffly, awkwardly, as if hinged at the waist, with his back quite straight and his hands hanging down in front of him. He had big powerful hands and he shook mine with a grip the like of which I'd never experienced. I asked him later about his grip and he explained it came from decades of shearing sheep by hand and building dry stone walls. He looked like a man who could endure a lot of pain.

Brasher, ever the romantic, had taken this tough, wiry fell farmer and popularised him in legend with journalistic clichés such as the 'King of the Fells' or the 'Iron Man'.

For a large part of his early life, Joss told me, he was practically immobile. From his childhood he had been hampered by a serious back injury and took no part in sports as a boy. He left school at fifteen to work on his father's farm and was reckoned to be unfit for national service. Along with almost everything else in Naylor's life, the origins of his back injury are lost or hidden under layers of legend and strange explanations.

Naylor never got on with his mother, an awkward and self-willed woman prone to bouts of short temper. Naylor's biographer, Keith Richardson, said that Joss had revealed to him rather emotionally that the real problem with his back started in his childhood.

'I had just turned nine when it happened,' said Joss. 'I got kicked in the bloody back. We shouldn't say, but it was my mother who kicked us. I maybe asked for it. I would have been up to some sort of mischief and I had gone out of the back door and I'd stepped down off the step and I was probably just at the wrong angle at the wrong time. You shouldn't say these things, but these things happen. I just got gradually worse and I went to see all sorts of specialists.'

This boyhood injury sentenced Naylor to wear corsets and special straitjackets in vain attempts to straighten his back. When he left school he started work on the farm, where they had sheep, cows and chickens. 'I never missed a day's work,' he said defiantly. In order to be able to walk properly, to get his stride right, Naylor scuffed the soles off his shoes, which helped his balance. He was already nineteen when he went to see a specialist in Manchester who removed two discs that had been at the root of the back problem for ten years or more. For a while surgery seemed to work. By 1958 he was pain free and his reflexes were fine.

'At that age,' said Naylor, 'I didn't need a dog to catch sheep.' Joss reckoned he could catch any sheep when he wanted. He would creep up on them and he could out-sprint them before they could get away. 'In those days I could catch bloody midges.'

Later Naylor aggravated his back problem with a fall. He was attempting to jump over a fence, his hand slipped and he landed painfully on slate on his back. This injury was followed by years of pain and it was not until he was in his late twenties that he was able to make tentative steps towards fell running. He ran his first race at Wasdale in a pair of working boots and a pair of old jeans clipped off around the knee. He went off too fast and got cramp. 'But I couldn't straighten up when I was running,' said Joss. 'I'm crouched over and that's to do with my back being wrecked.'

Naylor thought this crouching style had improved a bit over the years. 'I do a lot of work on exercises,' he said, but it's a very distinctive style and anyone could pick him out from miles away.

Even in his mid-seventies Naylor seemed to ignore age and injury and push himself as hard as ever. Now in retirement, he spent his summers in Wasdale, taking off for hours at a time to run on the fells, but when the winter snows came he took himself off to spend time in the warmth of Spain with his wife Mary. He found that the bitterly cold weather of a Cumbrian winter played hell with the circulatory problems in his legs and feet.

When I visited Joss it was misty and raining, weather not untypical of summer in Cumbria. Joss pulled on a battered pair of studs, a dark vest and shorts, and we ran.

Naylor's feet danced around the tussocks and he found paths that seemed invisible to me through bracken and heather, and sharp rocks that twisted and bruised your feet. He had a habit of whistling gently as he walked and ran, and for a moment I thought this snatch of music was some cruel form of gamesmanship. But other runners said he does it all the time.

Joss told me that he runs this way for hours – seven or eight at a time. Of course, when Naylor competes, he can endure not just for hours but for days at a time, pressing past exhaustion until, sleepless and swollen-jointed, he loses all appetite for food, the ability to swallow anything but baby-style food.

Naylor is a legend because for decades he has been able to absorb this treatment longer and faster than any before him. As well as a back injury, Joss told me that he had an operation at the age of eighteen to remove the cartilage from his right knee. It didn't work properly, so ever since he had had to adapt his gait even more, with slightly bent legs and a pattering, efficient movement that seems to work well for him over this uneven terrain. On runs of more than two days, Joss told me, he would often take just three hours' sleep a night on a mattress in the back of a van.

When the run was over Joss plunged into a stream, washing himself all over in the freezing cold fell water. The vision of Wilson of *The Wizard* hung in the drizzle.

It was easy to see why Chris Brasher admired Naylor so much.

The embodiment of Brasher's childhood dreams, in the flesh he was the best fell runner in the world. Brasher's love of competitive running and his passion for the hills came together like a marriage – and the honeymoon was fell running. He used to glory in its history and traditions, and would tell and retell stories of its heroes.

The origins of fell running have long since been lost in the mist; Scotland claims the first mention of the sport as far back as the eleventh century, when it is recognised as the precursor to the Highland Games – the Braemar Gathering. But the Lakeland fells are recognised as the historical and spiritual home of perhaps the oldest and most gruelling sport of all. Here local farmers would enjoy Cumberland wrestling and racing up and down the local peak – often for small cash prizes.

The first known formal race, the Grasmere 'Guides Race', took place in 1868 for a prize of £3 (it is still held each August). The course rose steeply from the village sports field to the 1292ft summit of the local peak, Silver How, and back again.

Today Cumbria hosts over fifty fell races every year. Often, like the 'guides races', these are short up-and-back romps over a single fell, though there are also marathons like the Borrowdale and Wasdale runs. But the ones that appealed most to Brasher were over more rugged terrain, especially if they required the ability to navigate between predetermined checkpoints, or solitary challenges like the Bob Graham Round that took the runner to deserted summits.

As well as the Lake District, fell races are now held in north Wales, the Highlands of Scotland, Peak and Pennines, Northumberland and North Yorkshire. The legendary Joss Naylor has been joined by names such as Kenny Stuart and Billy Bland, while alongside the Grasmere Guides Race and the Bob Graham Round in the calendar are a plethora of events such as the Three Peaks race, the Paddy Buckley Round in Snowdonia and the Ben Nevis race.

By 1963 the record for the Bob Graham Round had been

shattered by Eric Beard of Leeds City Athletic Club. The man known familiarly to Brasher and thousands of climbers, hill walkers, skiers and children as 'Beardie' completed a round of fifty-six peaks in twenty-four hours, a record that was to stand until Joss Naylor came along.

Brasher saw in Beard, as in Naylor, many echoes of the adventures that he had read about while a shy, stammering schoolboy. Beardie was killed in a car crash on the M6 on 16 November 1969 while returning from the Lake District and on 23 November, Brasher paid tribute in the *Observer*:

> The reason that I write about him is simple. He was a very special man, the simplest, kindest, most unselfish man that I have ever met. A hard man, yet hard only on himself, a man whose death diminishes everyone who knew him.
>
> He was 38 years old when he died towards the end of an incredible year which was to culminate in a 24 hour track run in aid of the Save the Children Fund, a project typical of the man. Beardie had little education and no formal qualifications whatsoever except for the greatest qualification of all – the ability to make people, especially children, happy when in his company.

Beard was born in Leeds and left school at fifteen, when he stood only 5ft tall and weighed just 5 st 11 lb. He had a variety of jobs – office boy, trainee salesman, conductor on the Leeds trams, greenkeeper at a golf club – before at the age of twenty-six, through the influence of the driver of his tram, he discovered distance running. Brasher continued the story:

> Beardie broke a leg in Easter 1958 while competing in a marathon. As part of his campaign to strengthen his leg he went into the hills to Snowdonia and then latterly to Chamonix. 'When I saw the big hills covered in snow I got the bug, the wanderlust,' he said. And a wanderer in the hills he became for the rest of his life.

I once asked him how much he needed to live on. He did not know exactly but it was a very small amount. 'I don't drink, I don't smoke, I haven't got a car or a house, just me, my skis, my climbing gear, my running gear, a tent and a rucksack.' That and the hills was enough for him.

Brasher concluded: 'His quality is hard to convey for it is the quality of a great human being and an utterly reliable man. A happy man, a man concerned with others.'

In the six months before he died Beard had run to the summit of Ben Nevis via Scafell to Snowdon, from John O'Groats to Lands End and across the roof of Wales from north to south. Most of Beardie's runs had been solo – a man challenging himself with the mountains. But the popularity of the sport was growing by the time of his death. The trails and the races were becoming crowded.

In the 1970s two separate bodies devoted to the promotion of amateur fell racing had emerged in the Lake District. These were the Fell Runners Association, formed in April 1970 following the Pendle Fell Race, and the Cumberland Fell Runners Association. The popularity of running produced ever-increasing fields which started to change the character of many of the races.

The prestige of challenges like the Bob Graham Round provided a tremendous upsurge in would-be competitors. The Bob Graham 24 Hour Club was founded in 1971 with Fred Rogerson of Windermere as its chairman, and only runners who had copleted the Round or a superior circuit based upon it could qualify for membership. At the end of 1971 there were only eight full members but their number increased rapidly as the sport became more popular and by the end of 1983 they had reached nearly 300.

There were already other fell running classics. One of the first of these was the Lake District Mountain Trial, established in September 1952 and 'open to YHA members wearing boots or stout shoes'. Once again Joss Naylor was triumphant, having run the event forty-eight times (in the 1970s he won the Trial seven times, as he put it, 'on the trot').

Another was the Karrimor International Mountain Marathon, which many see as a forerunner of modern adventure racing. Instigated and organised by Gerry Charnley, it was a two-day event in which two people as a team carried everything they needed for a weekend in the mountains and then ran or walked from control point to control point for thirty or fifty miles. Charnley did all the work involved in organising these events in the evenings from a desk under the stairs of his house in Preston. This do-it-yourself style was applauded by Brasher; he believed such events should be organised for the competitors and not for officials.

Now known as the Original Mountain Marathon (OMM), the event takes place in a different region of Britain every year. First held in 1968, it was designed to test orienteering skills in the most extreme circumstances. The full-length Karrimor course is a double-marathon length race the route of which is not disclosed until the race begins, so each team must have good navigation skills. It was guaranteed to appeal to Brasher.

Brasher competed in a Karrimor Mountain Marathon as early as 1969, coming fifth in the elite class with his partner Mike Wells-Cole. By 1973, the venue for the race being Snowdonia, Brasher emerged as a course planner, with Disley controlling the event. In 1976 the Mountain Marathon was held in the bogs and mountains of Galloway. That year Galloway had exceptionally bad weather with only a third of the field being able to complete the course. When asked in a BBC interview, 'Don't you think this event is too tough?' Gerry Charnley replied, 'Everybody knows this is the Karrimor Mountain Marathon, the toughest event on the calendar – it's not a Sunday afternoon picnic.'

In December 1982, at the age of fifty-three, Charnley was traversing the snow-covered slopes of Helvellyn in the Lake District when he slipped while trying to rescue his dog, and died instantly. Brasher wrote at the time: 'His tools were a telephone, a typewriter, a patient and orderly mind and a belief that sport was for participants and that an official's job was to ensure that everything was right for them.' The Charnley Way, a round of Eskdale, Borrowdale and Langdale totalling around 57km and 3600 metres of climbing, was devised by his friends following his death. The area chosen for the route was the scene of the 1981 Karrimor International Mountain Marathon.

Although the Bob Graham Round remained a true test of endurance and stamina for the fell runner, still other events were being developed. Paddy Buckley's classic round in Snowdonia, first completed in 1982, is generally acknowledged to be tougher by at least an hour than the Bob Graham Round. The route is a circuit just over 100km (61 miles) long with 28,000 feet of ascent, taking in some forty-seven summits. The aim is for participants to complete the route on foot within twenty-four hours. Most of the tops are in the well-known areas of Snowdon, the Carneddau, the Glydereau and the Moelwynion. Buckley devised the route with, he notes, 'helpful comments from Chris Brasher'.

Similarly, other records were being bettered. The Pennine Way record was first established by a team from Clayton-le-Moors Harriers, who set a relay record of 34 hours 54 minutes 7 seconds. Later in 1971 Bill Bird, a member of Brasher's club the Ranelagh Harriers, set a solo Pennine Way record in four days, eight hours and eight minutes.

Having enjoyed considerable success in setting up the British Orienteering Federation, Brasher and Disley wondered whether they might be able to employ the same template with fell racing. The reality of amateur fell running at this time was that it was both low key and low budget – for the first three years the Fell Runners Association charged its members just 25p. The spectre of the Amateur Athletic Association still haunted amateur fell running at this time and occasionally good club athletes wondered if they might jeopardise their amateur status with the AAA if they competed against so-called professionals. A Fell Running Association committee meeting in November 1974 passed a motion requesting the views of the AAA in an attempt to gain clarification of its attitude to fell racing as a sport, but the motion was never followed up.

Three years later, during the summer of 1977, Disley and Brasher called a meeting of fell runners at the Ullswater Hotel at Glenridding, on the eve of the Vaux Mountain Trial, at which they put forward a plan for the Fell Runners Association to break away from the AAA's jurisdiction altogether and form the Fell Runners Federation. This would become the sport's governing body, just like the British Orienteering Federation.

The proposal was linked to another agenda. Brasher wanted the fell runners to consider an invitation that had been extended to Joss Naylor to take part in the Pikes Peak Marathon in America. The possibility of a world fell running championship or festival was raised by Brasher. But Brasher and Disley's enthusiasm for the sport to break away from the AAA didn't meet with unqualified approval among the northern runners, who preferred not to have their sport completely revolutionised. Some traditionalists in the north were unhappy with the way the two southerners were trying to alter the sport of fell running. But the southerners were not easily put off.

The sport had clearly reached a crossroads. Brasher and Disley wanted to push it forward. Peter Knott, editor of *Fell Runner*, asked in his editorial in the autumn 1977 issue: 'Should the sport of fell running in the UK seek to become an accepted branch of amateur athletics or should it register as an independent sport with the Sports Council? Or should we simply carry on as in the past?'

The battle for the soul of fell racing was to be played out not just in the magazines and the committees but among the members whose votes really mattered. The debate over the sport's future came to a climax at the AGM of the Fell Runners Association on 1 April 1978. The situation was summed up by Norman Harris, himself an orienteer and someone who knew Brasher well. Harris wrote that members who wanted to stay with the AAA 'were anxious to protect all the members of athletics clubs who currently compete in fell running', while those who wanted to break away 'argued that fell running catered for a different breed and a mixed one and feared for the possible restricting influence of amateur athletic rules'. He continued:

> One of the arguments for remaining under the 'control' of the AAA was ironically that they are remote, far away in London and give fell runners the freedom they want. So in reality both sides wanted the same thing and at the recent meeting the fell runners made a decision to continue as before within the AAA whilst trying to secure their own best interests. These kindred souls wanted to stay just as they are: little, friendly, unbothered and unfettered to enjoy their 'fantastic' atmosphere.

But the battle continued and it was to be some years before Brasher and Disley managed to engineer a compromise. Disley explained, 'The British Orienteering Federation had a signed letter from Harold Abrahams stating that an orienteer would not lose his amateur status as a runner in the event of orienteering becoming an entity. But the northern lads would not take the plunge and ask the AAA and the British Amateur Athletic Board for the same deal that orienteering had made.'

Brasher was determined to get his own way. As Disley said, 'Chris Brasher and I believed that the dead hand of amateur athletics was still holding the sport back.' Brasher was impatient and there were some, as ever, who found his abrasiveness and enthusiasm counter-productive. One of the factors that bothered Brasher tremendously was that time was running out for his great hero Joss Naylor. He desperately wanted to see Naylor recognised as an international athlete and get him on to a wider stage. Like Brasher's other great hero, Abebe Bikila, Naylor was unheard of outside his native land. Brasher wanted to show what this man could do if the world was watching.

Fred Rogerson, chairman and founding member of the Bob Graham 24 Hour Club, did not welcome the publicity that Brasher had given to Naylor's record attempts. But very few beyond Cumbria had heard of Naylor, and Brasher, convinced that this shepherd was among the fittest athletes in Britain, was determined to change all that, whether Joss Naylor wanted it or not.

Naylor and his wife Mary speak fondly of Brasher. Mary is grateful for Brasher's support, his publicity and his generosity. 'Nothing,' she says, 'was too much trouble for him as far as Joss was concerned.' Ask Joss Naylor about Brasher's style, the stories and his famous abrasiveness and short temper, and Joss will pause. Then he'll add simply: 'I never quarrelled with him.'

'Ah,' I replied when I spoke to him in 2010, 'that's because you were one of his heroes. He never quarrelled with his heroes.'

Joss fell silent for a while and said, 'But he could be a bully. Ask Ken Ledward, they were often at it hammer and tongs.'

Ledward, who as a designer of mountain equipment for Brasher and Disley used to test their various running shoes, is a lively character with a gently wicked sense of humour and helped Naylor to organise his solo run over the Pennine Way in June 1974. Brasher, there to record the feat for the *Observer*, wrote:

> Every three hours there is Joss's mentor Ken Ledward with a meal ready, a change of clothes and shoes and some wintergreen to massage his legs. Joss will never be an international athlete, never wear a British vest, for if it were speed he could be beaten by many men in races of up to two or three hours.
>
> But once you venture beyond that time when ordinary mortals are wilting into exhaustion, Joss goes striding on covering the ground with a silky, effortless stride. What he does have is an outstanding ability to whisper over rough country without seeming to expend energy. It is the supreme quality of relaxation.

I have always believed that he is the toughest runner in Britain, which inevitably makes him the toughest runner in the world, for there is no other nation with such depth of talent in those events which really pull the stamina from a man's heart.

On this occasion, Brasher was all for attempting to pace Naylor over parts of this three-day run but couldn't keep with him and had to drop out within the first two miles. Later, getting ahead of him by car, Brasher set up a camera against a dry stone wall to await Naylor's arrival near a fell top. Sadly Brasher fell fast asleep propped up against the wall. Naylor sailed past him and Brasher and the *Observer* missed the photo opportunity.

Brasher was frustrated that whenever he wanted to move Joss on to the world stage, things seemed to go wrong. Brasher had been instrumental in starting the fund that was to send Naylor across the Atlantic to Colorado in 1975 to take part in the Pikes Peak Marathon, a race described as America's ultimate challenge. Once again though, it was not entirely successful. The problem was not just the heat but the altitude. 'There is a reason trees don't bother growing above 12,000 feet on Pikes Peak,' went the pre-race publicity for the event. 'They can't. Makes one wonder if trees are smarter than runners. Above the tree-line most runners take thirty minutes or more, some much more, just to cover a mile.'

Naylor reached the summit of Pikes Peak some forty minutes behind Rick Trujillo, the man who won it, but on the way down the 39-year-old Wasdale sheep farmer was the fastest of all. He ended up sixth but, nonetheless he was not happy to be beaten by a man who was acclimatised and understood the local conditions better than he did.

It always seemed to peeve Brasher that Naylor didn't have an international vest. In 1984 Brasher and others had arranged for Naylor to make an attack on a long-distance event – the 24-hour distance record – on the track at London's Crystal Palace. But things went badly awry.

'My knee went a fortnight before that track race,' said Naylor. 'I was shattered before I went because I knew that I was going to have problems. I was destroyed mentally before I went. I was geared up to do 170 miles and I would have done it. I was forty-eight years old and running well but my knee went. I knew that my knee was screaming, it had no cartilage and was full of bits of grime and stuff and if I'd had some anti-inflammatory tablets and taken something like that I would have got through without bother.' In the event Joss had to settle for a mere 134 miles.

People often ask Naylor what he might have achieved if he had stepped outside the world of fell running. Would he have been able to compete on the track or on the roads?

'I could have done, I had the pace,' said Naylor, 'but there was no sponsorship in athletics until I was about forty-three. I was running well but I couldn't have left the farm on a regular basis without sponsorship.'

So Joss remained what he always expected to be as a boy, a sheep farmer. Like Wilson of *The Wizard* he lived on his fells, discovered his own elixir of life. For all the efforts Brasher made, I doubt whether it made much difference to Naylor. He was awarded the MBE and a couple of honorary degrees from Manchester and Lancaster Universities; when, at Lancaster, he collected his degree from Princess Alexandra he said, speaking without notes, exactly what was in his heart: 'This was good for fell racing and the Lake District.'

The best fell runners are, as Brasher once ruefully observed, 'athletes of real world class. If their sport lent itself to being held in a stadium surrounded by television cameras they would be known the world over.' But the point about Naylor was that he was always a fell runner. He wasn't a 24-hour track runner. He wasn't a highly trained altitude runner who was likely to win in the rarefied conditions of the Pikes Peak Marathon. He wasn't a marathon runner, he hated running on the roads. But in his own environment on his own patch he was unbeatable.

There was no need to tempt Joss Naylor out. Fell runners are not hungry for prestige or profit; for them the joy throwing off the straitjacket of civilisation, pushing back the limits and sometimes doing the impossible is enough. For Brasher the answer to the Naylor enigma was there all the time. Brasher himself went to the Lakeland fells to get cold and wet and muddy, to get bruised and lost and very thirsty. This was his refuge, where he could relax.

But Joss Naylor pointed up the contradictions in Brasher. He was impatient to organise and codify the sport of fell running. He wanted to whisk Naylor out of the land of peaks and lakes and put him on the world stage. It was not until the second half of the 1980s that a world cup in mountain running was established. In 1988 the event was staged in the Lake District and was eventually sponsored by the Sports Council and Fleetfoot. Brasher said, 'I was only sad that it came too late for Joss Naylor to be awarded an England vest for competing for England in his native Lake District. By 1988 the great Joss Naylor was over 50 years old.'

Brasher wanted to take Naylor, as he had in his fantasy taken Wilson of *The Wizard* and his real-life hero Abebe Bikila, and turn the spotlight on them in the Olympic stadium. But Joss Naylor knew that even for Brasher this was beyond his grasp. It was just a dream.

19

Torment of a Decent Dreamer

'The reasonable man adapts himself to the world; the unreasonable one persists in trying to adapt the world to himself. Therefore all progress depends on the unreasonable man.'

George Bernard Shaw

AT 9.15 ON A Wednesday evening in March 1991, the telephone rang in the living room at Navigator's House in Petersham. Mrs Shirley Brasher turned away from the television screen and answered the call.

'I've just seen it,' said a man's voice. 'I'm a member of your husband's club. Tell him not to come anywhere near our club again, understand?'

The receiver was simply slammed down. Shirley Brasher returned to the living room where her husband was still staring at the credits as they rolled down the screen. She told him about the call but he didn't react. During the previous forty-five minutes Chris Brasher had been publicly accused of cheating charities, tax evasion and sharp practice. For him at this moment an anonymous phone call didn't seem that important.

The charges were made in the course of Channel 4's *Dispatches* programme by the investigative journalist Duncan Campbell. Essentially the programme alleged that Brasher, along with John Disley, had abused his position as a founding father of the London

Marathon to reap considerable financial rewards for himself and his sports shoe company. The article Campbell had already published in the *New Statesman* was the subject of libel proceedings and the programme now provoked further writs.

The years had not mellowed Brasher. He remained the abrasive, bloody-minded visionary whose battles with the athletics establishment had captured the sporting headlines in the 1950s. But for him there was sadness as he prepared to fight for his name, for his reputation.

'You can build up a reputation over the years and see it disappear in forty-five minutes,' Brasher told the journalist Pat Collins. 'I find myself wondering why we ever started the Marathon, why we set it up as a charity, why we just didn't make it a commercial operation and pick up the profits. But to hell with that, the Marathon has done the job we wanted it to do. It's given around a million pounds to recreational projects in the London boroughs and individual runners have raised close to £50 million for charities. Why should I apologise for something like that?'

Brasher had certainly made millions, a fact which some of his opponents found difficult to forgive. He was a man who made mistakes – and enemies. Ten years before this devastating broadcast, in a characteristic Brasher fashion, it was alleged that he had bawled out a marathon runner for arriving at registration without the proper credentials. Brasher gave his own account of that particular 'mistake'.

'If my memory serves me right,' said Brasher, 'Campbell entered for the 1983 Marathon and that year the registration of competitors took place in County Hall. Alan Sawyer, an employee of the GLC who gave considerable help to the Marathon, was manning the "trouble desk". This was where anybody in trouble with their entry came for advice. Throughout the years we have had all sorts of imposters trying to assume other people's identities. On my rounds of all the work stations I asked Alan if all was well. "Yes," he replied. "Except for one bloke who came without his proper documents and gave me a terrible time, insisting that he was a journalist and that I must issue him with a running number. He'll have to come back because he left his car keys here." At that moment Alan looked up and said, "And here he comes."

'Since I feel very strongly about those who abuse their power, particularly the power of my own trade as a journalist, I gave that person, whom I believe was Duncan Campbell, a dressing-down. It was after that incident that Campbell started his campaign against me in the *New Statesman*.'

For his part Campbell responds, 'None of Chris Brasher's recollections fit the facts. I'd started asking about his and John Disley's money from the Marathon in 1982, just when I started doing marathons myself – London '82 being my second. By the start of 1983, Chris had threatened to sue me four times for asking questions. The first time I actually did speak to him was three days after the '83 marathon when I was completing my *New Statesman* article.'

The television programme, its implications and what Brasher took to be smears deeply distressed him. 'I like to get things done,' he said. 'I like to go to the top people and almost without fail they have helped me. But what if they are influenced by this programme, what if they now regard me as a crook?'

Fellow journalists and friends of Brasher flocked to his defence. Ian Wooldridge, an old colleague and at the time the *Daily Mail*'s top sporting columnist, wrote after the programme:

Christopher Brasher is a mate of mine, has been for 25 years. As character references go that's probably as useful as earache, but I'm damned if I'm going to sit here speechless while he is being assailed by persons unfit to lace his Reeboks. Since I have not seen him for at least six months we have not discussed the contents of last night's Channel 4 documentary *Dispatches*, an alleged investigation into the finances of the London Marathon, but this much I can tell you: it struck me it has about as much to do with investigative journalism as a party political broadcast. It was more like another sword thrust in a running campaign and as such surpassed even this nation's capacity to run steamrollers over successful persons.

Frankly I don't give a toss whether Brasher cashed in by associating his shoe company with an event which has 50,000 legs pounding London's streets. They have to wear something. Nor do I care whether he was paid £9,000 in cash for running an event of such massive complexity. That is not even a filing clerk's wage. What staggers me is that in a forty minute documentary . . . there was not a single reference to one supremely positive aspect of the London Marathon. It is impossible to calculate exactly how much has been raised to help the sick, the crippled, the lonely, the desperate and the mentally handicapped – but £40 million is certainly a conservative estimate. I would have thought this worthy of passing acknowledgement. It was deemed unnecessary. Christopher Brasher conceived the idea of the London Marathon and nurtured it into the biggest event of its kind in the world. Without him that annual April event would leave London with just another bloody Sunday.

Such friends as Wooldridge, and Brasher had many, spoke of his vision, his tenacity and his idealism. His enemies, and he had his share of those too, told of a cantankerous autocrat who spared no feelings, accepted no excuses and made no allowances for those less able or less committed. As Brasher himself conceded, it had rarely been easy: 'We've had our bad times. And personally the worst time for me was when people challenged my motives for organising the Marathon. All sorts of nasty suggestions were made and they hurt me very much but I suppose that comes with the territory.'

Brasher's lengthy TV career had shown him the power of television to sway people's ideas and beliefs. He knew that one short item on a television news programme would be seen by more people and affect their ideas way beyond the most carefully researched and painstakingly written article. He believed that in March 1991 television was being used ruthlessly to murder his reputation and destroy his life.

'I sat there feeling as if I was being killed by knife wound after knife wound,' he said. 'Stab, stab, stab with blood pouring out of one side while the knife went into the other side.' One of those interviewed for the documentary was Alvar Kjellstrom, who not only accused John Disley of cheating the Silva company and its shareholders but also went on the record as calling Brasher a 'cheat and a liar'. Brasher believed that much of the bitterness stemmed from the loss of Kjellstrom's son, Jan, and that Kjellstrom had suffered a nervous breakdown following the tragedy of Jan's death.

It frustrated Brasher that he had supplied lawyers with evidence in an attempt to stop the programme by using a court injunction. It angered him that sitting in front of this 'tirade of invective', as Brasher saw it, was his wife Shirley, to whom he had been married for thirty-two years. Brasher described his portrayal in the programme as 'a sham, a thief and a crook', and he added, 'Shirley was being dragged through the mud with me, falsely labelled as a money grubber who is party to taking money from the Marathon on false pretences through some illegal tax avoidance scheme.

'Life,' reflected Brasher, 'is not the same when you are constantly reminded that there are those around you who have seen the programme and who could quite possibly believe that you are an unscrupulous and shady fraudster.'

He told of two experiences that he said were 'engraved into my memory'. The first was in 1992 when the then Minister of Sport, Robert Atkins, who was also the MP for South Ribble, came to visit Brasher and Disley in the offices of Reebok in Lancaster. Atkins was there at the request of the local MP, Dame Elaine Kellett-Bowman, to discuss the government's potential contribution to British sport.

'When Mr Atkins entered the room,' Brasher said, 'he told us that he had been advised by his office to have nothing to do with us.

In other words civil servants believed what the programmes had said about us and were advising one of Her Majesty's ministers not to consort with such unsavoury characters.'

Brasher's second engraved memory was that of a phrase tossed across the wind on a high mountain ridge in the Lake District. 'Ever since I was a teenager the mountains have been the places where I can go to renew my spirit, recharge the soul,' he said. 'Mountains are elemental, savage and yet beautiful, they seem to have the ability to wash away the cares of the world and to remind one of the eternal truths. One summer weekend in 1993 I climbed high on to the ridge between Buttermere and Ennerdale, knowing that somewhere along that ridge I would see fell runners taking part in one of the classic Lakeland races, a few of the old friends. Some would be from one of the athletic clubs to which I belong and I would recognise them by their club vests and cheer them on. Instead I heard a shout from one: "There is the man who has cheated us to get rich."'

One Sunday morning shortly after the programme's broadcast the phone rang and the caller introduced himself as a reporter from the Press Association. Did Brasher know, asked the reporter, that he was being investigated by the Fraud Squad? Papers from the programme had been deposited with the police, the Inland Revenue and the Charity Commissioners. Brasher was advised by his solicitors that he should carry their phone number in case the police arrived to take him away for questioning.

'I could not believe that anybody could attempt so viciously to destroy everything I had worked for, to destroy my whole life,' said Brasher. I kept asking myself, "Why?"'

In the hours and days that followed the *Dispatches* programme, Shirley said, 'It was obvious that he was fiercely hurt. For weeks afterwards his energy and enthusiasm for life vanished. He used to sleep remarkably soundly but since the programme he rarely sleeps for any length of time. He has spent many hours forced to think and go over a programme thoroughly distasteful to him. Stress can do very dangerous things to health and Chris has been under severe stress for a long time now. Only time will tell how much the programme and the legal proceedings have affected his health.

'The pressure that Chris had to face after the programme has been enormous,' she continued. 'He has not cracked. Certain people in business have stood by him because they know him well enough to know that the allegations must have been untrue. Above all as a top athlete Chris learned to survive and perform under pressure, disguising how much it affected him. If he hadn't done this he would have cracked and the opposition seized victory.'

Branded as a fraud and under investigation by the police and Inland Revenue, Brasher became at first subdued, even depressed. 'I felt I wanted to crawl away into a corner and hide from such a cruel and unjust world. But I could not do that because of my wife and my children, all three of whom were in their twenties. If I crawled away from the accusation they would be branded as the wife and children of a disgraceful cheat. I had to fight back.'

Both Brasher and Disley were concerned about the costs of the case. Brasher knew that the programme and its implications would 'haunt me day in, day out, night in, night out'. He developed a persistent sore throat. When over-the-counter medicines and antibiotics failed his doctor sent him to a specialist, who operated on his throat in March 1993. Brasher was advised to avoid all stress and tension and was given coaching on voice control at Charing Cross Hospital. He carried with him a sheet called 'Spotting Tension in Others and Ourselves' and he was told to relax whenever he felt tension coming on. At the foot of this stress sheet the specialist had drawn a man tied by a rope to a stake. The caption read, 'A person at the end of their tether'.

On Boxing Day 1994 Brasher took Andrew Sabisky, his first grandchild, to see *The Wind in the Willows* at the National Theatre. When Andrew, just three years old, hissed loudly at the evil weasels to make them run away, Brasher wondered: 'If only I could do that to Duncan Campbell and his allegations.' The strain ate further into his health. It disturbed his sleep. 'I will wake several times, sometimes every hour. It is simply that my body is tense because my mind is tense. Nowadays I only sleep well after a long day in the mountains which has tired my body and my mind. At other times I have to take anti-depressant tablets.'

He shelved plans for retirement while the lengthy legal case dragged on and he even brooded over whether his children's careers had been affected by the implications of the programme. By this time Brasher's son Hugh had taken over running the Sweatshop outlets. He was planning to expand, but business was bad. Brasher had to lend him £100,000 so that the shops would not go under.

At times, however, Brasher could be defiantly bullish. He didn't seem to worry whose noses he had put out of joint. He knew that the Marathon was now unstoppable, untouchable, and although he was anxious about many of the criticisms, he believed that he could fight them off; that he could fight back and he could win.

Nick Bitel, later chief executive of the London Marathon, first became involved with the event and with Brasher in 1985 when he was working for the family firm, of which Max Bitel, his father, was the senior joint partner. His evaluation of Brasher, his style and his ability to get things done was both shrewd and intuitive. During the early years of the London Marathon, he said, 'The management style was much coloured by Chris Brasher's own style. As far as legal matters were concerned this meant a distinct preference for a practical, pragmatic, informal approach rather than rigid formality. For instance the major sponsorship deals with the lead sponsors – Mars and ADT – were not dealt with by formal contracts drawn up by solicitors. The first major sponsor to have a proper contract was Nutrasweet in 1992. However, my experience is that when Chris Brasher consults lawyers and professional advisers he trusts them and acts upon the advice he receives.

'Chris Brasher is conceptually brilliant. He can be difficult to deal with. He is a hard taskmaster and demands skill and loyalty. He does not suffer fools gladly. This has sometimes given rise to difficulties in preserving business relationships but Brasher is an achiever and probably would not have been as successful had his character been different. When he has an aim in mind he will pursue it relentlessly. Without that single-mindedness the London Marathon would quite simply have never come into being.'

Bitel contrasted Brasher's style with that of his partner: 'John Disley is not so concerned with concepts and ideals. His strength is in the technical organisational side. He has been invaluable throughout the life of the Marathon as far as mapping the route, measuring, timing, analysing, checking road surfaces are concerned. He does also have a vast amount of experience in sports sponsorship which often proved valuable in board decisions on this subject. In many ways they have made a great team because their characters and their strengths complement each other rather than conflict with each other. They very rarely disagree.'

Shirley Brasher, with her background in world-class tennis, sports promotion and journalism, proved an invaluable ally to her husband. Money to Chris, it seemed to Shirley, was something to use if you had it and to earn by working hard if you needed it. His attitude, she notes now, meant that he was generous with money. She found that he was generous with his time too, but he always seemed to be rushed off his feet.

He tended to lack patience with formalities, she says, and could not abide red tape. After their marriage back in 1959, she reckoned that there was little alternative but to join in and start working for him and with him. She had a wide knowledge of sport and she knew that she could help take some of the pressure off him. He worked incredibly hard was never off the phone while travelling. She believes that where there were problems or mistakes in businesses or projects in which he was involved, they were invariably caused because he was trying to tackle too much.

Legal proceedings dragged on for four years, with Brasher and Disley growing increasingly anxious. And the costs, on both sides, were mounting alarmingly. Even though their businesses had prospered, Brasher was still prepared to fight this to the end. In securing the best barrister he had used his old tactic, of going straight to the top. In the spring of 1995 Brasher and Disley presented themselves at the chambers of George Carman QC to see whether he might take on their case. 'Don't ask him about the weather,' warned one solicitor. 'He'll charge you a fortune.'

Carman had successfully defended in 1979 the former leader of the Liberal Party, Jeremy Thorpe, who was charged with conspiracy to murder in a case which became the cause celebre of the decade. He became well-known for his celebrity clients, attracting headlines for his defence of the comedian Ken Dodd on charges of tax evasion and the overturning of the suicide verdict on Roberto Calvi, known to the press as 'God's Banker'. A colourful character, married and divorced three times, Carman was renowned for his robust cross-examination and for winning tricky cases against apparently insurmountable odds.

Carman read the papers and declared that he would take on the case. 'Of course, he said, 'as soon as they know it's me, they'll settle. Which is good news for you, but bad news for me.' Carman pointed out that he would miss out on his daily rate for any trial.

Carman's instinct proved true. In the days that led up to the settlement there was furious to-and-froing between the legal teams. Brasher and Disley favoured going easy on the damages claimed from the *New Statesman*, a magazine that they admired but was in financial turmoil itself at the time.

On 23 May 1995 it was reported that the founders of the London Marathon had accepted a libel settlement of more than £1.1 million over allegations that they had used the event to enrich themselves. Brasher and Disley were each awarded damages in the High Court in excess of £380,000, plus costs against Channel 4 and the *New Statesman*. Carman told Mr Justice Waller that the two men had been caused serious distress and damage by allegations made in the magazine and the broadcast.

'The defendants alleged that the plaintiffs had been consistently guilty of fraud, deception and dishonesty both in relation to a sports equipment company and in particular in relation to the London Marathon and that they had improperly enriched themselves to a considerable degree,' said Carman. 'It is entirely untrue that they have been guilty of any act of fraud, dishonesty or deception.' He added that Brasher and Disley could now consider themselves wholly vindicated.

The losers agreed to publish apologies and not repeat the allegations. Brasher said that he and his family had suffered 'Four years of hell. As a former sports editor our normal inclination is not to rush into a libel action, however these allegations were so outrageously untrue and hurtful that we had no choice but to seek retribution through the courts.'

Brasher and Disley went off to celebrate with eight other friends at Rules in Covent Garden, London's oldest restaurant. Brasher used some of the money that had been settled on them by the High Court to treat himself to a racehorse. He reckoned it was the nicest horse he had ever owned, a finely built and even-tempered chestnut.

Brasher knew what he wanted to call the animal. Sadly, the Jockey Club rules restricted the names to eighteen letters and spaces. Never a man to be put off by such restrictions, Brasher smiled and named the horse 'Dangerus Precedent'.

20

Save a Mountain, Save a Meadow: The Brasher Guide to Giving

'It is more agreeable to have the power to give than to receive.'
Winston Churchill

W HEN BRASHER SOLD the Brasher Boot Company in 1993 he transferred the funds, the best part of £1 million, to the Chris Brasher Trust. At last Brasher was able to fully back the dream of the 'wilderness' that had haunted him since his prep school days.

The trust had been established with the following objectives:

To provide or assist in the provision of facilities particularly facilities in the wild areas of these islands for the recreation of people of the United Kingdom with particular emphasis on those who have special need of such facilities by reason of their youth, infirmity or disability, poverty or social and economic circum - stances with the object of improving their conditions of life.

To conserve and protect for the public benefit wild areas of the United Kingdom in their natural condition so as to leave them unimpaired for future enjoyment, study in such a manner that the needs and aspirations of the indigenous population are acknowledged and respected.

Brasher gave the Trust 1000 of his Fleetfoot shares and transferred to it the ownership of a cottage in Snowdonia which the Trust sold for over £45,000, while for many years the Trust received all Brasher's royalties for the Brasher Boot.

Shirley Brasher believes that this behaviour was characteristic of her husband: 'I always suspected that Chris's attitude towards money was to have enough money to live comfortably by; he had no desire for excessive wealth. This went back to his childhood. His family had about enough money, I imagine, provided they were very careful and not extravagant. They did not have any obvious trappings of wealth or a luxury lifestyle that I could see. It never seemed that money was a motivation to his parents, and nor was it for CB.'

Her husband, says Shirley, wanted any staff he employed to be paid fairly and well, but he was likely to give away a generous proportion of the proceeds when he made a successful business deal. Only towards the end of his life, she recalls, when he bought racehorses (never very expensive horses) and two second-hand Bentleys did he spend any serious money on himself.

'The only really super car he bought was a new Aston Martin which he purchased around 1997. He had been on the waiting list for the Aston for about four years or more.

'When the car arrived at Navigator's House it really was superb. I was quite envious as my father and uncles had had Astons. CB's car had a racy and classy line. CB took all of six days to decide it wasn't him. The car was sold back – at a loss I expect. CB returned to his *Autocar* advert page and we resumed with his somewhat dodgy buys, makes and models. Our car journeys took their usual precarious path unless we went in my car, which was usually fast but of sounder stock.

'Upon reflection, the new Aston that I loved so much would have been useless for the boggy or woody areas into which I so often had to drive in order to rescue the orienteering ventures in his dodgy cars. Maybe that was why the Aston was returned so quickly. If I had been sharper at the time I could have struck a deal that I kept the Aston and that he bought a Land Rover. I am not sure the Land Rover would have been any use to me in London as my legs were too short and my skirt would usually be too tight to climb into it when he had borrowed the Aston.'

In the 1980s Brasher had been invited to give the Jubilee Lecture for the National Trust for Scotland. The title of his lecture was 'Happiness is a Wilderness'. During his preparatory researches he learned that two members of the National Trust's council were unhappy with the organisation's management of some of their mountain properties. So he approached the pair, Nigel Hawkins and Professor Dennis Mollison. Along with Brasher himself and a friend whom he had known for years, Nick Luard, the two set up the John Muir Trust. Its objective was 'To conserve and protect wild areas of the United Kingdom in their natural condition, so as to leave them unimpaired for future enjoyment and study in such a manner that the needs and aspirations of the indigenous population are acknowledged and respected.'

Very well known in the United States as a leading conservationist, John Muir was practically unknown in his native Scotland. He was born in 1838 in Dunbar, East Lothian, and his family left for America in the first half of the nineteenth century when he was eleven. In the latter half of the century, Muir was instrumental in the campaign to preserve the Yosemite area of California and in the formation of the United States National Parks.

Well-travelled author Nicholas Luard had first come to public prominence in 1961 when as an entrepreneur he founded the Establishment Club in Soho with comedian Peter Cook. A year later Luard and Cook bought the satirical magazine *Private Eye* and transformed it into a going concern. Luard had accompanied Brasher on the original trip to run the New York Marathon. Brasher's ally in setting up the John Muir Trust, he had long discussed the need for some of the world's finest wild land to be cared for in some way. Now, with the energy and funds provided by Brasher and Luard, the John Muir Trust was able to contribute substantially to the purchase of land around Ben Nevis and Snowdon. In particular, it would be able to secure the future of the Knoydart community.

Knoydart, one of the last wilderness areas in Great Britain, is a peninsula on the west coast of Scotland only accessible by boat from Mallaig or by a twenty-mile hike on foot. It is truly miles from any-where. You can't drive there, which greatly added to the fascination for Brasher. And to walk it you need a good map and compass, boots and a bivvy bag. No signs point the way. Most walkers take two days to cross it, breaking their journey at the campsite or bothy at Barrisdale.

Welcoming you in Knoydart is the Old Forge in Inverie – the most remote pub in mainland Britain. Wildflowers and wildlife surround you. It is home to the golden eagle, oyster catchers and herons, and here, too, you can catch a glimpse of minke whales, dolphins, sea otters and seals. Wild goats and red deer roam the rugged hills near the village. Knoydart was the scene of some intrepid adventures on the part of Brasher and the Oboe Club.

During his wanderings in the wilderness Brasher had gathered a loose group of companions who shared his enthusiasm and passion both for open-air adventure, for argument and for going into pubs and relaxing. He formed them into a club which he dubbed 'Oboe'. The name was provoked by a throwaway remark by Bill Tilman, an unconventional hobo of a man, a war hero in both world wars (he was twice awarded the Military Cross for bravery), explorer, sailor and above all mountain climber. As the expedition leader on Everest in 1938 Tilman had reached 27,200 feet without oxygen. He and the writer and explorer Eric Shipton had formed one of the most famed partnerships in mountaineering history.

Brasher revered Tilman as much for his legendary expeditions as for his unorthodox attitude to the establishment. The inspiration came at the first British Mountaineering Council Conference at Buxton in 1976.

The audience for this packed conference had become increasingly restless as mountaineer Chris Bonington explained the logistics of organising a Himalayan expedition. Talking with the aid of spreadsheets and computers, his technical presentation had failed to capture his listeners' imagination. Then Tilman bounded on to the stage. 'In my day,' he began with a grin, 'if you couldn't organise an expedition *on the back of an envelope . . .*'

The rest of his opening gambit was drowned by cheers and applause. Brasher savoured Tilman's phrase. Contracting it into 'OBOE', he labelled this group of travellers the OBOE Club.

He would occasionally pick up the phone or circulate members of this loose-knit pack and tempt them to go on walks, adventures, expeditions, sometimes by river, sometimes by sea and often over mountains. It was a couple of his closest OBOE friends, Paddy Buckley and Billy Wilson, that he called to celebrate his sixtieth year. Brasher later wrote about his OBOE companions' pilgrimage to Knoydart. This time he was writing in *The Times*, but he still employed the same emotional and reflective style he had used in his classic 'Breath of Air' columns:

> On my 60th birthday last August, with my youngest daughter in her last year at university, I determined that it was time to delegate, to pluck some of the fruits of my labour and to use them to enrich the sixth age of my life and to join the ranks of what the Americans describe as 'the golden oldies'. So now I snip cuttings from the travel pages and read tales of great but bygone adventures and contemplate a life devoted to exploring the beauty of this world.
>
> Throughout all my working travels I have found nowhere so wondrously changeable and beautiful as the highlands of Scotland, so it is to Doune that I have come and to the west coast of the Rough of Knoydart.

His reflections in the article on his early expeditions to Snowdonia and his later exploits reveal much about his life and the values he had shaped about life itself:

Thirty and more years ago, I ended my second age – the age of
the whining schoolboy – with an expedition to those fierce rock
mountains. Eighteen year olds – for that was our age – had little
to lose and we climbed hard and sometimes dangerously because
we were inexperienced. Then came the age of work in a dark and
dirty factory in Manchester and so to the age of a lover, and love
produced children and a mortgage and responsibility.

And this led me into my fifth age: building a business, writing,
organising the London Marathon – a regime that became
ridiculously a seven day week, 52 weeks in the year.

I have good companions with me. Paddy Buckley all the way
and Billy Wilson for the first quarter of our twelve day journey.
Paddy is a long time wanderer in the hills, a man of many talents
– forester, lab technician, librarian, handyman, clerk of works and
father of eight. He reaches the milestone of 60 on Tuesday.

Billy has honed his philosophies of life as a guardsman (a
Grenadier no less), a gardener, a racing cyclist, father of five
children and now a rescuer of abandoned and abused horses. He
is also a marathon organiser, the prickly conscious of road-race
organisers in Britain.

Billy Wilson was something of an eccentric even by Brasher's
standards. He ran the first London Marathon dressed as a
pantomime horse, opened a horse sanctuary and staged the Tough
Guy Challenge, which claimed to be the world's most demanding
one-day survival ordeal. Wilson once ran a hairdressing business in
the Midlands. He told Brasher and Disley that he had a plan to set
up a men's topless hairdressing salon. Sadly, he said, it was banned
by the city fathers of Wolverhampton.

Brasher continued:

I suspect that somewhere out there I shall have a flaming row with
Paddy Buckley. The cause will be fear – my fear. On steep ground
he is as confident as a mountain goat while I become tense and

terrified and start shouting, 'Paddy don't leave me. Paddy there must be an easier way.'

But that is a vital part of this new life that I have chosen. If it was easy, if the outcome was certain, there would be no adrenalin, no excitement pumping through our veins. It was Joss Naylor, the Lake District farmer, the greatest fell runner this century, who taught me that when embarked on a long mountain journey (and ours is 210 miles long) think only of the mountains on which your feet are treading – not of those that lie ahead.

That advice applies equally well to life itself – a life which I have spent dreaming dreams and then embarking on a voyage to turn them into reality. If I had known what obstacles were lying in wait, I doubt if any of my journeys would have begun. Certainly not the marathon journey, if someone had told me that we would have to handle more than 30,000 entries. Certainly not the journey into a business enterprise, if someone had told me that we would be responsible for the working lives of close on 200 men and women and a commitment financially that can rise in some months to £12 million.

But as Kipling said, triumph and disaster are both imposters and must be treated 'just the same'. It will not be a triumph if we traverse all the summits that we have planned. Nor will it be a triumph if we complete all 210 miles in 12 days – an average of 19 miles a day. But it will be a feeling of deep satisfaction, not least because it will tell us, the 60 year olds, that there is still strength in our bodies, determination in our minds.

Later, in the spring of 2000, Brasher went on yet another OBOE expedition with eight friends. They met up at Llandudno Junction and took a train south to Harlech, breaking the journey for a spin on the narrow-gauge slate railway at Blaenau Ffestiniog.

One of the team, whom Brasher described as 'a farming lady' called Paddy Hollington, had recently been fitted with a new hip and wanted to start early the next day so as not to hold up the rest

of the team. Paddy Buckley offered to be her guide. The rest of the
team poked around Harlech Castle before climbing the northern
tip of the Rhinog Range. By the time they were descending a gorge,
they were talking and arguing so furiously that they inevitably took
a wrong turning. Brasher remembered:

> We ended up more or less swinging from tree to tree, crossing the
> river at least three times before emerging into lovely country
> above Maentwrog. We stayed at the Grapes where the bar food is
> good and one of the barmaids is quite spectacular.
>
> The slow moving team of the two Paddys had already reached
> the pub and were relaxing over glasses of home-made sloe gin
> when the swingers arrived.
>
> We had an average age of over 60 and a large number of
> artificial hips among this OBOE group so we took just about the
> easiest way. But you can easily expand an OBOE group according
> to the fitness of your party to take in some of the summits. We do
> this whatever the weather – you've just got to take what it chucks
> at you.

'We all need,' concluded Brasher, '*a breath of air*'.

In 1999, the Knoydart peninsula was bought by the Knoydart
Foundation, a partnership of the local community, the Highland
Council, the John Muir Trust, the Kilchoan Estate and the Chris
Brasher Trust, set up to purchase the remains of the old Knoydart
estate. In so doing the Foundation became the guardian of over
17,000 acres of some of the wildest land in Britain. They also had
the responsibility for managing several properties, a bunkhouse,
numerous deer, and the supply and generation of electricity for the
local community. In the *Scotsman*, in March 2003, Brasher's friend
Nigel Hawkins wrote: 'Last July the Knoydart Community made
Chris their guest of honour at celebrations for the third anniversary
of the buy-out. We, like others, travelled to Knoydart sedately by
boat, but Chris – as always – did the journey the tough way

clambering over the mountains of the Rough Bounds of Knoydart and sleeping out overnight at 3,000 feet. He was in his 74th year.'

Brasher was also pouring money and energy into the Trees for Life campaign and the National Trust. Following an approach from the National Trust to buy the West Affric Estate when it was put up for sale in 1992, he made a large donation to the National Trust for Scotland which enabled them to buy the property. The condition which he attached to his donation was that Trees for Life should become a partner responsible for the restoration of native forest to suitable sites on the 4000 hectare estate. Then in 1996 he made a substantial loan towards the purchase of a field base for Trees for Life at Plodda Lodge.

Far from the Highlands and closer to his own home at Navigator's House in Petersham, Brasher fought a fierce battle to preserve the Petersham Meadows. In 1813 the painter J.M.W. Turner built himself a bolt-hole in rural Twickenham surrounded by fields and parkland stretching down to the River Thames and it was from here that he painted one of his best-known works, depicting the view from Richmond Hill taking in the broad sweep of the River Thames. To Brasher's horror this magnificent view of the London landscape was under threat from property developers.

With his usual energy, Brasher took the lead in organising resistance to the planned development. He raised money, held protest meetings and bombarded his friends in the press, urging them to run articles defending the landscape. A small watercolour painted by Turner around 1790, showing a view from the back windows of Joshua Reynolds' house on Richmond Hill, was used by *The Times* and other newspapers to illustrate the story of Brasher's battle with the developers.

Victory came when Richmond Council handed over ownership of the 30 acres of Petersham Meadows to a conservation trust headed by Brasher. The Petersham Trust was awarded an 125-year lease on the site, estimated to be worth at least £75 million for development, for the annual rent of a posy of wildflowers.

Brasher's acts of kindness and generosity didn't just extend to deserted highland acres of Scotland, or even to Wales and Richmond. Athletes and sportsmen who had fallen on hard times or who, in Brasher's judgement, had been badly treated were often the recipients of unrecognised acts of altruism. As Shirley Brasher says, 'This went back to his childhood. Chris was always likely to give away a generous proportion of his own proceeds when he made a successful business deal.

One man to receive such assistance from Brasher was Gordon Pirie. A giant of post-war athletics – his epic, but ultimately unsuccessful contests with Vladimir Kuts in the 1956 Olympic 5000 and 10,000 metres lived in the memory – as well as one of that band of 'retired athletes' who Brasher and Disley lured into the new sport of orienteering. In 1991 Pirie, was diagnosed with cancer and given just a few months to live. Dick Booth writes in his biography of Pirie, *The Impossible Hero*:

> For much of the time in the final weeks, Pirie was too weak to go out. Chris Brasher and John Disley had sat in the stands at Melbourne in 1956 after their own final and watched the battle with Vladimir Kuts. Ten years later they had introduced Pirie to orienteering and then been trounced by him.
>
> They visited him in October 1991 and Gordon found the energy just to accompany them to a pub for lunch. He was weaker and said something that suggested he knew there was not long to go, 'I'd like to go for a walk with you in the forest and not come back.'

On 10 November Brasher, who had been keeping in close touch with Jennifer Gilbody, a teacher in whose house Pirie had taken refuge, visited the clinic in Tunbridge Wells to which Pirie had been moved. Pirie was upstairs in bed, his face to the wall, a skeleton. He had had enough. 'Can you get me out of here, they're starving me to death,' he pleaded.

John and Sylvia Disley arrived to take him home to die. Pirie pleaded with them to drive carefully. Bills were presented for nearly £1000 for medicine but there was no money to pay them. 'Pirie was in fact a hostage,' wrote Booth. 'Gordon was not allowed to leave the clinic until the cheque had cleared.'

Once again (just as he had done at that long-ago reception in Kensington Town Hall), Brasher whipped out his cheque book. The account was settled. Pirie could go home.

Another recipient of Brasher's generosity was more obscure. Throughout the 1950s and 1960s Brasher had come across the story of the so-called 'Ghost Runner', both in races and in newspaper reports. John Tarrant was a long-distance runner, a legend, a folk hero, a real-life comic book hero. In the 1950s, Tarrant had been banned for life from athletics meetings because he once collected £17 expenses for a handful of fights as a teenage boxer.

The Amateur Athletic Association ruled that this made him a professional, and in 1952 banned him from all domestic and international competitions for ever. Frustrated and angry, Tarrant defied this ruling and gate-crashed events. Disguised in a cap and an old mac, he would leap from behind bushes and join in at the back of the field. Wearing no number, he would more often than not win. After he jumped from the crowd to run in the 1956 Liverpool marathon, newspapers asked: 'Who is the Ghost Runner?'

Tarrant had an appalling childhood. Born in Shepherds Bush in 1932, the working-class boy had none of the privileges that had guided Brasher. During the war, Tarrant's mother died of TB and he was shunted off to a pitiless and disciplinarian children's home, left to putrefy in a way that would shape his future. The experience turned out a man who was fiercely independent, obsessive and above all hated authority. Tarrant spent much of his brief life fighting a one-man crusade against the injustice of the treatment imposed on him by unbending bureaucrats of the athletic authorities.

Brasher's background could not have been more different – a privileged public school and Cambridge education, winner of an

Olympic gold medal, a man who rubbed shoulders with the rulers of British athletics – Jack Crump, Arthur Gold, Harold Abrahams. But Brasher shared important traits with Tarrant. The working-class rebel Tarrant was a maverick who shared Brasher's gargantuan self-belief that anything was possible; the captain of a running club that Tarrant wanted desperately to join in South Africa once described the Ghost Runner as 'arrogant, brash, selfish and unpopular'.

For years Brasher exchanged letters with Tarrant, and made it clear that Tarrant's predicament had angered and moved him. Tarrant wanted no reward, the only thing he longed for was that people should recognise his athletic ability and allow him to wear the vest of his country. No man trained harder than Tarrant; he would sacrifice everything – job, family, home – to pursue his campaign.

When Tarrant was diagnosed with terminal cancer in 1972, and badly needed money, it was to Brasher that he turned for help. Brasher immediately negotiated a £400 payment from the *Sunday People* for the Ghost Runner's exclusive story. Later that year Tarrant asked Brasher to look at the notes he had been gathering. In January 1975 Brasher phoned Tarrant's wife to tell her that he had found a publisher for Tarrant's remarkable autobiography. Within hours the Ghost Runner was dead at the age of forty-two. Brasher wrote in the *Observer* two weeks later: 'There are in this world very few utterly honest men. John Tarrant was one of them.'

The Ghost Runner (subtitled 'John Tarrant's Own Story') was eventually published by *Athletics Weekly* in 1979, selling for £4.95. It was masterminded by Mel Watman, the editor of the magazine at the time, and just 1000 copies were printed. All profits were paid to Tarrant's widow, Edie. Brasher began his foreword to the book: 'We, the people of Britain, are proud of our justice and yet there is still injustice in the land. This is the story of one injustice, one of the worst to have been meted out in sport in the post-war years. It is the story of a proud and honest man who, because he could not tell a lie, was banned from the sport he loved.'

Injustice was something that kicked Brasher into bouts of anger. He would attack it in print, kill it by argument and by action. He could be impossible, tenacious and aggressive in doing so.

'What would I be able to do for my country?' Brasher had asked himself as an eighteen-year-old, about to leave Rugby, when wondering at the legacy of Douglas Bader. Now, with his millions made, he could answer that question. Mountains, meadows and a hand on the wallet when injustice threatened meant, for Brasher, that there was a great deal he could do.

21

A Winner in the Sport of Kings

'No horse can go as fast as the money you bet on him.'

Nate Collier

AT THE AGE OF seventeen Chris Brasher, still a schoolboy at Rugby, put sixpence each way on a horse – Airborne – a grey not much fancied in the Derby of that year, 1946. The outsider romped home at 50 to 1, winning the race by two lengths with an amazing burst of speed past Tattenham Corner.

It was the first Derby after the war. Crowds flocked to Epsom for the occasion, the King and Queen were on parade and replays of the race were shown by Gaumont British News in every cinema. That was the year of victory parades in London, when Ernest Bevin was voted Pathé News Man of the Year – winning by a narrow margin from one of Brasher's heroes, the runner Sydney Wooderson – and all the talk was of the atom bomb.

The excitement of watching finely tuned horses race, straining every fibre, and the tension of gambling on them was something that stayed with Brasher throughout his life. 'When I have athletes like Coe, Ovett and Cram in a race my binoculars are steady as I watch,' Brasher told the *British Runner* in 2002. 'But for horse racing I have had to buy a new pair where if I press a button it takes the judder out of them.'

Following his libel case against Channel 4 and the *New Statesman*,

Brasher stayed on as president of the London Marathon, but his heart seemed no longer to be in the event. The strain of the court case, despite his victory, had taken its toll. As he relinquished day-to-day control of the Marathon, he was rumoured to be unhappy with certain elements of it. When asked what he was doing on race day in 1996 he told me: 'Nothing.' I arranged for him and my son William to attend in the company of Billy Wilson. William and Wilson joined Brasher and they leap-frogged as spectators around the course.

Instead of the London Marathon, which had consumed him day and night for over a decade, Brasher had already turned to another passion in his life, horse racing. He had long shared this love of racing with his wife Shirley, who had been brought up in Lincolnshire where her father often sold cars to wealthy racehorse owners. Shirley had been riding since childhood and understood the world of racing. So, having lived there for more than three decades, Brasher and his wife left their home in Navigator's House, Petersham, and attracted by the lure of the racing world they moved to Chaddleworth – a remote, close-knit village near Lambourn, deep in the border country between Berkshire and Oxfordshire.

For a while the Brashers bought a smaller house in Chaddleworth, a bolt-hole for the weekend close to racing country. But soon enough they had made the decision to move away from London altogether and they rented out the large family home in Petersham.

Their new home was first spotted by one of Brasher's racehorse trainers, Charlie Egerton. It had paddocks and stables and a room for Brasher's gym. By the mid-1990s Brasher and Shirley had a string of eight horses in training and a trainer on hand.

Nicknamed by the Brashers 'Edgy', Charles Egerton was one of the finest-bred among the ranks of racehorse trainers. He had been educated at Eton but sartorial elegance had never been a priority. When the Old Etonian was on hand to welcome back a winner, he would sometimes do so wearing a jacket with a rip right across the back. Like so many of Brasher's trainers, Edgy was chosen as much for his personality as for his ability to produce winners. As a member of the awkward squad himself, Brasher always liked the mavericks, the anti-establishment rebels. He enjoyed the bar-room gossip and the chance to challenge his trainers with his own ideas of how to produce a winning horse.

The legends about Edgy, who stuttered slightly, were legion. Shortly after leaving Eton he was invited to visit his bank manager. It was clear from the start that Edgy was in trouble. Grim-faced flunkies steered him to an inner sanctum and Edgy was told to sit down. The bank manager was studying some papers with a very serious look on his face. At length he spoke to the would-be race-horse trainer.

'Do you realise,' he said, in a voice intended to convey weariness and disapproval, 'that your overdraft is larger than my annual salary?'

Egerton sat for a moment quietly absorbing the information. At length he spoke. 'Have you ever thought,' he asked the bank manager, 'of changing jobs?'

As a trainer, Edgy found Brasher a difficult, though often inventive owner. But the difficulties seemed to dissolve with another of his racehorse trainers, Henrietta Knight. 'Henrietta really understood him,' said Shirley. 'Chris listened with respect to what Henrietta said and he never argued with her.'

Henrietta Knight had begun her career an assistant nursery teacher at a private school in Kensington. By her early twenties she was teaching at St Mary's School in Wantage, which allowed her to return home during her lunch break to check on her horses. 'Horses,' she said, 'got the better of me in the end and I gave up teaching for them.' In 1995, she married Terry Biddlecombe, having first met him in the 1960s when he was still one of Britain's top jump jockeys.

According to journalist Ian Wooldridge, Henrietta 'wears pearls and speaks like Princess Margaret at one of those now disbanded coming-out Balls'. 'In the racing world,' said Wooldridge, she and

Terry, a man the size of Mickey Rooney who speaks with a West Country burr, 'are known as the Odd Couple. But Henrietta is the most down-to-earth woman you could ever meet.'

Henrietta trained over 100 winners in point-to-point races and since 1989 she has trained racehorses on a farm in Lockinge, near Wantage in Oxfordshire. She is best known for training the triple Cheltenham Gold Cup winner Best Mate and Queen Mother Champion Chase winner Edredon Bleu. Both horses also won the King George VI Chase.

Henrietta took over the training of the Brasher-owned filly Heart from Michael Stoute, who could not seem to turn her into a winner. After a slow start in the first year, Henrietta's patience paid off and once Heart broke the winning tape for the first time, the wins just kept rolling along. Heart's finest triumph came in the Lanzarote Hurdle at Kempton, which she won in 2000. It cemented the firm friendship between Henrietta and the Brashers.

Brasher would delight, too, in naming some of his racehorses after champion athletes, runners he admired in his youth. One horse to be named this way was Dream of Nurmi, who raced in the yellow Brasher colours. 'Paavo Nurmi was simply the best and I had to name a horse after him,' Brasher said. 'It's great that the horse has managed a victory on the centenary of Nurmi's birth in June 1997.'

David Loder was the trainer of another fine horse, Maid for Walking, and noted that Brasher was 'very enthusiastic about his racing and very interested in the science of thoroughbred performance'. Brasher had long believed that racehorse training had not moved forward as much as the scientific training of athletes in his own discipline of running.

On one occasion Brasher and I were discussing the benefits of altitude training for athletes. Altitude, which played such a significant part in the Mexico Olympics, had produced enormous increases in the performance of human athletes. Athletes would train at altitude in order to condition their bodies to produce more red blood cells. In a sophisticated variant on this, by using an 'altitude tent' they could mimic sleeping at altitude but take their exercise at sea level. Lots of athletes were using this method, including Paula Radcliffe.

We had got through a couple of pints when Brasher said, 'Do you know what? We should have an "altitude stable" – do exactly the same thing as they do with this altitude tent. With a suitable investment we could really clean up.'

By the time the drinks were finished, Brasher had taken out his characteristic envelope and sketched out how much we could potentially invest and how much we could win. When I raised the concept rather flippantly with people in the racing world, they paused for a moment and then said, 'That's not such a crazy idea.'

Brasher also had a curious belief that he could convert nicotine into adrenalin. He confided this notion to Paddy Buckley. Adrenalin is one of the enzymes produced by the body that increases racing performance and speed. He tried it on himself, apparently with success, and reckoned it might work on horses. He repeated the pattern using himself as a guinea pig. In the bar before outings on the fells, Buckley reports, Brasher would rarely be seen without a cigarette or a pipe. 'I couldn't stand it,' says Buckley, 'I thought the smoke-filled bar would wreck my performance.' Nevertheless, the next day, Brasher would be running better than ever. 'He never got round to trying it on horses,' says Buckley, 'but it seemed to work for him.'

Back on the racecourse, Brasher began to notch up victories. In partnership with his wife Shirley, he won the 1994 Tote Two-Year-Old Trophy at Redcar with Prince Sabo and the mare Maid for Walking was runner-up in the 1994 Princess Margaret Stakes at Ascot.

Brasher began to haunt the racecourses and I joined him and Shirley at Epsom for a race meeting and a charity dinner. We placed our bets but it was perfectly obvious that Shirley was a much shrewder and better judge of horse flesh than Chris, and I soon learned to offset the bets by backing the horses that Shirley fancied. At the dinner, Brasher found it difficult to curb his enthusiasm.

Auctions for prizes, all for charity, had him raising his hand for almost everything.

Shirley would lean across and whisper: 'Stop him bidding, he's buying anything.' He bought paintings, holidays, shirts, jockeys' outfits, and on one occasion paid a small fortune for a boat that was going to be crewed anywhere in the world, all food provided.

Brasher was a member of the Travellers Club, a gentlemen's club in Pall Mall, and he started a syndicate among the members to buy and race a horse. He had a one-twentieth share in a two-year-old called Telemachus and pointed out to fellow club members that Telemachus was the son of that greatest of mythical travellers, Odysseus.

In July 1996 Brasher was elected to the Council of the Racehorse Owners' Association (ROA) and before too long he was stirring up that once sleepy body. This was Brasher's last venture into the politics of sport, but once again as soon as he had identified a cause he would fight for it with gusto and an almost unstoppable stamina.

The ROA president, Jim Furlong, said: 'It was Chris's idea that the ROA should promote partnership-ownership, and he attacked the issue with such enthusiasm that it was always going to work.' As soon as Brasher had identified a cause to fight for, said Michael Harris, the ROA's chief executive, he would attack it with unbelievable energy, 'And one of these causes was waving the flag for racehorse owners.' As an owner Brasher knew himself how much he was putting into the sport and what return he was receiving. This upset him greatly and was the underlying reason why he joined the ROA.

Brasher had been wary of how much money the bookmakers made when he was passing on bets as an illegal bookmaker's runner at the engineering works in Manchester. 'I was apprenticed to the factory bookie. Each week my 'master' took an £80 wad out of his dungarees. That was my pay for more than half a year. Bookmakers and the government still take too much out of racing.

'Mysilv won £50,000 for being second in the French Champion Hurdle,' he said. 'Our prize money is desperate by comparison.

A Tote monopoly would be the answer. Or the Australian system; bookies on the track, all Tote off it. Racing is living off subsidies – ours, the owners'. Prize money is decreasing and our costs increasing. Stable staff and jump jockeys are paid far too little – but not for much longer. It's extraordinary that racecourses contribute less to prize money than owners.

'Now they claim copyright for pictures from the course. That has to be wrong. Where do other sports get their money from? TV and sponsorship. There'd be no London Marathon without sponsorship. And no sponsorship without TV. TV is the most powerful tool – it brought down the Berlin Wall. I can't accept that racecourses own the TV rights.'

Brasher maintained that he was going to fight this as he had fought for other basic rights in the world of sport. 'Look,' he said, 'the MCC has now given up all its power. The Jockey Club representation on the British Horse Racing Board will have to be reduced. In every other sport the disciplinary side is all done by the governing body, but that isn't so in racing. Yet. We've the world's best racing but we're in danger of losing it. That's close to my heart because we made the London Marathon the best in the world.' For Brasher it was another cause, another race, and once again he was up to the challenge.

Charlie Egerton, who saddled Brasher's last runner Krzyszkowiak to defeat by a short head at Hereford just days before Brasher died, said: 'One of the greatest privileges I had was meeting Chris and getting to know him. He was an amazing and very wise man. He taught me a lot about attitude to sport. He was same in defeat as in victory.

'To be honest, I didn't want to run the horse in that last race, but Chris insisted and I simply couldn't refuse.'

22

A Life Worth Living

'It is said an Eastern monarch once charged his wise men to invent him a sentence to be ever in view, and which should be true and appropriate in all times and situations. They presented him the words: And this, too, shall pass away.'

Abraham Lincoln

DESPITE NEARING SEVENTY, Brasher shrugged off the advancing years as he continued to walk, climb, ski and sail with an energy that would have put a man half his age to shame. Finally recognised for his contribution to charity and British sport through the founding of the London Marathon, he accepted the CBE from John Major in 1996. On his OBOE trips, meanwhile, with his friends grouped around him, Brasher still maintained the whirlwind pace of his life.

On one such sailing voyage in 1996 Brasher enlisted the support of the round-the-world yachtsman Sir Robin Knox-Johnston. The crew was a mixture of marathon runners and sailors in a race that took four or five days and involved around 350 miles of sailing, including a cross-channel voyage to Alderney, a loop around its coastal path, followed by a run across most of the Isle of Wight. The runners would stagger ashore now and then to cover sixty miles of hills and coastal paths.

The abrasive interplay between Sir Robin and Brasher was a

wonder to behold. When Sir Robin growled, 'There can only be one skipper on a boat, I give the orders,' Brasher gave the most disarming of mutinous grins. But it ended as always with late-night tumblers of Scotch and tales that grew ever more outrageous in the moonlight. In these races Brasher often made up the rules as he went along, which was certain to guarantee him and his team victory in whichever class he had invented for the events. He still had a taste for winning and manhandled the rules robustly but with good humour.

I had got to know Chris Brasher well in the late 1970s, after he set up the Sweat Shop in Teddington. I knew all the runners he employed there and often used to meet him to talk about shoes and training. I occasionally ran and raced with his club, the Ranelagh Harriers, and inevitably any running session would end in the bar at the Dysart Arms.

At the time I was running the features department of the *Daily Mail* and we started running together to discuss plans and publicity for the London Marathon. Brasher believed that I was the best person to produce the programme for the event, which I did for the first five years, happily, with no payment. Following that first race, I managed to get the London Marathon pictured and headlined on the front page. The friendship grew as Brasher and I started to plan other adventures, involving running, sailing and cycling – all of which ended up, cold and wet, but in some bar. I got to know the family well – Chris's wife Shirley; I ran with Kate and Hugh, and went on holiday with them.

In the late 1980s I persuaded Brasher that he should rejoin the Thames Hare and Hounds, and for a decade or so he would hold court during riotous evenings in the Fox and Grapes at Wimbledon. Brasher got to know my family well, particularly my oldest son Matthew who seemed to share his delight in running and the wilderness.

On occasions Matthew would join Brasher in a two-man canoe that he had shipped over from Canada. They would paddle great stretches of the Thames. At night Brasher would sleep in the canoe under a canopy while Matthew had to make use of the river bank. One afternoon Chris had invited me up to run along the towpath, daring me to see if I could keep pace with the canoe. What I didn't know was that he had brought a miniature outboard electric motor; when I was running flat out they went flying by, nonchalantly paddling and whooping with delight.

Brasher took a similar childlike delight in the cycle rides that we tackled. In his *Observer* days he had interviewed Tommy Simpson, who in 1962 became the first Briton to wear the yellow jersey as leader of the Tour de France, so he was steeped in the lore and tales of France's greatest race. But then in mid-July 2002, when Matthew was due to get married, something odd happened.

Matthew organised a most unusual stag run, partly inspired by Brasher. He planned to run from Bryants Bottom in Buckinghamshire to Bryants Piddle in Dorset as a relay with his friends. The baton for the relay was the wedding ring that his wife would wear on their wedding day. Brasher and I had been invited along to take part and Brasher joined in on the third day on a mountain bike as we were nearing Bryants Piddle.

Brasher had been told by his doctor that he needed to lose weight. This he found difficult because to round off a day spent walking, running or cycling he would invariably head for a pub. There his log-fire personality would warm up his companions and soon enough he would be reaching for the menu and pints of beer.

Brasher turned up at Matthew's wedding characteristically late, explaining that his car had blown up en route. Once again he protested that he couldn't drink or eat much because of his weight problem. His weight issue seemed to have caused him stomach problems and he complained that he did not have the energy to exercise properly.

Just a few weeks later Brasher called me at my office at the *Daily Mail*, told me that he was in St Thomas' Hospital in London and asked me if I could come to see him. He told me the news that he had just heard from his doctors. They said that he had pancreatic cancer and that it was incurable. I tried to reassure him with all the usual platitudes – how wonderful the treatment was these days and so on. But Chris was realistic. He told me that he didn't want to end his life undergoing chemotherapy and all tubed-up in a hospital. Quietly he returned to Chaddleworth, and although there were rumours that he was ill, no real word got out of just how ill he was.

A few friends used to visit him and spend time with him. In a matter of months Brasher lost an enormous amount of weight and I vowed that I would take him on a walk, perhaps his last, to the pub. Shirley, his wife, had gone out and left the house to us; Chris said that it would be good to walk to the pub and he knew of a footpath. We set off slowly and then we found that our way was blocked by a five-barred gate. Brasher said that Shirley had probably locked it to stop him using the footpath. He had lost so much weight that I managed to heave him up to the top bar of the gate and clamber over myself and lower him down gently.

In the pub I asked him if he would like a pint of beer and he said, 'No, I'd like water.' I got him a beer anyway. I asked what he would like to eat and he told me that he didn't eat anything, wasn't hungry.

A week later he was back in a central London hospital getting yet more treatment for his cancer. Brasher owned a racehorse that was due to run and the family joined him at his bedside to watch the meeting on television. Hugh picked up his sister Amanda on his motorbike from her home in Twickenham and Amanda was anxious that they should make it to the hospital in time for the race, which was scheduled to begin at 2.15 p.m.

There was a delay while Hugh rushed to a betting shop to back the horse. Amanda, clinging to Hugh on the pillion, kept shouting to Hugh because the bike was making a spluttering sound. By the Chiswick roundabout the engine failed. 'Not a hope of getting a taxi,' noted Amanda. Hugh flagged down a passing motorcyclist, found a spare bike from home, picked up Amanda and, she says, 'drove at around ninety miles an hour to make the hospital. We got there at 2.14.'

Their father was by this stage on heavy doses of morphine. But a nurse reduced the dose so that he would have an outside chance of staying awake for the race. Sadly the horse didn't win, but as the nurse approached Brasher with yet more morphine he gave a smile. 'Anyone for gin and tonic?' he announced.

The next time I visited Brasher he was home again, but far too ill to get out of bed. He was being looked after by nurses round the clock. A basket of ski sticks stood propped by the front door and I asked Shirley if Chris was up or awake. On the way to his bedroom I passed his study. The door was open and there was a large desk. Books and papers were scattered everywhere. I caught a few of the titles – *Spirit of the Hills*, *The Heart of a Champion*; a few of the writers: Eric Shipton, John Hunt.

On the desk were photos of his children and Brasher himself in an ill-fitting tracksuit beaming over the winners of the London Marathon. And there in the corner was a little slag-heap of running shoes, among them a battered pair of Brasher Boots.

Upstairs Chris was lying in bed with his eyes closed. The clutter here was different: bottles, paper bags and medicines, tubes and cylinders – the paraphernalia of death.

'Last time I was here we managed to walk to the pub. In the end you managed a beer. We'll do that again when you're better,' I said to him.

'Give me some water now,' said Chris, 'my throat is so sore this isn't good.' I looked helplessly at him. This was no way to go; this was a man who should have met death falling off a mountain or crashing his car rushing flat out to make some impossible ski rendezvous.

But we chatted on about old times. 'I've had a good life,' said Brasher, 'but there was never enough time.' What do you talk about? I wondered, and I took him back to the Olympics and Melbourne.

'Remember those stories you used to tell, how you collected a medal breathing fumes of gin over the officials? You used to tell wonderful stories in the pub about an American who you called the Vaulting Vicar.'

'Great man,' said Chris. 'Bob Richards the American; won gold at the pole vault in '52 and '56. I liked him and I liked what he believed. He was a minister, the Vaulting Vicar. He would say that you could only go as high in life as you dared to believe you could go. Hitch your wagon to a star he would tell me, and then he would repeat that great line from Browning:

'"Ah, but a man's reach should exceed his grasp, or what's a heaven for".

Sporting fame is an ephemeral blessing, bestowed one day and barely remembered the next. There seemed to be few reminders in the house of Brasher's victory in the 3000 metres steeplechase; no trophies, no photos, no great hints of his past. 'I don't know where the medal is,' said Brasher. 'I could ask Shirley, maybe she remembers or maybe Hugh borrowed it.' The Melbourne gold medal may be long forgotten, but there was one race that millions will remember.

When he was fifty-one Brasher took part in the 1979 New York Marathon and was overwhelmed by the atmosphere of the city and its citizen runners. He came back to London with his dream of the Marathon and refused to take 'No' from anyone. 'Apart from helping to bring up my family the Marathon is the most satisfying thing that I have ever been involved with.'

'I won that race in Melbourne,' said Brasher, 'but I never won the Crick.' He went over the incident again and again, sometimes closing his eyes as the morphine kicked in – that far-off race as a schoolboy in Rugby, the race that he never won. Nearly sixty years later it still rankled with him.

'I never did win the Crick, I should have done, but I didn't.' He closed his eyes and the muttering stopped. I sat by the bed awhile, whispered a silent goodbye and then I drove away, still wondering about the race Chris Brasher didn't win.

On 28 February 2003 I took a phone call from Shirley Brasher telling me that Chris had died. The obituaries were plentiful and full of praise for a man who had achieved so much.

'My enduring memory of Brasher was his absolute focused determination,' said journalist and fellow athlete John Goodbody at the time. 'I wrote a piece in *The Times* recalling the 1977 World Athletics Cup Final in Düsseldorf. We went out running together and did some long repetitions in the woods. As I was much younger and by my running standards relatively fit at the time, I fancied my chances, particularly when he gave me a start of at least thirty seconds. But every time just as we came towards the finish I would hear him thundering up to my shoulder like a bull, and each time he just caught me. It was the mentality of an Olympic champion.'

In *The Times* in March 2003, meanwhile, John Cleare paid tribute to Brasher's work to preserve his beloved wilderness:

> Brasher's business success enabled him to finance all manner of good works in the outdoors, the mountains and the wild places of Britain. In central Snowdonia he secretly purchased a run-down eyesore of a petrol station and returned the site to green hillside. Word of this somehow leaked abroad and in 1994 in Florence a very embarrassed Chris Brasher was presented with a special award by Italian mountain lovers as being 'the individual who had done most for mountain conservation anywhere in the world over the previous decade.'
>
> Brasher was greatly respected by hikers and climbers, and many involved in the outdoors feel that a knighthood was long overdue – he had been a far more worthy recipient than most – but alas he has died before lobbying could take effect.

Brasher's old friend Roger Bannister said simply: 'Chris was gallant and brave right to the end. He had won so many battles in his life. We had more than fifty years of friendship.'

Other groups of friends took their own memories of Brasher and celebrated his life in their own way. In the 1990s, Brasher had decided to provide plentiful wine for the annual match between his two running clubs, Thames Hare and Hounds and the Ranelagh Harriers, and for the riotous supper that followed. When he was far too ill to run (or buy bottles) I bought the wine myself and passed it off as Brasher's. To keep the tradition going, his friends, led by my son Matthew, organised the Chris Brasher Memorial Relay on 20 September 2003 to provide funds to buy the 'Brasher wine'. Members of the two clubs ran the length of the Thames towpath, from the river's source to Navigator's House where Brasher spent most of his life. The baton for the relay was a flask of Brasher's favourite Scotch whisky. A low-key, very English, slightly bizarre tribute, it will keep the wine flowing for years to come.

I ran with Chris Chataway and a few friends along the stage of the course that passes through Oxford. We diverted from the river to include a lap of the Iffley Road track, where the first four-minute mile was run and where Brasher achieved a little immortality. The black cinder track on which the young Brasher ran is red rubber now. We swung back to the towpath to complete the relay; waiting in the sun at the riverside pub where the stage ended, buying us drinks, was Roger Bannister.

Memories and mourning filled the silences as we sipped our beers. At dinner later Chataway paid tribute to Brasher and to Franz Stampfl, the mentor who long ago had shared their dreams.

'Half an hour with Franz Stampfl,' said Chataway, 'convinced you that to break a world record really was as good as painting the *Mona Lisa* – and we believed it then. Chris Brasher was a man of no moderation. He was dogmatic, irrational, infuriating; but he left no scars. His life was all about creative passion.'

Brasher's OBOE friends, those he took on his crazy expeditions, took matters quietly in hand, led this time by John Disley. On 7 June 2004 at Black Sail Youth Hostel, high in the mountains of the Lake District, they unveiled a plaque of Honister green slate engraved in Brasher's memory. It read:

Chris Brasher CBE
1928–2003

Olympic athlete, mountaineer, journalist, businessman and philanthropist
   'Ah, but a man's reach should exceed his grasp, or what's a heaven for?'

                                                                Robert Browning

A lifetime of love and support for outdoor sport and for the world's wild places.
   A benefactor to the YHA and outdoor activity in the Lakes.
   Spent his last nights hostelling, with friends, at Black Sail on 29 June 2002 – 'a disgraceful episode at which we devoured 14 different curries and consumed nine bottles of good Australian wine!'
   This plaque erected by his friends in OBOE – 'On the Back Of an Envelope' – the way Chris believed any worthwhile expedition can be planned.

At the dinner that followed, John Disley read a poem that he had written for his old friend. It was a moving tribute and spoke much of the partnership that had lasted a lifetime since he and Brasher had climbed and run together in the 1940s.

   To a 74-year-old friend who died in winter

   I wanted him to have another living summer,
   To walk in the sun and share the company of tired legs.
   Just one more adventure with his friends on a less beaten path,
   Another debate about where we are and the best route forward.

I needed time to hear him rehearse old epics, glass in hand,
Stories that were known by heart but that with each telling
    pleased again.
Another chance to watch him delight in playing Richard
    Hannay,
Or dispute why his route was better than mine through a sun-lit
    forest.
That last departure should be paced through the heat of long
    days
And warm evenings in some small hostelry or sat beside a two-
    man tent.
It should give time to say 'well-met and Godspeed', without
    haste.
And to part company content that a friendship endured.
But it was not to be, what memories I have — are all I have.
Winter visits to that neat white bed-side traced with tubes and
    wires,
Did little to prolong that affinity, except to note,
That I was standing and he was lying — quietly dying.

Just over a week after Brasher died there had been a private cremation and a small, intimate memorial service at St Peter's Church in Ham. There was a poignant moment in the small church when Sir Christopher Chataway, who had delivered the address, clasped arms with Sir Roger Bannister, who had read the first lesson.

However, for the thousands of runners who had completed the London Marathon and who wished to salute Brasher for his writing and his powers of inspiration, there was an opportunity to pay tribute to him. His son, Hugh, organised a memorial 10,000 metres run on Sunday 20 June 2003 in Richmond Park, close to where Brasher had lived most of his life and where he ran with the Ranelagh Harriers and the Thames Hare and Hounds.

The event was to raise money for the Petersham Trust to

preserve the Petersham Meadows beside the Thames, that scene painted by Turner and described by Brasher as 'one of the best in the world – a herd of cows grazing beside a majestic river. It's a view that epitomises what England is all about.'

That Richmond Park race was started by Roger Bannister. I ran every step of the way with Chris Chataway, the two of us swapping tales about Brasher and comparing memories from the obituaries we had read.

A couple of months before he died, while discussing his medical treatment, Brasher told me he'd had 'a good life, a life worth living'. He had no wish to spend time in hospital having highly invasive treatment.

Somehow the shy, Corinthian, public-school and Oxbridge amateur had unearthed the Herculean self-belief to reshape himself into a successful businessman, racehorse owner, journalist, broadcaster, adventurer and conservationist; he had won an Olympic gold medal and guaranteed the creation of the London Marathon.

Chataway and I agreed, as we clocked off the miles, that, love him or scorn him – and there seemed to be plenty in both camps – there was one ambition Brasher had fulfilled; he had drunk very deep of 'a life worth living'.

ACKNOWLEDGEMENTS

This book could never have been written without the help of Chris Brasher's family. First and foremost I must thank Shirley Brasher, Kate, Hugh and Amanda Brasher, and Chris's sister, Margaret Brasher, for giving me so much of their time and providing me with such wonderful access to his story

Many others have played an invaluable part in turning this project from a labour of love to a sporting biography. I must acknowledge the exceptional contribution made by John Disley and his wife Sylvia and those athletes who shared with Chris Brasher the magic of making the four-minute mile a reality. Sir Roger Bannister, Lady Bannister and Sir Christopher Chataway and Lady Chataway. Special thanks must go to Paddy Buckley, who shared so many of Chris Brasher's expeditions and his wife Sally, for their constant help.

Many runners, those of the Thames Hare and Hounds, Ranelagh Harriers, Achilles and other athletic and orienteering clubs kept me running and writing when I might have ground to a halt.

My thanks here to Joss Naylor, Tommy MacPherson, Steve Rowland, Donald Macgregor, Eric Shirley, Paul Wilcox, Lord Archer, Dick Beardsley, Will Cockerell, Bill Bird, Amby Burfoot, George Hirsch, Jeff Bull, Ronnie Williams, Steve Cram, Brendan Foster, David Coleman, Mike Farmery, Jim Forrest, Mike Gratton, Hugh Jones, Charlie Spedding, John Hanscomb, Norman Harris, Martin Hyman, Bruce Tulloh, Tony Barnes, John Landy, Wes Santee, Ken Ledward, Rex Lofts, Veronique Marot, Eamonn Martin, Carol McNeil, David Rosen, Miriam Rosen, Mike Peace, Andrew Ronay, Joyce Smith, Allan Storey, Billy Wilson, Mike Allen, Dennis Porter, Geoff Tudor, Mel Watman, Dave Wright,

Steven Downes, Randall Northam, Michael Hubbert, Bill Wheeler, Rainer Burchett, Chris Finhill, Jeffrey Gordon, Doug Gillon, Dr Dan Tunstall-Pedoe, Sir Ranulph Fiennes, Sir Robin Knox-Johnson and (Lord) Sebastian Coe.

Donald Trelford, for many years editor of the Observer, gave many valuable insights into Brasher's journalistic life, and I would like to thank among others Steven Downes, Ron Atkin, Neil Allen, Pat Collins, Duncan Mackay, Pat Butcher, Keith Dovkants, Neil Wilson, John Goodbody, Allan Hubbard, Hugh McIlvanney, Peter Corrigan, Peter Nicholls, Terry O'Connor, Tom Clarke, John Samuel, Tom Knight and Stan Greenberg

I gained the most privileged insight into the schoolboy life at Oakley Hall from Jocelyn Letts, Dick Letts and Quentin Letts and my thanks for details of Brasher's time at Rugby go to Rusty MacLean and Sir Peter Miller.

The London Marathon team have been supportive throughout and I must thank David Bedford, Nick Bitel, Nic Okey, Lisa Thompson, David Golton, Jim Clarke and Andrew Torr.

I would also like to acknowledge the assistance I received from, among others, Duncan Campbell, Matthew Parris, Gary Waller, Mark Shearman, Graham Robson, George Band, Dick Booth, Tony Wale, Marco Ellerker , Heather Kemp, Lloyd Scott and John Cleare. From the world of racing I owe much thanks to many, including Charlie Egerton, Henrietta Knight, Charlie Brooks and John Maxse.

My own efforts would have remained a dream without the skill and encouragement of Graham Coster and his excellent team at Aurum Press, Louise Tucker, Melissa Smith, Liz Somers, Jodie Mullish, Steve Gove and my literary agent Mark Lucas.

Above all, for their unwavering support through the time it took to research and write this book, my thanks go to my wife Carol, and to my family, Matthew, Kirsten, William and Lucie Bryant, who have paced me throughout this long journey in the footsteps of Chris Brasher.

Index